Essential LISP

John R.
Anderson
Carnegie-Mellon
University

Albert T.
Corbett
Carnegie-Mellon
University

Brian J.
Reiser
Princeton
University

ADDISON-WESLEY PUBLISHING COMPANY, INC.

Reading, Massachusetts ▪ Menlo Park, California
Don Mills, Ontario ▪ Wokingham, England ▪ Amsterdam ▪ Sydney
Singapore ▪ Tokyo ▪ Madrid ▪ Bogotá ▪ Santiago ▪ San Juan

Sponsoring Editor Keith Wollman
Developmental Editor Darlene Bordwell
Production Supervisor Laura Skinger
Production Coordinator Helen Wythe
Manufacturing Supervisor Hugh Crawford
Cover Designer Marshall Henrichs
Designer Melinda Grosser

Library of Congress Cataloging-in-Publication Data

Anderson, John R. (John Robert), 1947-
    Essential LISP.

    1. LISP (Computer program language) I. Corbett,
Albert T., 1950-   II. Reiser, Brian J., 1955-
III. Title.
QA76.73.L23A53   1986   005.13'3   86-3536
ISBN 0-201-11148-9

ABCDEFGHIJ-HA-89876

Contents

7
Introduction to Recursion   111

8
List Iteration   129

9
Advanced Recursion   143

Preface

To the Student

LISP, a programming language developed in the 1950s by John McCarthy, is one of the oldest programming languages in use today. LISP is used principally in the field of artificial intelligence. It is an extremely powerful yet simple language that can be learned easily — even as a first programming language. Indeed, LISP was once confined to artificial intelligence applications, but now it is more widely used, thanks to the development of more efficient and flexible versions of LISP that can be used on a wider variety of machines.

How to use this book

This book attempts to teach what we call essential LISP — that is, all the basic func-

tions and programming techniques in LISP. As such, the book is appropriate as a first programming course or as an introduction to LISP for more advanced programmers. The text is also designed to enable self-study, provided you have access to a LISP system.

This text is written with a strong philosophy about how you learn to program — you learn to program through practice. The psychological evidence for this learning-by-doing principle is overwhelming, and we have written the textbook to facilitate that learning process. We have organized each chapter into sections, each of which gives the knowledge relevant to a particular feature of LISP. After each section, we provide problems, called LISP Exercises, which are denoted by the special symbol

These LISP Exercises enable you to practice the knowledge you gained in reading each section. It is essential that you actually work through these LISP Exercises, or exercises like these, before continuing to read the text. Occasionally, we provide optional, more difficult LISP Exercises, which you can try for a challenge.

Virtually all the LISP Exercises ask you to write LISP code. These problems should be done in a LISP environment — in other words, while using your LISP system. You can obtain LISP systems for almost all mainframe computers and minicomputers and for many personal computers. It is absolutely essential that the student have access to a LISP system before trying to use this book.

In addition to LISP Exercises, we provide several other features to aid you in learning LISP:

- Programming templates — abstract descriptions of LISP functions;
- A glossary of key terms at the end of each chapter, with key terms boldfaced within the text;
- A summary of LISP functions at the end of each chapter, serving as a quick review of the functions covered in the chapter.

The LISP Intelligent Tutoring System

This book is intended to be used with a standard LISP environment. However, as an additional aid to learning, we have developed a special system for learning LISP called the LISP Intelligent Tutoring System — an artificial intelligence system that actually monitors students' progress as they go through the LISP Exercises in the text. The LISP tutor provides immediate feedback on errors and advice on correct solutions. If you encounter substantial programming difficulties, the tutor will provide you with practice problems in addition to the material in this text. We have found that students who work with our LISP tutor are at an advantage over students who do not. At the time of this writing, the LISP tutor is just beginning to be commercially marketed as an AI system.

Some Notes on LISP Systems

There are numerous dialects of LISP available. Recently, there has been an effort to standardize these dialects to something that is called "Common LISP." Because this text is concerned with teaching only basic LISP competence, most of the features we describe are common to all LISP systems. Where there are deviations among systems, we follow the conventions in Common LISP. We also explain in footnotes what the deviations are in other dialects of LISP so that you will be able to use this book with your own particular LISP system. Most LISP systems contain capabilities beyond those described in this book, although this text is sufficient for many purposes. You should obtain a user's manual for your LISP system that describes the system's full capabilities. Such a manual differs from a textbook in that it will tell you what your LISP system is capable of, not how to get it to do what you want it to. If you successfully master this text, you will have a sufficient grasp of the capabilities of LISP to meet the challenge required by more advanced aspects of your LISP system.

To the Instructor

This book is intended for use in a LISP programming course, although students have managed well with it on a self-study basis. We used drafts of this book to teach LISP as a first language, or as a later language, with and without our LISP Intelligent Tutoring System. (See the comments to the student for more details on the tutoring system.) We find our role in such courses largely one of explaining how LISP is used in actual applications, dealing with residual student confusion, and producing interesting illustrations of concepts. You will discover that the sequence of topics is fairly tight, although there is some room for deleting and rearranging chapters (as we have done in our classes). We strived to create a book that enables the instructor to focus on the fun of LISP, leaving the mechanics to the text.

The Basis for this Book

We base this text on a careful analysis of the knowledge required for introductory LISP, and on a set of (we believe) well-motivated assumptions about how to learn LISP. This analysis derives from our research on how students learn to program in LISP, analysis of the errors they make, structure of simulations of their behavior, and creation of a LISP tutoring system based on these simulations.* At the core of our LISP tutor is a

production-system model of ideal student programming behavior. Our text is largely devoted to explaining (in English) the knowledge behind these rules, and then asking the student to practice that knowledge.

One of our strong assumptions, as explained in the preface to the student, is the power of practice. Therefore we include a special learning tool called LISP Exercises so the student can practice each concept. You should not feel compelled to use only these exercises, but we strongly urge you to assign the student exercises that cover all the material.

Some Notes on the Book's Organization

We have also given a great deal of thought to the sequence of material, particularly with respect to how to teach iteration and recursion. Iteration and (more particularly) recursion, are notoriously difficult for students to

*For a sample of this research see:
- Anderson, J.R., Farrell, R.G., Sauers, R. (1984) Learning to program in LISP. *Cognitive Science*, 8, 87–130.
- Anderson, J.R., Jeffries, R. (1985) Novice LISP errors: Undetected losses of information from working memory. *Human-Computer Interaction*, 1, 107–131.
- Katz, I.R., Anderson, J.R. (1986) An exploratory study of novice programmers' bugs and debugging behavior. (In revision.)
- Kessler, C.M., Anderson, J.R. (1986) Learning flow of control: Recursive and iterative procedures. *Human Computer Interation*, in press.
- Pirolli, P.L., Anderson, J.R. (1984) Learning to program recursion. In: *Proceedings of the Sixth Annual Cognitive Science Meetings*, 277–280.
- Reiser, B.J., Anderson, J.R., Farrell, R.G. (1985) Dynamic student modelling in an intelligent tutor for LISP programming. In: *Proceedings of IJCAI-85*, 8–14.

learn, and our research has been focused here. We have found that students learn recursion much more readily after an introduction to iteration (Kessler and Anderson, 1986). Therefore our first chapter on this material (Chapter 6) covers iteration, and the next (Chapter 7) covers recursion. The one thing students find relatively easy to understand is a simple looping structure in which familiar LISP expressions are evaluated sequentially, so Chapter 6 is devoted to this method. With this information as background, Chapter 7 covers basic recursion. The next three chapters are devoted to refining the knowledge of the two constructs. Chapters 8 and 9 contrast situations when iteration and recursion are useful. Chapter 10 introduces the advanced iterative constructs of *dos* and *mapcars*, which we find students understand only after they have a good grasp of iteration.

As mentioned in the comments to the student, our LISP Intelligent Tutoring System will aid students in doing the LISP exercises in the text. This tutor currently runs on a number of larger computers with FRANZ or Common LISP, and we are trying to increase its availability. For current information about availability, write to the authors.

Acknowledgments

The book still shows its origins in a research project. This research on LISP programming was funded for the past five years by the Office of Naval Research (most recent contract, N00014-84-K-0064). Our early research involved studying students' learning behavior as they used the Siklossy text and the first edition of Winston and Horn.* Some of the exercises from these sources were adapted for our LISP tutor, and were further adapted for this text. Also, Chapter 14, on search, evolved from research done with Irvin Katz, which in turn evolved from class lectures, which in turn evolved from Winston and Horn. Many of the ideas from Winston and Horn were preserved in this evolution.

A great many people besides the authors contributed to the LISP tutor on which this text is most directly based. Robert Farrell deserves special mention, as he put together the initial LISP tutor code and saw it through its first year of development. Other individuals involved in various aspects of our LISP research include Peggy Galdi, Robin Jeffries, Irvin Katz, Claudius Kessler, Jean McKendree, Peter Pirolli, and Ron Sauers. All contributed to the knowledge base from which this book developed. Peggy Galdi also played a major role in the preparation and coordination of this book. Special acknowledgment should be made of Peter Pirolli, who actually wrote the initial drafts of the recursion chapters (Chapters 7 and 9). A number of academic reviewers offered valuable comments on the manuscript at various stages in its development. We would like to acknowledge the contributions of James Hendler, University of Maryland; Michael Lebowitz, Columbia University; Christopher K. Riesbeck, Yale University; Greg W. Scragg, Williams College; Jerry D. Smith, University of Tennessee at Chatta-

---

*Winston, P.H., Horn, B.K.P. (1981) *LISP, First Edition*. Reading, Mass.: Addison–Wesley.
Siklossy, Laurent (1976) *Let's talk LISP*. Englewood Cliffs, N.J.: Prentice-Hall.

nooga; Richard Wojcik, Hofstra University; Jerrold H. May, University of Pittsburgh; Douglas D. Dankel II, University of Florida; and Gautam Biswas, University of South Carolina at Columbia.

We would also like to thank Addison–Wesley. Our sponsoring editor, Keith Wollman, has been stellar in his support of the book, and the developmental editor, Darlene Bordwell, has succeeded beyond our expectations in getting us to face up to all the issues of exposition.

Pittsburgh, PA   J.R.A.
                                    A.T.C.
                                    B.J.R.

Introduction to LISP

For some of you, this will be your first introduction to computer programming, so perhaps it would be appropriate to start with a brief description of what a computer program is. A **computer program** simply is a set of instructions that a computer can follow step by step to accomplish a task. (Words that appear in boldface type throughout this book are key words that you should try to understand and remember.) The task might be to compute profits and losses for a business, it might be to print out mailing labels for envelopes, or it might be to play a game of chess with a human being. Of course, the instructions, or program, must be written in a language that a computer can process. As you probably realize, LISP is only one of many languages that are available for writing computer programs; other well-known languages are Fortran, Pascal, Basic, and Cobol (unfortunately, English is not one of the choices). Each of these is a general-purpose computer language, although each was designed to emphasize certain applications. For example, Fortran is an efficient language for numerical computation; Pascal encourages good programming style and is also efficient for numerical computation; Basic is easy to learn as a first language; and Cobol was designed for business applications.

Programming in LISP

LISP is also a general-purpose language, but it was developed specifically for use in artificial intelligence. That is, it has been developed for use in writing programs that approximate certain types of human thinking and reasoning processes, and it is the most common language used by cognitive scientists (e.g., computer scientists, psychologists, linguists, philosophers) who are writing such programs. LISP has been used to write programs that perform "expert" tasks — for example, programs that can make diagnoses and prescribe treatments, given descriptions of medical symptoms. It has also been used to write programs that not only can perform "reasoning" tasks, but are actually intended as theoretical models of how humans perform those tasks. Finally, LISP has been used to write programs that can play games or solve problems.

You might well ask what it is about LISP that makes it appropriate for artificial-intelligence applications. LISP is designed to facilitate symbolic processing, the key to many aspects of intelligence. Unfortunately, it is not immediately obvious just what it means to process a symbol. However, we hope that by the end of this book you will not only understand LISP but have insight into the nature of symbolic processing and how it underlies intelligent behavior.

Getting Started: Functions

Most programs in LISP are **functions**. In this first chapter you will learn about some basic functions provided by LISP, and you will learn how to **call** functions (that is, to get them to execute). In Chapter 2 you will learn how to define your own functions. In the remaining chapters you will learn about more functions that are defined in LISP and how to use them to write your own functions to accomplish tasks.

In order to run LISP programs we need to enter the **LISP environment** on the computer. That is, we need to start up a program called the **LISP interpreter**, which can execute programs written in LISP. The LISP interpreter is an interactive system, (like Basic, but unlike most other computer languages). This means essentially that when you are in the LISP environment you can type in function calls and LISP will immediately execute them and respond by putting the result on your screen.

Table 1.1. Arithmetic functions

Function calls	Value returned	Operation
(+ 8 12 3)	23	Add the arguments
(− 12 4)	8	Subtract the second argument from the first
(* 4 3)	12	Multiply the arguments
(/ 12 3)	4	Divide the first argument by the second

When you start up the LISP interpreter, it tells you it is ready to accept a function call by printing a prompt on the screen. In the examples in this text, we will use = ⟩ as the LISP prompt, but different LISP systems may use other prompts. In order to clarify the interactions between the user and LISP in these examples, the input typed by the user is printed in italics to differentiate it from the output from the interpreter (LISP's response to the input). On an actual terminal screen, however, there is frequently no distinction in font or brightness between the user's input and LISP's response.

How to Write LISP Function Calls: Arithmetic Functions.

The following is an example of a LISP function call.

```
= ⟩ (+ 9 5)
14
= ⟩
```

In this example, the prompt = ⟩ appeared, the user typed (+ 9 5), and LISP responded with 14. Then the prompt character appeared, indicating that the interpreter was ready for more input. Of course, it is difficult to portray the actual interaction on a page in a book and you may be having trouble picturing exactly what happened. If at all possible, you should go into the LISP environment on your computer and, after the prompt appears, type (+ 9 5) to see what happens. In this example, + is a function and 9 and 5 are called **arguments**. So, the user called the function + with the arguments 9 and 5, and LISP **returned** the result 14. It is no doubt apparent to you what the function + does; it adds together its arguments and returns the sum. Table 1.1 presents some other examples of LISP function calls and the value returned by each.

Since you already know arithmetic, you are familiar with what these functions do, and you know how to perform each of these operations in your head and on a calculator. So, what you really need to learn from this table is the general form of a function call in LISP, and the specific symbols that LISP uses for these four arithmetic functions (+, −, *, /).*

Notice some of the things that are common to each of these four function calls. First, each function call is enclosed in parentheses. The first element within the parentheses is the function name. The other elements within the parentheses are arguments. The function name designates an operation or computation that is performed on the arguments. Functions differ in how many arguments they accept. For example, − and / take two arguments, while + and * can take two or more arguments. Some functions accept only one argument and a few functions that we will discuss in future chapters take no arguments!†

Thus, when we call a function, we tell the LISP interpreter to apply the function to its arguments and return the value. In general, to type a function call, you

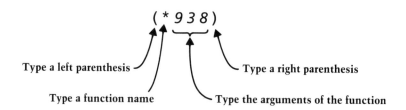

Type a left parenthesis

Type a function name

Type a right parenthesis

Type the arguments of the function

---

*In some LISP dialects the functions are called *plus, difference, times,* and *quotient,* respectively.

†Actually, (+) and (*) can take 0 or 1 argument. The sum of no numbers is 0, and the product of no numbers is 1. You will not have cause to call these functions with 0 or 1 argument until the more advanced chapters. Also, − can take 1 argument in which case it returns the additive inverse of its argument, i.e., (−3) = −3. In some LISPs a function *minus* exists to calculate additive inverses.

Another complication is that LISP will produce somewhat different results depending on whether you call it with floating-point numbers or integers. Floating-point numbers are represented with a decimal (6.0, 5.431, etc.) while integers are simple whole numbers (1, 412, −31, etc.). Note that the same value can be represented either as an integer, 3, or as a floating-point number, 3.0. LISP does what you would expect it to in most cases, but it does behave peculiarly in the case of division. (/ 3.0 2.0) = 1.5, but (/ 3 2) = 1 or 3/2, depending on the LISP implementation with which you are working. In the first case, it rounds down to 1, while in the second it produces what is called a rational number. Common LISP produces a rational number, but most other LISPs round down. In general, you have to consult the details of your LISP implementation to see how it deals with the peculiarities of integers versus floating-point numbers.

We can also characterize the general form of a function call in the following template notation:

(⟨function-name⟩ [arguments ...])

This template is not a LISP function call itself, but it is an abstract description of the components of a LISP function call. Each template presented in this book will give you a general pattern for a particular type of LISP operation. This template indicates that every function call begins with a left parenthesis and ends with a right parenthesis. The symbol ⟨function-name⟩ that follows the left parenthesis indicates that a function name is required. The angle brackets ⟨ and ⟩, however, indicate that we do not literally type "function-name," but rather type an actual function name (+, −, * and / are our choices so far). Square brackets around a symbol represent an optional component, and the three dots indicate that there may be one or more such components. Since some functions accept no arguments, and other functions accept different numbers of arguments, the template indicates that arguments are optional and the maximum number is unknown. Keep in mind, however, that some LISP functions require a specific number of arguments.

LISP Exercises

This is the first of many exercises for you to do in LISP. You should not read any farther before you have actually tried to do these problems in your LISP environment. You will find the answers to all the exercises at the end of this book.

1.1 Write a LISP function call that adds the numbers 3 and 2. You should call a particular LISP function with the arguments 3 and 2.
1.2 Write a function call that will divide 6 by 2. Do this just as you did in the previous problem, but use the function that divides numbers.
1.3 Write a LISP function call that multiplies together the numbers 2, 3, and 5.

Combining LISP functions

Suppose you want to add together 38 and 85 and divide the result by 41. We could do it this way:

```
=> (+ 38 85)
123
=> (/ 123 41)
3
```

LISP allows us to do the same thing more efficiently, as follows:

```
=> (/ (+ 38 85) 41)
3
```

In this example, we have again called the function / with two arguments, but now the first argument is itself a function call, *(+ 38 85)*, while the second argument is the number *41*. Notice that the form of the call *(+ 38 85)* has not changed at all even though it is **embedded** in another function call (i.e., it appears as an argument of another call). The form of the outer function call to / has not changed either, but one of its arguments is now another function call rather than a number.

The ability to embed function calls in other function calls is important, since it allows us to create complex function calls. Notice that for the first time in this example, we have a ''program'' that consists of two instructions instead of one: an instruction to add two values, and an instruction to divide two values. It is very important to understand the order in which LISP executes these instructions. Whenever a function is called, any embedded function calls will be evaluated before the function is applied to its arguments. (Evaluating a function is synonymous with ''calling'' or ''executing'' the function, and getting the value returned by the function.) In our example, before the function / is applied to its arguments, the function call *(+ 38 85)* will be evaluated and will return *123*. Then the function / will be applied to the arguments *123* and *41*, just as if we'd typed *123* into the function call in the first place. Notice, by the way, that the value *123* returned by the embedded function call never appears on the screen. Only the final value of the outermost function call is printed by LISP.

This is an example of an important general principle in LISP that we will come back to.

> The arguments of a function call are **evaluated** before the function is applied to the arguments.

LISP Exercises

1.4 Multiply together the number 5 and the result of 3 minus 2. To do this you must write a LISP function call that multiplies two things. One of these things will itself be a LISP function call.

1.5 Write a function call that will divide 100 by 4. But do not just type the number 100 — instead, you should get 100 by adding 60 and 40.

Atoms and lists

The four functions we have discussed so far accept only numbers as arguments (or function calls that evaluate to numbers) and perform mathematical operations. Remember, though, that LISP was designed for artificial intelligence, and programs that can perform reasoning tasks must be able to perform non-numerical computations. For example, a program that can process natural language must be able to represent the words in a sentence and their meaning. The type of representations used for such purposes are referred to as **symbolic expressions**.

The two basic types of symbolic expressions in LISP are **atoms** and **lists**; all legal expressions in LISP consist of these two entities. An atom is a simple element. Here are some examples:

george
16
b10
+
first-part
we-can-have-very-long-atoms

As you can see an atom is a string of letters, numbers and/or punctuation marks.* Atoms begin to provide us with the flexibility to represent non-numerical information. For example, if we want to represent chess pieces we could just use atoms such as *king*, *queen*, and so on. Notice that numbers are atoms, but they are special atoms. We can use the atom *king* to stand for anything we want in our programs, but a number always represents its corresponding numerical value.

---

*In some LISP dialects there are some restrictions on the name of an atom. For example, *6a* is not a legal atom name in some LISPs. In addition, atoms usually cannot include parentheses or single quote marks.

The second basic entity, the list, is an important structure that gives LISP much of its power. Indeed, the name LISP stands for list processing language. The following are examples of lists:

(2 4 6 8)	[1]
(cat dog canary goldfish hamster)	[2]
(george)	[3]
(feb (apr jun sep nov) (jan mar may jul aug oct dec))	[4]
(x tsv lan)	[5]
(b b (egg) 67 (h g (f)) house (r))	[6]
(+ 3 2)	[7]
()	[8]

A list is a sequence of items or **elements** enclosed in a pair of parentheses. Each element in a list can itself be either an atom or a list. Thus, in example 6, the atom *67*, and the lists *(egg)* and *(h g (f))* are all elements of the list *(b b (egg) 67 (h g (f)) house (r))*. The atoms *h* and *g* and the list *(f)*, however, are not considered elements of the list. Instead, they are elements of the list *(h g (f))*, which is embedded in the larger list. Lists can consist of a single element (as in example 3), or many elements; there can even be lists with no elements (as in example 8). A list with no elements is called the **empty list** or *nil*. Finally, note that the order of the elements in the list is important. We can talk about which element is first or second and the list *(2 4 6 8)* is different from the list *(6 2 8 4)*, because the order of the elements in the list is different.

Lists are extremely important in symbolic processing because they provide a mechanism for grouping symbols together. Lists can be of any arbitrary length and since we can embed lists within lists, they can be used to represent information of arbitrary complexity. As we will see shortly, LISP provides functions that make it easy to add items to lists and remove items from lists — operations that are necessary if we wish to update lists and retrieve information from them. Notice that by our definition of lists, function calls, such as example 7 above, are also lists. This is just one example of how lists can be used to group symbols into meaningful structures. Shopping lists, mathematical sets or any collection of a finite number of things can be represented as lists.

Balancing lists

It is important to balance the left and right parentheses in a list; that is, there must be one right parenthesis for each left parenthesis in the list. If you examine the following list, you will see that it has balanced parentheses; that is, there is one right parenthesis for each left parenthesis.

(A (B (C)) D)

Now consider the following "unbalanced" version of the preceding list:

(A (B (C) D)

If you compare this to the preceding list, you can see that in this unbalanced list a right parenthesis has been omitted after *C*. Rather than treating *(B (C))* as an embedded list in the whole list, LISP will treat *(B (C) D)* as the sublist, using the right parenthesis after *D* to balance the left parenthesis before *B*. If you tried to type this into most LISPs, they would not respond until you typed one more right parenthesis to balance the remaining unbalanced left parenthesis.
   Now consider a second "unbalanced" version of the original list.

(A (B (C))) D)

This one has too many right parentheses after *C*. LISP would treat the third right parenthesis after *C* as the one that balances the left parenthesis before *A*. Therefore it would treat *(A (B (C)))* as a complete list and would treat *D)* as an illegal expression because there is no left parenthesis to pair with the right parenthesis.

LISP Exercises

1.6 How many elements does each of the eight example lists on p. 8 have?
1.7 i) Can a list have more right parentheses than left parentheses?
    ii) Can a list have more left parentheses than right parentheses?
1.8 Consider the list: *((a (b c)) d (e (f (g)) (i j)))*
     i) What is the first element?
     ii) What is the second element?
     iii) What is the third element?
     iv) What is the second embedded list?
     v) How many elements does the first embedded list have?
     vi) What is the second element in the second embedded list?

Functions for Operating on Lists

Lists enable us to represent complex information, but we need functions that can operate on lists in order to make use of that information. For example, if

Table 1.2. List functions

Function calls	Value returned	Operation
(car '(c d f))	c	Return the first element in the list
(cdr '(c d f))	(d f)	Return the list with the first element removed
(cons 'c '(d f))	(c d f)	Insert the first argument at the beginning of the second argument
(list 'c '(d f))	(c (d f))	Make a list out of the arguments

we have a list that represents the positions of the pieces on a chessboard, we need functions that will allow us to examine the contents of that list in order to choose our next move. Then we will need functions that can modify lists to represent the results of that move. LISP provides many functions that operate on lists. Table 1.2 introduces four basic functions that perform list operations. These functions are extremely important; you should not go beyond this chapter until you understand how they work. If you have questions after doing the exercises that follow, you should experiment with the different function calls in your LISP environment to make sure you understand how each function works.

Before we discuss these functions, notice that each of the arguments in the function calls is quoted. The quote mark tells the LISP interpreter to treat an expression as a **literal expression**. For example, the quote in '(c d f) tells LISP not to evaluate this argument as a function call, but rather to treat it simply as a list of three atoms. We will discuss quotes in more detail in a later section to clarify when they are needed.

Extracting information from lists: car and cdr

The first two functions, car and cdr allow us to examine the contents of lists. The function car always takes one argument, which must be a list, and returns the first element in the list. Remember, that first element may be a list rather than an atom. For example, the first element in the list ((a b) c (d e)) is the list (a b), so (car '((a b) c (e f))) returns (a b).

The function cdr performs a complementary operation. It also accepts one argument, which must be a list, and returns the **tail** of the list. That is, it returns a version of the list with the first element deleted. LISP provides other functions that extract information from lists, but as will become clear when you begin doing exercises, these two functions are actually sufficient tools to examine all the information in a list.

Finally, consider one more example. What is the value of the expression

(car (cdr '((a b) c d)))

This can be confusing. Does LISP apply *car* to *((a b) c d)* first, which yields *(a b)*, and then apply *cdr* to yield *(b)*? Or, is *cdr* applied first, yielding *(c d)*, followed by *car* to yield *c*? This is not confusing if we remember the point made earlier: LISP evaluates the arguments to a function before it evaluates the function. In this example, *(cdr '((a b) c d))* is the argument to *car*, so the expression *(cdr '((a b) c d))* will be evaluated, yielding *(c d)*, and then *car* will be applied to that value, yielding *c*. This is an important point:

> LISP evaluates expressions such as these "inside out"; it evaluates the embedded function call(s) before the outer function calls.

If we wanted to take the *car* of the list before the *cdr*, we would write

(cdr (car '((a b) c d)))

and LISP would return *(b)*.

Building lists: *cons* and *list*

The function *cons* inserts an item at the front of a list. This function takes two arguments; the second argument must be a list, but the first argument can be either an atom or a list. The function *cons* returns a new list in which the first argument has been inserted at the beginning of the second argument. If you understand *car*, *cdr*, and *cons*, the following example should be clear.

> = ⟩ *(cons (car '(cat dog fox)) (cdr '(cat dog fox)))*
> (cat dog fox)

The first step in evaluating this function call is to evaluate the arguments. The first argument, *(car '(cat dog fox))* returns *cat*. The second argument, *(cdr '(cat dog fox))* returns *(dog fox)*. When we apply *cons* to these arguments, we insert *cat* at the beginning of *(dog fox)*, yielding *(cat dog fox)* again.

Notice, you can *cons* together an atom and a list, or you can *cons* two lists.

> = ⟩ *(cons 'x '(1 2 3))*
> (x 1 2 3)
> = ⟩ *(cons '(a b) '(f g))*
> ((a b) f g)

In either case, you make a new list where the first argument to *cons* becomes the first element of the resulting list.

Finally, the function *list* allows us to create new lists. This function can take any number of arguments, which can be atoms or lists, and returns a new list by "wrapping" parentheses around the arguments. It is important to see the difference between *cons* and *list*:

```
=> (list 'a '(b c))
(a (b c))
=> (cons 'a '(b c))
(a b c)
```

The call to *list* creates a new list, with *a* and *(b c)* as elements, while *cons* actually "opens up" the list *(b c)* and inserts *a* at the front. You can also use *cons* to put an item into a list by itself. That is, we can use *cons* to create the list *(piano)* from the item *piano*. To do this, you must start with the empty list, which can be coded as *nil* or *()* in LISP. Here is how *cons* and *list* work with *nil*.

```
=> (cons 'd nil)
(d)
=> (list 'd nil)
(d nil)
```

Quoting arguments

LISP can interpret lists and most atoms in more than one way. We have already seen that lists can be interpreted literally or as function calls, and, of course, it makes a big difference which way a list is treated. Consider the following example in which we try to take the *car* of the list *(+ 2 3)* under both interpretations:

```
=> (cons '(+ 2 3) '(4))
((+ 2 3) 4)
=> (cons (+ 2 3) '(4))
(5 4)
```

In the first case, the argument *(+ 2 3)* is quoted, so LISP treats it as a literal list, and the function *cons* inserts it as the first item of the list. In the second case, the argument is not quoted, so the list is treated as a function call, and that function call returns the value *5*, which is inserted by *cons* as the first element of the list.

LISP Exercises

1.9 Write a function call that will take the list *(c d e)*, and return the first element, which is c.

1.10 Write a function call that will take the list *(1 2 c)* and return it with the number *1* removed. The resulting list, *(2 c)*, is sometimes referred to as the tail of the original list.

1.11 Write a function call that inserts the atom c into the the front of the list *(e f)*. The result will be the list *(c e f)*.

1.12 Write a function call that takes the lists *(3 2)* and *(b c)* and produces the complex list *((3 2) (b c))*.

1.13 Make a list of transportation vehicles out of two lists. The first is a list of nonmotor vehicles, *(bike feet)*, and the second is a list of motor vehicles, *(car bus)*. Your final list should be *((bike feet) car bus)*.

1.14 Write a function call that adds 4 to 2 and produces 6. However, you cannot just type the number 4. Instead, you must get 4 from the list *(4 3)* so that you can add it to 2.

1.15 Write a function call that returns the second element, *dog*, from the list *(horse dog cat)*. You will need to use more than one LISP function.

Variables

Like lists, atoms can be interpreted in two ways by LISP. As with a list, an atom will be taken literally when quoted. LISP will treat an unquoted atom as a variable. **Variables** are symbols that stand for another LISP expression. Variables play an important role in any programming language.

If you look back at earlier examples, you will see that numbers and *nil* are not quoted. Numbers are atoms, but they cannot serve as variables. They always represent their numerical value, and so they do not need to be quoted. Similarly, *nil* is a special symbol (which LISP treats as both an atom and a list) and does not need to be quoted. Except for numbers and a few special symbols like *nil*, all unquoted atoms are treated as variables.

The expression that a variable stands for is called the **value** of the variable. We can assign a value to an atom with the LISP operator *setq*. For example, we can **assign** the value *100* to the atom *x* as follows:

```
= > (setq x 100)
100
```

As you can see, *setq* takes two arguments. When *setq* is called, it evaluates the second argument, assigns the result to the first argument and returns the value of the second argument. The first argument must be a non-numerical atom. That argument is not evaluated. Now we can use the atom *x* in LISP expressions to stand for the value 100. Here are some examples of how *x* can be used:

```
=⟩ (cons 'x '(a b))
(x a b)
=⟩ (cons x '(a b))
(100 a b)
```

In the first case, *x* is quoted, so LISP treats it literally, even though it has been assigned a value, and *x* is inserted into the list *(a b)*. In the second case, *x* is not quoted, so when *x* is evaluated, LISP treats it as a variable and returns its value, which is *100*. Thus, in the second case, *100* is inserted into the beginning of the list *(a b)*.

In everyday life we think of values as numbers, but remember, a value can be any LISP expression. A variable can only have a single value at any time, but we can still use a variable to stand for a collection of things by putting those things in a list. Thus we can assign the variable *hold* the value *(fork knife spoon)*, and then use it like this:

```
=⟩ (setq hold '(fork knife spoon))      [1]
(fork knife spoon)
=⟩ hold                                  [2]
(fork knife spoon)
=⟩ 'hold                                 [3]
hold
=⟩ (car hold)                            [4]
fork
=⟩ (cdr hold)                            [5]
(knife spoon)
=⟩ (list '(plate bowl glass) hold)       [6]
((plate bowl glass) (fork knife spoon))
```

In the first line of the example, we assigned the value *(fork knife spoon)* to the variable *hold*. Then, when we typed *hold* without a quote in line 2, LISP evaluated it as a variable, and returned its value *(fork knife spoon)*. When we typed *'hold* in line 3, however, LISP treated it as a literal atom and returned *hold*. Since the unquoted atom *hold* now stands for (or has the value of) the list, we can use it as an argument for list processing functions like *car*, *cdr*, and *list* in lines 4 through 6.

As you can see in line 6, if we *list '(plate bowl glass)* and *hold*, LISP returns *((plate bowl glass) (fork knife spoon))*. This example suggests one of the advantages of variables. If we have a long complex list such as *'((The boy) (with a red hat) (started to run) (down the street))* that we want to use repeatedly, we can avoid typing the list repeatedly by assigning the list to a variable, such as *sentence*. Then we can use the variable *sentence* to refer to the list. Thus a program written to understand natural-language texts might have a variable whose value is a list of individual sentences, each of which is a list of phrases, where each phrase is a list of words (atoms).

Assigning a value to a variable is frequently referred to as **binding** the value to the variable or **setting** the variable, so you should be familiar with those terms. For example, if you type an atom without quoting it and that atom has not been assigned a value, LISP will respond with an error message as shown:

```
=> egg
Unbound variable: egg
```

This error message indicates that the variable *egg* has not been bound to a value.

Resetting a Variable's Value

If we set a variable (i.e., bind a value to it), the variable will keep that value until we **reset** it. That is, the variable will keep the value until we explicitly assign it a new value. We can use the variable as an argument in other function calls, but those function calls will not change its value. For example,

```
=> (setq data '(a b c))
(a b c)
=> data
(a b c)
=> (cdr data)
(b c)
=> data
(a b c)
=> (setq data (cdr data))
(b c)
=> data
(b c)
```

Note that the variable *data* did not lose its value when we used it as an argument to *cdr*. Using *car*, *cdr*, +, or any of the other functions you will learn in the first part of this book will not change the value of a variable. We had to explicitly reset the variable *data*, to *(cdr data)* with *setq* to achieve this.

LISP Exercises

1.16   i) Can an atom be a variable?
ii) Can a number be a variable?
iii) Can a list be a variable?
iv) Can an atom have no value?
v) Can an atom have more than one value at the same time?
vi) Can a variable have itself as a value?
vii) Can an expression such as *(a b c)* be the value of more than one variable?

1.17 Write a LISP function call that sets the variable *x* to the list *(c (d e))*. Before you set *x*, it will be unbound. After you set *x*, it will have the value *(c (d e))*.

1.18 Write code to give *y* the value *(a b)*. Instead of writing *'(a b)*, use a LISP function to put *a* and *b* in a list.

1.19 Make the list *(d b)*. You should get *b* from the variable *y*, which has the value *(a b)*.

1.20 (a) Set *num* to have the value *4*.
(b) Now reset *num* to have the value *5*. You should do this by adding *1* to the current value of *num*.
(c) Set *w* to have the value *(a b c)*.
(d) Now *num* has the value *5* and *w* has the value *(a b c)*. How can you get a list that is the result of replacing the first element of *w*'s value with *num*'s value? You should write a function call that returns *(5 b c)*. Note that the value of the variables will not change when you type this function call.

1.21 (a) Now *x* has the value *(c (d e))* and *y* has the value *(a b)*. Using the variables *x* and *y*, produce the list *(c a b)*.
(b) Now modify the function call you just wrote to reset the variable *y* to have the value *(c a b)*.

1.22 (a) An accounting firm keeps track of the top two soft-drink manufacturers by setting the variable *neworder*. Set the variable *neworder* to have the initial value of *(coke pepsi)*.
(b) Recently Pepsi has increased sales and is ahead of Coke. So you need to write a LISP function call that will store the new list *(pepsi coke)* in the variable *neworder*. You have to get both the atom *pepsi* and the atom *coke* individually by using the old value of *neworder* — the list *(coke pepsi)*.

1.23 Set *z* to the result of dividing *18* by the square of *3*. Use a function call to calculate the square of *3*.

1.24 (a) Set a variable called *data* to contain the number of deposits, 5, and withdrawals, 6, of a bank customer for December.

(b) Up through November the bank customer had 10 deposits. Add the number of deposits for December (get it from the variable *data*) to the number of prior deposits.

In this chapter we have learned some of the basic functions that LISP provides to perform operations, and we have learned how to call those functions. We have also begun to discuss how we can use lists to represent complex information and how we can use variables to store those lists. This is the first step toward writing "intelligent" programs. In the next chapter we will take another step in the direction of writing, or creating, such programs.

Summary of LISP Functions

+ This function accepts one or more arguments and returns the sum of the arguments. The arguments must be numbers. This function can be called with no arguments, in which case it returns 0.

Example: *(+ 14 22 5)* returns *41*

− This function accepts one or two numerical arguments. If it is called with two arguments, it returns the difference of the two arguments. If this function is called with one argument, the negative of the argument is returned.

Example: *(− 14 6)* returns *8*

* This function accepts one or more numerical arguments and returns the product of the arguments. If this function is called with no arguments, it returns 1.

Example: *(* 3 8)* returns *24*

/ This function accepts two arguments and returns the result of dividing the first by the second.

Example: *(/ 100 25)* returns *4*

car This function takes one argument, which must be a list. It returns the first element in the list.

Example: *(car '(a b c))* returns *a*

cdr   This function takes one argument, which must be a list. It returns the tail of the list; that is, it returns a version of the list in which the first element has been deleted.

Example: *(cdr '(a b c))* returns *(b c)*

cons   This function takes two arguments, the second of which must be a list. It inserts its first argument as the first element of its second argument.

Example: *(cons 'a '(b c))* returns *(a b c)*

list   This function accepts one or more arguments. It places all of its arguments in a list. This function can be called with no arguments, in which case it returns *nil.*

Example: *(list 'a '(b c))* returns *(a (b c))*

setq   This function takes two arguments, the first of which is an unquoted variable. It binds the value of the second argument to the first argument. It returns the value of its second argument.

Example: *(setq x '(a b c))* causes *x* to have the value *(a b c)* and returns the value *(a b c)*

Glossary   **argument**   A value passed to a function.
assign   Make a variable stand for a specific value.
atom   A string of letters, numbers, or punctuation marks.
bind   Make a variable stand for a specific value.
call   Cause a function to execute.
computer program   A set of instructions, written in a computer language, that a computer can follow to perform a task.
element   An atom or list that is a member of a list.
embedded function call   A function call that appears embedded as an argument to another function call.
empty list   A list with no elements, denoted *nil.*
evaluation   The process by which LISP assigns a value to an expression.
expression   An atom or a list.
function   LISP procedures that operate on arguments to produce a value.
function call   A request to the LISP interpreter to apply a function to a list of arguments.

LISP environment   The system on a computer used to evaluate LISP expressions.

LISP interpreter   A system that executes programs written in LISP.

list   A sequence of items or elements enclosed in parentheses.

literal expression   An expression that is not evaluated by LISP.

reset   Change the value of a variable.

returning a value   When a function call evaluates to an expression, it is said to return a value.

set   Make a variable stand for a specific value.

symbolic expression   Atoms and lists.

tail   All but the first element of a list.

variable   An atom that has been assigned a value.

value   What a variable stands for.

Defining LISP Functions

In the last chapter, you learned about some LISP functions, and you learned how to call those functions. You also learned how to combine those functions to accomplish a variety of tasks. In this chapter you will learn some new built-in LISP functions, and how to define your own functions when there are no built-in LISP functions to do exactly what you want.

Why Define Functions?

Let us consider why you might want to define your own functions. One of the functions you learned about in Chapter 1 was *cons*. That function inserts its first argument at the beginning of its second argument. Suppose, however, that you wanted to insert two items at the beginning of a list. LISP does not have a built-in function to accomplish this, but we can accomplish it by combining functions we already know.

Think about how you could do these insertions with the functions you know, then consider the following examples:

```
=> (setq fruit '(apple cantaloupe grape))    [1]
(apple cantaloupe grape)
=> (cons 'orange (cons 'plum fruit))         [2]
(orange plum apple cantaloupe grape)
=> fruit                                     [3]
(apple cantaloupe grape)
```

We began by assigning the list to the variable *fruit* in line 1. That saves some typing in the subsequent function calls. In these function calls, the atom *fruit* is not quoted, since it is a variable, but the atoms we want taken literally are quoted — *'orange* and *'plum*.

Now consider how we accomplished the insertion task. In line 2, we added two items to the beginning of a list. We *cons*ed one item into the list, and then *cons*ed the second item in. The items were added to the front of the list in the order that the two function calls were evaluated. Since the embedded *cons* was applied first, *plum* was added to the front, and then the outer *cons* put *orange* at the front of the list. After performing the task, we typed *fruit* in line 3 to demonstrate that the value of *fruit* has not changed. If we wanted to save the new list, we would need to use *setq* to assign the result of our function call to a variable.

We have figured out how to add two items to the beginning of a list, but suppose we want to perform this operation repeatedly with different elements and lists. Each time, we would have to type the same pattern, with whatever arguments we wanted. For example:

```
=> (cons 'train (cons 'truck '(bus boat car plane)))
(train truck bus boat car plane)
=> (cons 'dress (cons 'shirt '(jacket (shoes socks))))
(dress shirt jacket (shoes socks))
```

It would be far more convenient if we had a function, perhaps called *cons-two*, that did what we wanted. For example:

```
=> (cons-two 'train 'truck '(bus boat car plane))
(train truck bus boat car plane)
```

In this chapter, you will learn how you can define your own functions in LISP such as *cons-two*. After you have defined a function, you will be able to call it just as you do built-in LISP functions. So, when you define a function such as *cons-two*, you can use it again and again to add two elements onto a list, saving you from typing the same long function calls over and over again.

Defining Your Own LISP Functions

To define a function, you need to do three things:

1. Give a name to the function, so that you can use it later in a function call.
2. Specify how many arguments the function accepts.
3. Specify what you want the function to do.

LISP provides a special form, *defun*, that allows you to define new functions. A call to *defun* takes three arguments, one for each component of the function definition: (1) the **function name**, (2) the **function parameters**, and (3) the **function body**. Here is the template for a call to *defun*:

```
(defun ⟨function-name⟩ ([parameters...])
    ⟨function-body⟩)
```

To illustrate the use of *defun*, consider the following example. Suppose we wanted to define a function that accepts one number as an argument and multiplies that number by two. A good name for that function would be *double*. We can define this function with the following call to *defun*:

```
= ⟩ (defun double (num)
       (* num 2))
double
```

As indicated in the template, this call contains three arguments (an atom followed by two lists). None of these three arguments is quoted, because *defun* automatically treats each of its arguments as literal. Let us examine each of these three arguments in more detail.

The Function Name

The first argument of a *defun* must always be an atom, which will serve as the name of the new function. Thus the name of our new function is *double*.

The Function Parameters

The second argument in a *defun* is the **parameter list**. The elements in this list are the **parameters** of the function we are defining. In our example, there is just one element in the list, *num*, so the function *double* has just one parameter. Parameters are necessary so that you can describe in general terms what the function is going to compute. To do this, you need to be able to refer to whatever argument or arguments the function will be passed. Parameters are actually variables. When you call a function you have defined, each parameter in the definition of the function is assigned the value of one of the arguments in the function call. For example, if you call *(double 15)*, the argument, *15*, is assigned to the parameter *num*. These parameters are used as variables in the function body.

The Function Body

The third argument in our example call to *defun* is also a list, called the **function body**. The function body is a LISP expression that uses the function parameters to specify what the function should compute. When the function is called, the function body is evaluated like any LISP expression. The value that the function returns is the value returned by the function body.

As you can see in the example, the parameters of a function appear in the function body. They serve as variables in the body, so they are not quoted. Recall that when the function is called, each parameter is bound to an argument. As a result, when LISP evaluates the function body, it essentially replaces each parameter with the value of its argument. In our example, the body of the function consists of the function call *(* num 2)*. When we call *(double (+ 5 10))*, LISP assigns the value *15* to the parameter *num*, and then computes *(* 15 2)*.

After we define the function *double*, we can use it like any predefined LISP function. For example,

```
=)(double 7)
14
=)(setq hold (double (+ 5 10)))
30
=)(double hold)
60
```

Table 2.1 includes a detailed example to demonstrate how the parameters of a defined function get their values from the arguments of the function call.

Let us consider a second, more complicated, example. Let us define a function that will insert an item into the second position of a list. First, we need to choose a name for the function; we will call it *insert-second*. Then we need to choose parameters. When we call *insert-second*, we will need two arguments — the item to be inserted and the list into which it is inserted. So, we will need two parameters. We can call them *item* and *oldlist*. Finally, we need to figure out the body of the function. The body will be

```
(cons (car oldlist) (cons item (cdr oldlist))).
```

So, we can define *insert-second* as follows:

```
(defun insert-second (item oldlist)
     (cons (car oldlist) (cons item (cdr oldlist))))
```

Table 2.1. An example of how function parameters get their values from function arguments

Function definition

=> *(defun double (num)* *(* num 2))*	The parameter in this function definition is *num*.

Function call

=> *(double (+ 5 10))*	The argument in this function call is *(+ 5 10)*

Steps in evaluating the function call *(double (+ 5 10))*:

1) The argument of the function call, *(+ 5 10)*, is evaluated.
   The result of *(+ 5 10)* is *15*.
2) The function *double* is applied to the value *15* as follows:
   a)   The value of the argument *15* is assigned to the parameter *num*. (Remember, *num* is a variable.)
   b)   The body of the function, *(* num 2)*, is evaluated as follows:
      i)   The variable *num* is evaluated. *num* was assigned the value *15*, so *num* evaluates to *15*.
      ii) The number *2* evaluates to itself: *2*.
      iii) The function * is applied to its arguments *15* and *2*, and returns *30*.
      iv) The function *double* returns the value *30*.

LISP Exercises

2.1 Let us consider a call to *insert-second*. Assume that the variable *units* has been assigned the value *(inches yards miles)*. Answer the following questions about what happens when you call *insert-second*.
   i) What are the parameters in the following function definition?
      => *(defun insert-second (item oldlist)*
         (cons (car oldlist) (cons item (cdr oldlist))))
   ii) What are the arguments in the following function call?
      => *(insert-second 'feet units)*
   iii) The first step in evaluating the function call is to evaluate the arguments. What does each of the arguments evaluate to?
   iv) Then the function *insert-second* is applied to the arguments. First the argument values are assigned to the parameters; then the body of the function is evaluated.

a) What value is assigned to each parameter?

b) What is the value of *(car oldlist)*, the first argument to *cons*?

c) What is the value of the second argument to *cons*, *(cons item (cdr oldlist))*?

d) Now that you have evaluated the arguments, apply *cons* to its arguments. What is returned by this call to *cons*?

e) Finally, what value is returned by the call to *insert-second*?

Local and Global Variables

Parameters are typically the hardest thing to grasp in defining new functions. Remember that parameters are actually variables. However, we do not assign them values with the function *setq*. Instead, each parameter is assigned a value automatically when the function is called. Specifically, each variable is assigned the value of one of the arguments in the function call. Since parameters are variables, parameters are always atoms, regardless of whether the value of the argument that will be assigned to them is a list or a number or a non-numerical atom.

There is another important distinction between parameters and the variables we discussed in Chapter 1. Parameters are **local variables**, while the variables in Chapter 1 are **global variables**. Parameters are called local variables, because they only have values within the context of the function. Consider the following example:

```
= ) (defun double (num)
        (* num 2))
double
= ) (double 7)
14
= ) num
Unbound variable: num
```

When *double* was called in this example, the parameter *num* was assigned the value 7. But, after the function call has been evaluated, if you try to get the value of *num*, you get an error message, because that value was only assigned to the parameter during the execution of *double*. After *(double 7)* was evaluated and returned *14*, the parameter *num* lost the value it was given — it again became unbound. The value a parameter acquires is therefore local to the function using the parameter. The variables in Chapter 1 are called **global**, because they are not set just within the context of a specific function defined by us.

Recall that when we set a variable in Chapter 1, it retained its value until that value was changed with another call to *setq*.

Printing a Function Definition

It is often necessary to check to see how you have defined a function. One important reason is that functions do not always work quite the way we want them to, and we need to examine their definitions to discover why. Most LISP dialects have a function that allows you to print a function definition on your terminal screen. For example, in Franz LISP, this function is *pp*:

```
= ) (pp cons-two)
(defun cons-two (item1 item2 oldlist)
   (cons item1 (cons item2 oldlist)))
```

This function prints the function definition just as they have been displayed throughout this chapter, with the name and parameters on the first line and the function body on the next line. This is called "pretty-printing" (hence the name of the function), and is designed to make it easy for people to read the function.*

An analogous function in MacLISP is called *grindef*. Common LISP does not come with a function as convenient as *pp*, but you can define your own *pp* function. (This definition uses the LISP operator *defmacro* that you won't encounter until Chapter 13. Don't worry about how it works for now).†

```
(defmacro pp (fun)
      (list 'pprint
         (list 'quote (list 'defun fun
                 (cadr (symbol-function fun))
                 (caddr (caddr (symbol-function fun)))))))
```

Now do the following five problems in your LISP system. After you define each function, print it out to make sure the definition is correct, and try it out with some arguments.

---

*It is not necessary to type function definitions in this format. LISP only checks the way the parentheses balance. It does not treat the return key any differently than it does the space bar in processing function definitions.

†In some Common LISP variants (e.g., Golden Common LISP) you need to define *pp* as

```
(defmacro pp (fun)
      (list 'pprint
         (list 'quote (append (list 'defun fun)
                 (cdr (symbol-function fun))))))
```

LISP Exercises

2.2 Define a function called *first-elem*. Given any list, it returns the first element of that list. For example,

(first-elem '(a b c)) returns *a*.

2.3 Define a function called *second-elem*. It returns the second element of a list. For example,

(second-elem '(a b c)) returns *b*.

2.4 Write a function called *replace-first* that replaces the first element of a list with a new element. This function takes two parameters — the new element and the list. For example,

(replace-first 'rings '(ties hats pants)) returns *(rings hats pants)*.

2.5 Define a function called *ftoc*, which takes as its argument a degree reading in Fahrenheit and returns the Celsius equivalent. First you should translate the scale by subtracting 32, since 32° Fahrenheit = 0° Celsius. Then you need to change the scale by dividing the result by 1.8. For example,

(ftoc 68) returns *20*.

2.6 Define a function called *sqr* that returns a list of the perimeter and the area of a square, given the length of one side. For example,

(sqr 2) returns *(8 4)*.

Algorithms

Now you have learned to define your own functions. The remainder of this chapter introduces some new LISP functions and gives you practice putting together combinations of functions in order to accomplish more complicated tasks. As mentioned in Chapter 1, a substantial part of learning to program involves learning not just how functions work, but how to use them to compute desired results. The procedure by which a function computes a result is called the **algorithm** for the function. For example, our algorithm for inserting an item as the second element of a list was to insert the first element of the list into the list that results from inserting the new element into the rest of the original list. Notice that we can describe the algorithm without referring to function names. The LISP function, *insert-second*, that we wrote earlier, is said to **implement** the algorithm.

Additional List Manipulation Functions

Below are three new functions useful for manipulating lists.

Function calls	Value returned	Operation
(append '(a b) '(c))	*(a b c)*	Merge two or more lists into a single list
(reverse '(c d e))	*(e d c)*	Reverse the order of the elements in the argument
(last '(g h i))	*(i)*	Return the list consisting of the last item in the argument

There are some important points to be made about each of these functions. The function *append* is used to construct lists. It takes two or more arguments, each of which must be a list. The function constructs a new list containing the elements of each of the arguments. Consider the following examples:

```
=> (append '(peas) '(carrots celery) '(broccoli))
(peas carrots celery broccoli)
=> (append '(Dave (Jack Sue)) '((Anne Ted) Mandy Richard))
(Dave (Jack Sue) (Anne Ted) Mandy Richard)
```

Notice that the elements in the argument lists are not changed. That is, the elements *Dave*, *(Jack Sue)*, *(Anne Ted)*, *Mandy*, and *Richard* were combined into a new list, but the atoms *Jack* and *Sue* were not taken out of the embedded list *(Jack Sue)*.

Study the following example to see how *append* is distinguished from *cons* and *list*. It is important to be able to choose the right function from among these three in constructing a list.

```
=> (list '(a b) '(c d))
((a b) (c d))
=> (cons '(a b) '(c d))
((a b) c d)
=> (append '(a b) '(c d))
(a b c d)
```

The function *cons* always takes two arguments and inserts the first argument at the beginning of the second. The function *list* can take one or more arguments, and makes a new list by "wrapping parentheses" around its arguments.

The arguments may be atoms or lists, and *list* preserves the arguments; that is, if an argument is a list, it remains an embedded list in the new list. The function *append* makes a new list by "removing the parentheses" from around each of its arguments and putting all the elements into one long list.*

The function *reverse* takes one argument, which must be a list. It returns a list in which the order of the elements has been reversed. However, it does not reverse the order of elements within any embedded lists.

```
=> (reverse '(shirt dress socks shoes jacket))
(jacket shoes socks dress shirt)
=> (reverse '(shirt dress (socks shoes) jacket))
(jacket (socks shoes) dress shirt)
```

The function *last* also takes one argument, which must be a list. It returns the tail of the argument consisting of the last item. That is, it does not return just the last item. Instead, it returns a list with one element, which is the last item of the argument. Calling *last* is equivalent to taking successive *cdr*s of a list until only one element remains.

LISP Exercises

2.7 Define a function called *listone*. It takes an atom, and returns a list containing that atom. For example,

(listone 'a) returns *(a)*.

Try to code this function without using the function *list*.

2.8 Write a function called *back* that returns two copies of a list, where each copy is the original reversed. For example,

(back '(a b c)) returns *(c b a c b a)*.

2.9 Define a function called *ends*, that has one argument and returns a list containing the first and last items in that argument. For example,

(ends '(a b c d)) returns *(a d)*.

---

*Actually, *list* and *append* can be called with no arguments, in which case each would return the empty list, *nil*. In addition *append* can be called with one argument, in which case it returns only that argument. The occasions for calling these functions in this way are rare. On the other hand, *list* can be quite useful with one argument, because you might want to make a list containing that argument.

2.10 Define a function called *pal* that takes a single list as an argument and returns a palindrome that is twice as long. A palindrome is a list that reads the same forward and backward. For example,

(pal '(a b c)) returns *(a b c c b a)*.

2.11 (a) Write a function called *snoc* that is the opposite of *cons*. Instead of inserting an item into the front of a list, it inserts the item at the end. For example,

(snoc 'd '(a b c)) returns *(a b c d)*.

Use the function *append* in your definition of *snoc*.
(b) Write another version of *snoc*, but this time do it without using the function *append*.

2.12 Define a function called *rotater*. It rotates its argument list one element to the right. For example,

(rotater '(a b c d)) returns *(d a b c)*.

In this chapter you have acquired an essential tool for writing programs; you can now define your own functions. This chapter demonstrates a second reason why variables are extremely important in programming languages. By using variables (parameters) to stand for arguments, we can define general programs to perform computations. Then, having defined them, we can call them repeatedly with specific values (arguments), without having to type the function definition each time. In future chapters we will introduce additional LISP functions that can give the functions we write still greater flexibility.

**Summary
of LISP
Functions**

append   This function accepts one or more arguments, each of which must be a list. It merges the elements of the arguments into a single list. The function can be called with no arguments, in which case it returns *nil*.

Example: *(append '(a b) '(c) '(d e f))* returns *(a b c d e f) defun*   This special form is used to define functions. It takes three arguments: an atom which serves as the function name, a list of parameters, and an expression which is the function body.

Example: *(defun half (num) (l num 2.0))*

last   This function accepts one argument, which must be a list, and returns a list containing the last element in the argument.

Example: *(last '(a b c d e f))* returns *(f)*

pp   This function accepts a function name as an argument and prints the definition of the function. It must be defined in Common LISP.

Example: *(pp half)* prints
(defun half (num)
*   (l num 2.0))*

reverse   This function accepts one argument, which must be a list. It returns a list containing the elements of the argument in opposite order.

Example: *(reverse '(a b c d e f))* returns *(f e d c b a)*

Glossary

algorithm   The general method or plan for achieving the desired result in a function.

function body   The LISP expression in the function definition that specifies what the function is to do.

function parameters   The variables in a function definition that take the arguments as values when the new function is called.

global variable   A variable that is assigned its value by *setq* outside of any function definition and retains the value until it is explicitly reset.

implement an algorithm   Write LISP code that performs the algorithm.

local variable   A variable that retains its value only during the execution of a particular function.

parameter list   A list of the parameters the function will use.

Predicates and Conditionals

3

In Chapters 1 and 2 we discussed a variety of built-in LISP functions, and you defined some functions of your own. One property that all these functions have in common is that each time they are called they perform the exact same operations. That is, *car* always returns the first element in its argument, and *double* always multiplies its argument by 2. However, in programming it is also important to be able to write functions that do **conditional processing**, that is functions that perform different actions under different circumstances. To give just one example of why such functions are important, it would be nice if we could define *double* so that it tries to multiply its argument only after ensuring that the argument is a number. If we inadvertently give the function a non-number, we could code the function so that it simply returns an answer such as *non-number*. In this chapter we will discuss the LISP functions that allow us to do conditional processing.

Conditional Processing

In order to do conditional processing, a function needs to be able to perform **tests**, and to perform actions depending on the outcome of those tests. In the case of *double*, for example, we need to be able to test whether the value of the argument is a number. If it is, we want to perform multiplication; if not, we want to return *non-number*. LISP provides a number of functions, called **predicates** that are designed specifically to perform tests. In this chapter we will learn how to employ predicates in conditional processing.

Predicates

Predicates take arguments like other functions, but they return information about their arguments. For example, the predicate *atom* takes one argument and tests whether the argument is an atom or not. If the argument is an atom, *atom* returns *t*. If not, *atom* returns *nil*. The predicate *listp* also accepts one argument and performs a test with a *t* or *nil* result — it returns *t* if the argument is a list and *nil* if the argument is not a list.

Here are some examples:

```
=> (atom 'dog)
t
=> (atom '(dog))
nil
=> (listp 'dog)
nil
=> (listp '(dog))
t
```

Technically, a predicate is a function that returns one of two values — ''true'' or ''false.'' The special symbol *nil* is used to represent ''false,'' and the special symbol *t* is often used to represent ''true.'' However, as we will see, the important distinction in LISP is between *nil* and non-*nil* values, hence any non-*nil* value is really considered to be ''true.''

Note that neither *t* nor *nil* needs to be quoted, because, like numbers, they evaluate to themselves. Both *t* and *nil* have the form of atoms, and if we test them with the predicate *atom*, we get the expected result:

```
=> (atom t)
t
=> (atom 'nil)
t
```

However, if we test them with the *listp* predicate we get a surprising result:

```
= ) (listp t)
nil
= ) (listp nil)
t
```

The *listp* predicate reports that *nil* is a list! Remember that in Chapter 1 we stated that *nil* is synonymous with the empty list (). Since *nil* essentially plays two roles, as the symbol for false and as the empty list, LISP considers *nil* or () to be both an atom and a list.

Like other functions, predicates can take arguments that are literal atoms, literal lists, variables, or function calls. Here are some examples with variables and function calls:

```
= ) (listp (cons 'a '(b)))
t
= ) (atom (list 'a 'b 'c))
nil
= ) (setq x '(a b c))
(a b c)
= ) (listp x)
t
= ) (atom (car x))
t
```

LISP provides many other predicates that take a single argument and test the nature of that argument. Three of these predicates that are very useful are *numberp*, *zerop*, and *null*. As its name suggests, *numberp* tests whether or not its argument is a number. Here are some examples:

```
= ) (numberp 10)
t
= ) (numberp '(10))
nil
= ) (numberp 'chris)
nil
= ) (numberp -6.5743)
t
```

The function *zerop* tests whether its argument evaluates to zero. For example:

```
= ) (zerop 5)
nil
= ) (zerop nil)
nil
```

```
= ) (zerop 0)
t
= ) (zerop (- 5 5))
t
```

Finally, *null* tests whether its argument evaluates to *nil*. Thus it returns *t* if its argument is *nil* and it returns *nil* otherwise.

```
= ) (null nil)
t
= ) (null '(a b c))
nil
= ) (null (car '(x y z)))
nil
```

Note that the predicates *zerop* and *null* test for a specific value, while the predicates *atom*, *listp*, and *numberp* test for categories of LISP expression. These categories are called **data types**. When you use these data-type predicates, you must keep in mind that these data types are not mutually exclusive. In particular:

- Nil is a list, but it is also an atom.
- All numbers are also atoms.

A second type of predicate takes two or more arguments and tests the relationship between those arguments. For example, the predicate *equal* takes two arguments and tests whether they have the same value. If so, *equal* returns *t*; if not, it returns *nil*.

```
= ) (equal t t)
t
= ) (equal 5 6)
nil
= ) (equal 'g '(g))
nil
= ) (equal (car (cdr '(a b c))) 'b))
t
```

Three more functions that are useful for checking the relationship between LISP expressions are introduced in this section. Unlike the predicates we have introduced so far, there are restrictions on the type of arguments these functions will accept. Be sure to note these restrictions: if you call these functions with inappropriate arguments, LISP will be unable to perform the test and will give you an error message. Two of these functions are the predicates ⟨ (pronounced "less-p") and ⟩ (pronounced "greater-p"). These predicates take two numbers as arguments and test the relative size of those arguments. The

predicate ⟨ returns *t* if the first argument is less than the second argument.*
Here are some examples:

```
= ⟩ (⟨ 5 6)
t
= ⟩ (⟨ 5 5)
nil
= ⟩ (⟨ 6.5 5)
nil
```

The predicate ⟩ does just the opposite of ⟨: it returns *t* if its first argument
is greater than its second argument.†

```
= ⟩ (⟩ 5 6)
nil
= ⟩ (⟩ 5 5)
nil
= ⟩ (⟩ 6.5 5)
t
```

The final function we want to introduce in this section is *member*. This
function takes two arguments: the first can be any LISP expression, but the
second must be a list. This function checks whether the first argument is an
element of the second argument. If not, *member* returns *nil*. If the first argument is an element of the second argument, *member* returns the tail of the
second argument, beginning where the first argument appears.‡ As with the
other predicates, a non-*nil* value for a *member* test indicates the test is true, and
nil indicates the test is false. However, *member* is a somewhat different type of
predicate from those we have encountered so far, because it does not return *t*
for success. It returns something that is more useful than *t*, because frequently
we need the tail beginning with a target item. Here are some examples of
member:

---

*The predicate ⟨ is spelled out as *lessp* in some LISP dialects. Technically, it can take one or
more arguments, and returns *t* if, from left to right, each succeeding argument is less than the
next argument. If there is only one argument, ⟨ simply returns *t*.

†The predicate ⟩ is spelled out as *greaterp* in some LISP dialects. Technically, like ⟨, it can take
one or more arguments, but it returns *t* if, from left to right, each succeeding argument is
greater than the next argument. If there is only one argument, ⟩ simply returns *t*.

‡In most LISP dialects, *member* will recognize embedded lists — e.g., *(member '(c d) '((a b) (c d)
(e) (f)))* = *((c d) (e) (f))*. However, it does not recognize embedded lists in Common LISP — i.e.,
(member '(c d) '((a b) (c d) (e) (f))) = *nil*. To get *member* to recognize embedded lists, type *(member
'(c d) '((a b) (c d) (e) (f)) :test 'equal)*, which advises the function to use the *equal* test.

```
=> (member 'a '(d f a g h))
(a g h)
=> (member 'y '(l k z))
nil
=> (member 'b '(d (b) g))
nil
=> (cons 'x (member 't '(s t u v)))
(x t u v)
```

LISP Exercises

3.1 Define a function called *compare*. It takes two arguments that are numbers. If the first number plus 10 is greater than twice the second number, then *compare* returns *t*. Otherwise *compare* returns *nil*. For example,

(compare 5 5) returns *t*.

3.2 Define a function call *palp*. This predicate takes a list and tests whether that list is a palindrome. Recall that a palindrome is a list that reads the same backward and forward. If the list is a palindrome, *palp* should return *t*, otherwise it should return *nil*. For example,

(palp '(a b c c b a)) returns *t*
(palp '(dog cat)) returns *nil*

3.3 Define a function call *numline*. It takes one argument that is a number and returns a two-element list. The first element of the list is *t* if the number is 0 and *nil* otherwise. The second element of the list is *t* if the number is negative and *nil* otherwise. For example,

(numline -5) returns *(nil t)*.

Conditionals

Recall that our goal in this chapter is to write functions that do conditional processing, in which actions are performed depending on the outcome of some tests. In the last section we described nine predicates that allow us to perform tests, and we already know how to perform actions with function calls. Only one question remains then: How do we make actions depend on test results? LISP provides the special form *cond* for this purpose.

Let us consider a silly example. Suppose that we wanted to write a function that returned *good* if its argument was *pizza*, *bad* if its argument was *peas*, and *ok* otherwise. The following function *testfood*, which employs *cond*, will do what we want:

```
(defun testfood (food)
      (cond ((equal food 'pizza) 'good)
            ((equal food 'peas) 'bad)
            (t 'ok)))
```

Let us consider the structure of a *cond*. A *cond* can take one or more arguments, each of which must be a list. The arguments of a *cond* are called **cases**, and each one contains at least two elements. The first element is a test to perform, and the remaining elements are conditional actions; that is, they are LISP expressions to evaluate if the test is "true." It is important to remember that LISP considers any non-*nil* value to be "true," not just the atom *t*. Whenever a LISP expression used as a test evaluates to a non-*nil* value, then LISP will evaluate the corresponding actions.

In our example, the *cond* has three cases:

[1] *((equal food 'pizza) 'good)*
[2] *((equal food 'peas) 'bad)*
[3] *(t 'ok).*

LISP evaluates the cases of a *cond* one at a time, from first to last. As soon as a test is true, LISP evaluates the action(s) in that case. Then evaluation of the *cond* terminates (no further cases are evaluated), and LISP returns the value of the final action in the case.*

Let us consider some sample calls to the function *testfood*:

```
= ) (testfood 'peas)
bad
```

In this example, the parameter *food* is assigned the value *peas*, and then the first case in the *cond* is evaluated. The test, *(equal food 'pizza)* returns *nil*, so the action for that case is not evaluated, and instead, the second case is evaluated. The test in the second case, *(equal food 'peas)*, returns *t*, so the corresponding action is evaluated, and LISP returns that value without evaluating any more cases. The action in this case is the literal atom *'bad*, which evaluates to itself, so the function returns *bad*.

---

*Again, to be totally accurate, a *cond* case may contain just one element, a test, with no actions. If that test is true, LISP returns the value of the test. However, it is much clearer always to write out both the test and the action, even if they are the same.

Let us consider a second example:

```
=> (testfood 'carrots)
'ok
```

In this case, the parameter *food* is assigned the value *carrots*, and the test in the first case returns *nil*, as does the test in the second case. As a result, the third case is evaluated, but here we encounter a strange "test." The first argument in the third case is *t*, but *t* always evaluates to itself. As a result this test always returns *t*, which is of course a non-*nil* value. So, if we get as far as evaluating this third case, the corresponding action will always be evaluated.

When the first element (the test) in a case is *t*, the case is referred to as an **else case**, because it is the case where the action is performed if all the previous tests have failed.* If we get as far as evaluating an else case, the action(s) will always be evaluated, and the result will be returned. So, when an else case appears, it should always be the final case in the *cond* (since any case that follows the else case can never be evaluated). Since the test in our else case will always return a non-*nil* value, we are essentially saying to return the result in this case if anything else is true, other than the tests in the earlier cases. (Notice that the test in the else case does not have to be *t*. It can be any LISP expression that always evaluates to a non-*nil* value, such as *'else*, or *100* or *'xyz* or *(cdr '(a b c))*. The symbol *t* is used by convention, just so that it will be easier for people to read the code and recognize when an else case appears.)

Recall that earlier in this chapter we discussed writing a version of the function *double* that guards against an inappropriate argument. We can now write such a **guarded** version of *double* as follows:

```
(defun guarded-double (num)
    (cond ((numberp num) (* num 2))
          (t 'non-number)))
```

We can summarize our discussion of *cond* with the following template:

```
(cond ( ⟨test⟩ [⟨action⟩...] )
      ( ⟨another test⟩ [⟨other action⟩...] )
                .
                .
                .
      ( ⟨last test⟩ [⟨some other action⟩...] )
)
```

---

*If an else case is not included in a *cond*, and tests in all the cases return *nil*, then the *cond* will return *nil*.

LISP Exercises

3.4 Define *carlis*. It takes one argument. If the argument is a nonempty list, then *carlis* returns the first element of that list. But if the argument is the empty list, then *carlis* returns the empty list. If the argument is an atom, *carlis* returns just that atom. *Hint*: Be careful how you order your tests. Remember that *nil* is both an atom and a list. For example,

(carlis '(cat rabbit)) returns cat
(carlis 'george) returns george
(carlis nil) returns nil

3.5 Define a function called *checktemp*. It takes one argument, a temperature, and returns an atom that serves as a temperature indicator. A global variable, *hightemp*, stores a high temperature. Another global variable, *lowtemp*, stores a low temperature. If the temperature is above *hightemp*, return the atom *hot*. Return the atom *cold* if the temperature is below *lowtemp*. If it is between the extremes, return *medium*. The variables *hightemp* and *lowtemp* should be set to *90* and *30*, respectively. For example,

(checktemp 100) returns hot

3.6 Define a function called *make-list*. It takes one argument. If that argument is an atom, it puts that atom into a list. If the argument is already a list, it leaves the argument the way it is. If the argument is an empty list, it returns the empty list. For example,

(make-list 'x) returns (x)
(make-list '(a b)) returns (a b)

3.7 Define a function called *classify* that will determine the type of its argument. If the argument is a nonempty list, return the word *list*. If the argument is a number, return *number*. If the argument is an atom, return *atom*. If the argument is *nil*, return *nil*. Be careful to order your tests properly. For example,

(classify 'a) returns atom
(classify '(x y)) returns list
(classify nil) returns nil
(classify 5) returns number

3.8 Define a function called *numtype* that takes one argument, a number. It returns an atom that indicates what type of number the argument is. If the argument is a positive number, the function returns the atom *positive*. If it is a negative number, the function returns the atom *negative*. If the argument is equal to zero, then the function returns the atom *zero*. For example,

(numtype 3) returns *positive*
(numtype -2) returns *negative*

Logical Functions

So far we have discussed several predicates that LISP makes available for testing, and we have discussed conditional processing. In this last section of the chapter we will discuss three functions, *not, or,* and *and,* that can be used in conjunction with predicates to perform more powerful tests. These functions are called **logical functions**.

Let us consider the predicates ⟩, ⟨, and *zerop*. We can use these to test whether a number is greater than 5, equals zero, or is less than −10. But suppose you wanted to perform some of the following tests:

1) Is a number greater than 5 or less than −5?
2) Is a number both greater than 0 and less than 100?
3) Is a number not 0?

LISP does not have any single predicates that will allow us to perform these tasks. However, we can use the logical functions *not, or,* and *and,* along with the predicates ⟩, ⟨, and *zerop,* to do these tests. For example,

```
= ⟩ (setq x 250)
250
= ⟩ (or (⟩ x 5) (⟨ x -5))
t
= ⟩ (and (⟩ x 0) (⟨ x 100))
nil
= ⟩ (not (zerop x))
t
```

Let us consider each of these three logical functions more carefully.

The simplest of the logical functions is *not*. It accepts a single argument, which can be any LISP expression (the argument does not have to be a predicate). If the argument evaluates to *nil*, *not* returns *t*. If the argument evaluates to *any* non-*nil* value, *not* returns nil. Thus *not* returns *t* if its argument is *not* true. Here are some examples:

```
=> (not nil)
t
=> (not t)
nil
=> (not '(a b c))
nil
=> (not (atom '(a b c)))
t
```

The logical function *or* accepts one or more arguments. It evaluates its arguments from left to right and returns the first value it encounters that is non-*nil*. If all the arguments of an *or* evaluate to *nil*, then *or* returns *nil*. Here are some examples. Note that, just like *not*, the arguments to *or* do not have to be predicates. Any legal LISP expression can be employed as an argument.

```
=> (or t nil)
t
=> (or nil nil)
nil
=> (or (numberp 'a) '(a b c) (+ 6 5))
(a b c)
```

So, *or* returns a non-*nil* value if at least one of its arguments is non-*nil*, otherwise it returns *nil*. As a result, *or* can be used to combine tests and determine whether *at least one* of the tests is true. Thus *(or (> x 5) (< x −5))* will return *t* if the value of *x* is either greater than 5, *or* less than −5. Notice the third example in particular. When a non-*nil* argument is encountered in an *or*, LISP does not automatically return *t*, but rather, returns the value of the argument. Once it encounters such a non-*nil* value, none of the other arguments to the right are evaluated.

The logical function *and* also takes one or more arguments and evaluates them from left to right. If it encounters an argument that evaluates to *nil*, *and* immediately returns *nil* without evaluating any more arguments. If every argument evaluates to a non-*nil* value, *and* returns the value of its final argument (the one farthest to the right).

Here are some examples:

```
=> (and 5 nil)
nil
=> (and 'a 'b)
b
=> (and (listp nil) (atom nil))
t
```

So, *and* returns a non-*nil* value if every one of its arguments is non-*nil*; otherwise it returns *nil*. As a result, *and* can be used to combine tests and determine whether *every one* of the tests is true. Thus *(and (> x 0) (< x 100))* will return *t* if the value of *x* is greater than 0 *and* less than 100. Once again, keep in mind that *and* does not just return *t* if all of its arguments are non-*nil*; it returns the value of the last argument. As in the case with *or*, that feature will be useful for some simple conditional processing.*

LISP Exercises

3.9 Define *lisnump*. It takes one argument. If the argument is a number, like 5, or a list, like *(a b c)*, it returns *t*. Otherwise it returns *nil*. Although you could implement this with a *cond* structure, implement it with *or*.

3.10 Define *samesign*. It takes two numbers as arguments, and returns *t* if both arguments have the same sign. That is, if both arguments are 0, both positive, or both negative, the function should return *t*. Again, use an *or* rather than a *cond* structure. For example,

(samesign 0 0) returns *t*
(samesign − 2 − 5) returns *t*
(samesign − 2 3) returns *nil*

3.11 Define *classify-sentence*, which will take as an argument a list encoding of a sentence. It will classify sentences as either questions, active sentences, or passive sentences, making three assumptions that will simplify the task: (1) questions will always begin with "why" or "how"; (2) any sentence that contains both "was" and "by" will be passive; and (3) every list we pass to the function will contain a legal sentence. For example,

(classify-sentence '(mary threw the snowball at steve))
returns *active*

(classify-sentence '(why did mary throw the snowball?))
returns *question*

(classify-sentence '(steve was hit by a snowball))
returns *passive*

3.12 Define *not* using a *cond* structure. Call your function *my-not*, just so you do not destroy the *not* already implemented in your LISP.

---

*To be precise, *and* and *or* can each be called without arguments — *(and)* returns *t* because none of its arguments are nil, and *(or)* returns *nil* because none of its arguments are non-*nil*.

3.13 Define *or* using a *cond* structure. Call the function you are defining *my-or*, and assume it takes just two arguments.

3.14 Define *and* using a *cond* structure. Call the function you are defining *my-and*, and assume it just takes two arguments. *Hint*: To do this you want to take advantage of the fact that a *cond* that may be embedded as the action of a *cond* case.

Simple Conditional Processing with Logical Functions

Logical functions also enable us to do some types of conditional processing without using *cond*. First, consider this function that uses *cond*:

```
(defun guarded-car (lis)
    (cond ((not (atom lis)) (car lis))
          (t nil)))
```

This function takes the *car* of its argument, but only after checking that the argument is not an atom, since it is not possible to take the *car* of an atom. If the argument is not a list, the function just returns *nil*. It is actually possible to do this conditional processing without employing a *cond*. Consider the following example that uses *and* instead of *cond* to guard the *car*.

```
(defun guarded-car (lis)
    (and (not (atom lis)) (car lis)))
```

Consider what happens when this function is called. If the value of *lis* is an atom, *(not (atom lis))* will return *nil*. As a result, no further arguments to the *and* will be evaluated, and the function will return *nil*. On the other hand, if the value of *lis* is a non-*nil* list, *((not (atom lis))* will return *t*, and the next argument of the *and*, *(car lis)* will be evaluated. Since that is the final argument, the function will return the value of *(car lis)*, whatever it is. So, this function will yield the value of *(car lis)*, whenever the value of *lis* is a list, and will yield *nil* otherwise.

Here is one more example of a guarded function. It employs *and* to do two guard tests before performing a ⟩ test.

```
(defun safe-greaterp (x y)
    (and (numberp x)
         (numberp y)
         (⟩ x y)))
```

If *x* and *y* are both numbers then LISP will evaluate *(⟩ x y)* and *safe-greaterp* will return the result of the ⟩ test. However, if either *x* or *y* is not a number, the *and* will immediately return *nil* and in that way guard against what would be an illegal call to ⟩.

LISP Exercises

3.15 Define the function *addbag*. It takes two arguments, an item and a "bag" (a list). If the item is in the bag, it returns the bag unaltered. If the item is not in the bag, it returns the bag with the item in the first position. For example,

(addbag 'b '(a b c)) returns *(a b c)*
(addbag 'x '(a b c)) returns *(x a b c)*

3.16 Define a function called *safediv*, which takes two arguments, and returns the result of dividing the first argument by the second, if this is possible. It returns *nil* if this division is not possible. Division is only possible if the first argument is a number, the second argument is a number, and the second argument is not equal to 0. For example,

(savediv 6 3) returns *2*
(savediv 6 'a) returns *nil*

3.17 Define a function called *successor*. It takes two arguments, a target and a list. If the target is not in the list, the function returns *not-there*. If the target appears only in the final position of the list, the function returns *no-successor*. Otherwise, it returns the item that immediately follows the first occurrence of the target in the list. For example,

(successor 'x '(w x y z)) returns *y*
(successor 'q '(a b c)) returns *not-there*

3.18 Define a function called *addit*. It takes two arguments, an item and a list and searches for the item in the list. If it finds the item in the list, it returns *found*. If it does not find the item then it adds the item onto the end of the list. But, if the first argument is an empty list, avoid adding it to the end of the old list and just return the old list untouched. For example,

(addit 'a '(c d e)) returns *(c d e a)*
(addit 'a '(a b)) returns *found*
(addit nil '(a b)) returns *(a b)*

3.19 Write a function called *combine* that takes two arguments and does the following.

☐ If either argument is *nil*, it returns *nil*.
☐ If both arguments are numbers, it returns the sum of the numbers.

□ If both arguments are atoms (but the conditions above do not apply —
i.e., neither argument is *nil* and at least one argument is not a number),
then the function returns a list of the arguments.

□ If both arguments are lists (but neither one is *nil*), the function appends
them and returns the resulting list.

□ Otherwise, it inserts the argument that is an atom into the argument
that is a list and returns the resulting list.

Hint: Do not assume that your function will have five cases or that they
should be coded in the order of the five statements above.

In this chapter we have discussed conditional processing, a technique that
allows us to write functions that perform different actions under different
circumstances. As we have seen in the examples and exercises, this capability
is extremely useful, indeed, essential in a programming language. As we
discuss more powerful programming techniques in later chapters, we will see
even more clearly how useful this capability is.

Summary of LISP Functions

and   This function takes zero or more arguments, and returns that value of
the final argument if all the arguments have non-*nil* values. Otherwise,
and returns *nil*. If it is called with zero arguments, it returns *t*.

Example: *(and (listp '(a b)) (cdr '(a b)))* returns *(b)*

atom   This function takes one argument. It returns *t* if the argument evaluates to an atom and returns *nil* otherwise.

Example: *(atom 'a)* returns *t*
Note: *(atom nil)* returns *t*

cond   This special form is used for conditional processing. It takes zero or
more arguments, called cases. Each case is a list, whose first element is
a test and whose remaining elements are actions. The cases in a *cond* are
evaluated one at a time, first to last. When one of the tests returns a
non-*nil* value, none of the remaining cases is evaluated. Instead, the
actions in the case are evaluated and the value of the final action is
returned. If none of the tests returns a non-*nil* value, *cond* returns *nil*.

Example: *(cond ((listp x) (cdr x))   (t x))*
If *x* has the value *(a b c)*, this *cond* returns *(b c)*

equal This function takes two arguments and returns *t* if the the two arguments have the same value. Otherwise, *equal* returns *nil*.

Example: *(equal 'a (car '(a b)))* returns *t*
Note: *(equal 1 1.0)* returns *nil*

listp This function takes one argument. It returns *t* if the argument evaluates to a list and returns *nil* otherwise.

Example: *(listp '(a b))* returns *t*

member This function takes two arguments, the second of which must be a list. If the first argument is an element of the second, *member* returns the tail of the second argument beginning where the first argument appears. Otherwise, *member* returns *nil*.

Example: *(member 'b '(a b c))* returns *(b c)*

not This function takes one argument. If the argument evaluates to *nil*, *not* returns *t*. If the argument evaluates to a non-*nil* value, *not* returns *nil*.

Example: *(not (atom '(a b c)))* returns *t*

null This function takes one argument. It returns *t* if its argument evaluates to *nil*, and returns *nil* otherwise.

Example: *(null nil)* returns *t*

numberp This function takes one argument and returns *t* if the argument evaluates to a number. Otherwise, *numberp* returns *nil*.

Example: *(numberp 14)* returns *t*

or This function takes zero or more arguments and returns the value of the first argument with a non-*nil* value. If all the arguments evaluate to *nil*, *or* returns *nil*. If it is called with zero arguments, it returns *nil*.

Example: *(or (listp '(a b)) (cdr '(a b)))* returns *t*

zerop This function takes a numeric argument and returns *t* if the argument evaluates to 0. Otherwise, the function returns *nil*.

Example: *(zerop (difference 5 (plus 2 3)))* returns *t*

⟨ This function takes one or more numeric arguments and returns *t* if they are ordered from lesser to greater. Otherwise, the function returns *nil*.

Example: *(< 10 15)* returns *t*

> This function takes one or more numeric arguments and returns *t* if they are ordered from greater to lesser. Otherwise, the function returns *nil*.

Example: *() 15 10)* returns *t*

Glossary   **case**   An argument of a *cond*, which must be a list. The first element in a case is a test followed by one or more additional elements, which are actions that are performed if the test evaluates to a non-*nil* value.

conditional processing   Processing in which the actions performed depend on the outcome of tests.

data types   Types of LISP expressions. The three data types we have discussed are atoms, lists, and numbers (which are a subset of atoms).

else case   A *cond* case in which the first element (typically, the atom *t*) always evaluates to a non-*nil* value. If an else case is evaluated, the action(s) will always be evaluated.

guarded function   A function that is called only after its arguments have been tested to ensure that they are appropriate.

logical function   A function that combines or reverses the results of predicates in order to create more powerful tests. Logical functions are *not*, *or*, and *and*.

predicate   A function that performs a test and returns a result that can be interpreted as either ''true'' or ''false.''

test   Examines whether a property holds true for a single LISP expression, or whether some relationship holds true among two or more expressions.

Programming Style

In Chapter 3 you learned how to write functions with conditional processes. In the following chapters you will learn new techniques and more built-in LISP functions that will allow you to write still more complex and powerful functions. As early as Chapter 2, however, you may have noticed that there is frequently more than one way to write a function to perform a particular task. In the last section of Chapter 3, we saw examples of how we can write two different functions, one with *and* and one with *cond* that perform the same task. In fact, any function can be coded in a virtually unlimited number of ways. The simple functions you have coded so far have only a few reasonable variations. We have tried to show the different versions in the answers at the end of this book. As the functions you code get more complex, though, you may begin to think about many different ways to go about coding a particular function. Therefore it is important to discuss some guidelines for selecting among the alternative ways of coding a function. In this chapter we will make some recommendations on this topic.

Coding Style

There are essentially two considerations that influence coding style. One is computational efficiency — how quickly can LISP evaluate the functions we write? Determining the efficiency of function definitions can be complex, but one rule of thumb for the types of functions we have considered so far is that the fewer function calls that are evaluated when the function is called, the better. The following example demonstrates two function calls that delete the second element of a list. Both are effective, but the one involving *cons* is somewhat more efficient than the one involving *append* because it involves one fewer function call.

```
=> (setq x '(a b c d))
(a b c d)
=> (cons (car x) (cdr (cdr x)))
(a c d)
=> (append (list (car x)) (cdr (cdr x)))
(a c d)
```

Computational efficiency is not the only concern in programming style, however. The difference in execution time for the two function calls above would be extremely small. An equally important consideration is how easily a person can understand the code. It is not possible to write functions that "confuse" the computer. No matter how complicated the code is, the LISP interpreter will never be perplexed. It will simply execute the function calls one at a time as indicated by the program until it is finished, or until it encounters a function call that cannot be executed. However, it is notoriously possible to write code that is difficult for people to follow.

You need to write understandable code for two reasons. First, once you learn LISP and start writing programs to accomplish tasks, you will find that it is necessary to go back and revise those programs, frequently after you have forgotten how the programs work. Moreover, you may have to go in and revise a program that someone else has written. As a result, it is important to write functions in a way that makes it easy to follow what is happening.

Secondly, once you start writing your own long programs, you will find that you make errors and write programs that either cannot be executed at all by the LISP interpreter, or programs that do not do what you want them to. Programs that do not execute as planned are said to contain **bugs**, and it is up to the programmer to **debug** them. Indeed, it would be surprising if you managed to code all the exercises up till now without any bugs in your code. As a result, you need to write functions in a way that you can trace through in your head as easily as possible, in order to track down bugs and fix them. In this chapter, we will discuss some topics that make code somewhat easier for human beings to read (and to write) and we will introduce the topic of debugging programs.

Helping functions

One important principle in making functions easy for people to read is to make them short. So far all the functions that you have defined have been fairly short, and as a result, relatively easy to read. However, it may already have crossed your mind that a program that does something really useful, like playing tic-tac-toe, would require considerably more code. As you write longer and longer programs, it remains equally important to continue to define fairly short functions. As a result, when you are coding a new function, you will find it necessary to define additional functions to perform subtasks. Functions you define to do a subtask of a problem are often called **helping functions** or **sub-functions**. This section will cover some suggestions about when to create helping functions.

Suppose we wanted to write a function that returned a list of the positive and the negative roots of a quadratic expression. (A quadratic expression is a mathematical expression with the form $ax^2 + bx + c$, and the roots of a quadratic expression are the values of the variable x for which the expression equals zero. For example, the roots of $-3x^2 + 3x + 6$ are 2 and -1, because if we substitute either of those values for x, the value of the whole expression is zero.) We can compute the two roots of any quadratic expression with the following equations:

$$\text{positive root} \; = \; \frac{-b + \sqrt{b^2 - 4ac}}{2a}$$

$$\text{negative root} \; = \; \frac{-b - \sqrt{b^2 - 4ac}}{2a}$$

Given these equations, it is fairly easy to write a function *quadratic* that accepts three arguments (the values of the coefficients a, b, and c), and returns a list of the positive and negative roots. To do this, we will need the function *sqrt*, which takes the square root of a positive number. Here is the code for *quadratic*:

```
(defun quadratic (a b c)
    (list (/ (+ (- b)
                (sqrt (- (* b b)
                         (* 4.0 a c))))
             (* 2.0 a))
          (/ (- (- b)
                (sqrt (- (* b b)
                         (* 4.0 a c))))
             (* 2.0 a))))
```

(Note that $(- b)$ is used here to get the additive inverse of b — it is the same as subtracting b from 0.)

This is certainly a rather complicated piece of code. It would be fairly difficult for a person to figure out what the function is doing. The code becomes
easier for a person to read if we break it up with helping functions as follows:

```
(defun quadratic (a b c)
    (list (pos-root a b c)
          (neg-root a b c)))

(defun pos-root (a b c)
    (/ (+ (- b)
          (determinant a b c))
       (* 2.0 a)))

(defun neg-root (a b c)
    (/ (- (- b)
          (determinant a b c))
       (* 2.0 a)))

(defun determinant (a b c)
    (sqrt (- (* b b)
             (* 4.0 a c))))
```

The function *quadratic* simply returns a list of the positive and negative
roots. The positive and negative roots are computed separately by the functions *pos-root* and *neg-root*. Both of these functions use another function *determinant* to calculate $b^2 - 4ac$, which is called the determinant of the expression
and which must be calculated in computing both roots.

In this example, *quadratic* is called the **top-level function**, because it calls
helping functions to do part of its work, and there are no higher-level functions
that call it. There are several advantages to using helping functions when we
code in LISP.

1. It is easier to read and understand the shorter functions (i.e., a top-level
   function and one or more helping functions) than one long, complex
   function. It may not seem important now, but it will become more
   important as you write more-complex functions. Many programmers
   have had the experience of looking back at old programs and not being
   able to figure out what the functions do!
2. When we create a helping function we can give it a name that indicates
   what the function does. Notice that when we used helping functions it
   became extremely easy to see what the top-level function *quadratic* does;
   it returns a list of the positive and negative roots. Moreover, it becomes
   easier to read the code for each of the helping functions, because the name
   of each helping function gives us a clue about what it is supposed to do.

3. Frequently, the initial code for a function contains bugs. It is easier to test shorter functions in order to find and correct these problems. Also, we have written the code for *determinant* just once and do not have to debug two separate copies of that code.
4. Any helping functions we create in coding one function are available for use in other functions as well.

Guidelines for Helping Functions

Below are some guidelines for deciding when to create helping functions, and what kinds of helping functions to create.

1. *Useful chunks*: Helping functions should be sensible "chunks" of code. We would not want to create a helping function that does an arbitrary combination of operations. For example, it is doubtful that a function to return the tail of a reversed list would be very useful, even if you needed to do such an operation as a piece of a larger problem. The job done by a helping function should be easily describable. The helping functions shown below are reasonable:

   - square of a number
   - third item of a list
   - last item of a list

2. *Repeated code*: It is a good idea to create a helping function when you see that you have to perform the same operation more than once in a function. So, in the function *quadratic*, it is a particularly good idea to create a helping function to calculate the determinant.
3. *Depth in the code*: You should think about creating a helping function if the top-level function contains three or more levels of embedded functions. For example, the original code for *quadratic* was six levels deep.

Local Variables

There is one more point to note about helping functions. All the helping functions for *quadratic* above use the variables *a*, *b*, and *c* for parameters. This is to make them easily understandable; they could be named differently in different functions.

One might be tempted to omit parameters in a helping function and write *determinant*, for instance, as

```
(defun determinant ()
    (sqrt (- (* b b)
          (* 4.0 a c))))
```

under the assumption that *a*, *b*, and *c* will inherit the values they are assigned in the top-level function. This is extremely poor style because it means you cannot tell what a function does by looking at it — you have to find the context from which it is called. Also, in many LISP implementations such as Common LISP this will not even work and will generate an error. It is usually a very bad practice to use variables from a higher-level function without making them parameters of the helping function.

The LISP Functions *abs*, *mod*, and *sqrt*

There are three more functions that you will need for the problems in this chapter. The function *abs* takes a number and returns the absolute value of that number. That is, if the number is 0 or positive, it returns that number, while if it is negative, it returns its additive inverse. For example,

```
=> (abs -5)
5
=> (abs 5)
5
```

The function *mod* takes two numbers and returns the remainder of dividing the first number by the second. For example, (mod 5 2) = 1, because 2 goes into 5 twice, with a remainder of 1. Here are more examples:

```
=> (mod 6 3)
0
=> (mod 6 5)
1
```

The function *sqrt*, as mentioned earlier, takes the square root of a positive number.

```
=> (sqrt 25)
5
=> (sqrt -1)
error
```

LISP Exercises

4.1 Define the function *eqends*. It takes one argument, a list, and returns *t* if the list has the same first and last elements. However, if the list is empty, then *eqends* should return *nil* before trying to compare the first and last elements. Finally, *eqends* should return *nil* if the first and last elements are not the same. You should write *eqends* using a helping function *lastitem* that returns the last element of a list.

4.2 Define *trim*. It takes one argument, a list. The function *trim* should return a copy of the list minus its first and last elements. For example,

(trim '(a b c d)) returns *(b c)*.

4.3 Define *switch*. It takes two arguments, each of which should be a list. The function *switch* should return a new list that is the same as the first list, with one difference: The new list should not contain the last element of the first list, instead this element should be replaced by the last element of the second list. For example,

(switch '(a b c d) '(cat dog)) returns *(a b c dog)*.

4.4 Define *endsp*. This function takes two arguments, a target item and a list. The function *endsp* returns *t* if the item is the same as either the first or the last element of the list. For example,

(endsp 'a '(a b c)) returns *t*.
(endsp 'a '(c b a)) returns *t*.
(endsp 'a '(c a b)) returns *nil*.

4.5 Define *radius*. It takes two arguments, *x* and *y*. These arguments are the *x* and *y* coordinates for a point on a given circle, which has its center on the origin. The function *radius* should compute the radius of that circle given the *x* and *y* coordinates using the equation: $x^2 + y^2 = radius^2$. For example,

(radius 3 4) returns *5*, because 9 + 16 = 25.

Note: You will have to define your own squaring function for this problem.

4.6 Define the function *evendiv*. It takes two positive numbers as arguments. The function should return *t* if one of these numbers is evenly divisible by the other argument, and return *nil* otherwise. You should write your function so that it makes no difference whether the first number is larger than, smaller than, or equal to the second number. For example,

(evendiv 3 6) returns *t*.
(evendiv 6 3) returns *t*.
(evendiv 6 4) returns *nil*.

4.7 Write a function called *rightp* that takes three arguments, *side1*, *side2*, and *side3* — which represent the lengths of three sides of a triangle, where *side3* is the longest side. This function returns *t* if the three sides form a right triangle, and returns *nil* if they do not. In a right triangle, the square of *side3* (the longest side) equals the sum of the square of *side1* and the square of *side2*. However, the function *rightp* should allow for a measurement error of 2%. That is, your function should return *t* if the sum of squares of the first two sides is within 2% of the square of the third side. For example,

(*rightp 3 4 5.01*) returns *t*, because $3^2 + 4^2 = 25$, which is within 2% of 5.01^2.

Abbreviating *cars* and *cdrs*

LISP provides a scheme for abbreviating a series of embedded function calls to *car* and *cdr*. For example, the call (*car (cdr (cdr lis)))*, which returns the third item in *lis*, can be replaced with the single function call (*caddr lis*). To generate such an abbreviated function name, each call to *car* or *cdr*, from left to right, is represented by a single letter, ''a'' for *car* and ''d'' for *cdr*. This string of ''a''s and ''d''s is preceded by a ''c'' and followed by an ''r.'' Thus (*caddr lis*) stands for (*cAr (cDr (cDr lis)))*.* Here are some other examples:

(*car (cdr x))* can be replaced by (*cadr x*).
(*car (cdr (cdr (car x))))* can be replaced by (*caddar x*).

This option is provided primarily to make it easier to write LISP code, rather than to make it easier to read LISP code. A contraction that consists of a single ''a'' followed by a string of ''d''s is fairly easy to understand, because it is simply returning an element of a list. For example, *cadddr*, which has three ''d''s following an ''a,'' returns the fourth item from the list. However, contractions that consist of three or more ''a''s and/or ''d''s, are not as easy to read; that is, it may not be so apparent what they are extracting from the list. So, if you have occasion to write a complicated extraction, such as *cadadr* (which extracts the second item of the second item in its argument), it is a good idea to put it into a helping function that has a more meaningful name, particularly if you will be using the contraction at several points in your code. For example, consider the function *make-active*. This function takes one argument, which is a list containing a sentence with a relative clause. (Note in the example below that the structure of the list corresponds to the structure of the sentence.) The

*Different dialects of LISP differ as to how many ''a''s and ''d''s you are allowed to string together. In most implementations of Common LISP, you are limited to a combination of four ''a''s and ''d''s. In Golden Common LISP you can use only three.

function returns a new sentence, which it constructs from the main subject of the original sentence and the verb phrase of the relative clause.

```
= ) (setq s '((The zebra) (that (escaped from the circus))
                (crossed the road)))
((The zebra) (that (escaped from the circus)) (crossed the road))
= ) (defun make-active (sentence)
        (list (car sentence) (clause-phrase sentence)))
make-active
= ) (defun clause-phrase (sen)
        (cadadr sen))
clause-phrase
= ) (make-active s)
((The zebra) (escaped from the circus))
```

Note that *clause-phrase* is a somewhat more mnemonic name for a function than *cadadr*, since the function is intended to return the verb phrase of the relative clause. Of course, the name *clause-phrase* is still a bit cryptic. We could have named the function *find-the-relative-clause-verb-phrase*, but then the name becomes too long. Function names can be as long as you want to make them, but long names are somewhat difficult to read. So, in defining functions, you want to strike a balance between names that are descriptive and names that are relatively short.

LISP Exercises

4.8 Define a function called *compute* that accepts one argument, which is a list. The list will consist of three items, the second is an arithmetic operator (+, −, *, or /), and the first and third elements will be numbers. The function should return the value of the expression. For example,

*(compute '(3 * 6))* returns 18.

> *Hint:* The function should test the second element of the list to see which operator it is, and then call the appropriate function with the first and third elements of the list.

4.9 Define a function called *compound-sentence* that takes two arguments, which are lists. Each list consists of two elements: an embedded list (which contains a sentence), and a number (either 1 or 2). For example,

((The sailor climbed the rigging) 2)
((The sailor read a book) 1)

The function should check whether the subjects of the two sentences are identical (i.e., whether the second word of the two embedded lists is identical). If so, the function should return a list that contains a compound sentence of the form

(The ⟨subject⟩ ⟨verb phase 1⟩ and ⟨verb phrase 2⟩).

The numbers in the list indicate the order in which the verb phrases should appear in the sentence. That is, the first verb phrase in the compound sentence should come from the list that contains a 1, and the second verb phrase should come from the list containing a 2.

So, in the case of our example, the function should return

(The sailor read a book and climbed the rigging).

If the two subjects are not identical, the function should return *nil*. Here are some example calls.

```
=> (compound-sentence '((The lawyer made a sandwich) 2)
                       '((The lawyer went to the kitchen) 1))
(The lawyer went to the kitchen and made a sandwich)
=> (compound-sentence '((The sailor climbed the rigging) 2)
                       '((The lawyer read a book) 1))
nil
```

4.10 (Optional) Write a function *winner*, which will tell whether xs or os have won a tic-tac-toe game. The function takes a single argument, which is the tic-tac-toe game encoded as a list of three lists. Each embedded list encodes one row of the puzzle, and *nil* denotes a blank cell. Here are some examples of *winner*.

```
=> (winner '((o nil x)(nil o nil)(x nil o)))
o
=> (winner '((x nil o)(x o o)(x o x)))
x
=> (winner '((x x o)(o o x)(x o o)))
nil
```

Debugging

In this section, we will discuss techniques for debugging or fixing errors in your functions. There are actually two types of errors we need to be concerned about, which you will realize as you start coding. If we call a function with the wrong number of arguments, or with the wrong type of argument, or if we have an undefined function or variable, LISP will be unable to evaluate the call, and will return an error message. We can call these **syntactic errors**, since we have broken the rules of LISP syntax. On the other hand, we can write functions that do not violate the rules, and run to completion without generating an error, but do not do what we want to do. These are called **functional errors**, since the function does not perform the planned task.

Functional errors can be both more insidious and more difficult to debug. After all, a syntactic error is not difficult to recognize when a function grinds to a halt and an error message is returned. However, it is not always apparent when a function call is returning the wrong result.

Debugging Syntactic Errors

It is somewhat easier to debug code in LISP than in other languages, because it is an interactive language — you immediately see the result of each function call you type. Moreover, LISP handles syntactic errors in a helpful way. In most LISP systems, when the interpreter encounters code that cannot be evaluated, it not only returns an error message, it also calls up some functions to help you debug the code. In some versions of LISP, it calls up a **debugger**, while in other versions it puts you into a **break loop**. These serve similar purposes, and in either case they allow you to do things to determine the nature of the error. In this book, we assume that a syntactic error will put you into a break loop. However, you will be able to perform essentially the same actions (and more) if your version of LISP has a debugger.*

Consider the following function definitions and function call:

```
=> (defun pair-off (lis)
      (list (outer-pair lis) (inner-pair lis)))
pair-off
=> (defun outer-pair (x)
      (cons (car x) (last x)))
outer-pair
=> (defun inner-pair (y)
      (list (second y) (second-to-last y)))
inner-pair
=> (defun second (z)
      (car (car z)))
second
```

---

*You should be warned, however, that the exact behavior of the system varies from one LISP implementation to another. You will have to consult the specifics of your own implementation.

```
=> (defun second-to-last (w)
      (second (reverse w)))
second-to-last
=> (pair-off '(a b c d))
ERROR: Bad arg to car a
1>
```

The error message indicates that *car* was called with the argument *a*. The prompt "*1>*," in addition, indicates that we are in the break loop. In the break loop, processing of the function call has been suspended, but we are not returned to the top level. This fact is important, because if we had returned to the top level, we would lose all information about the processing that went before, and the exact point at which the error occurred. For example, since parameters are local variables, if we simply returned to the top level, those local variables would no longer retain their values. By placing us in the break loop when the error occurred, the current bindings of those variables are preserved, so we can inspect them, or any other information about the current state of the function, in order to try to discover the error. Thus when LISP encounters a syntactic error, it immediately suspends evaluation, notifies us that there is an error, and preserves the information we need to debug the error. Unfortunately, LISP cannot do this for functional errors, because it does not "know" what your functions are supposed to do.

Let us go back and examine the error now. Notice that the error message indicates that we called *car* with an illegal argument. However, there are three different calls to *car* that might have caused that error. How can we determine which one it was? LISPs provide a facility to get what is called a backtrace of the function calls. In some LISPs this can be obtained by invoking a function called *backtrace*, but consult your own LISP implementation. The following example demonstrates a call to *backtrace*:

```
=> (pair-off '(a b c d))
ERROR: Bad arg to car a
1> (backtrace)
(backtrace)
(car (car z))
(second y)
(list <**> (second-to-last y))
(inner-pair lis)
(list (outer-pair lis) <**>)
(pair-off '(a b c d))
nil
```

The function *backtrace* prints a list of all the functions that LISP has begun evaluating, but has not finished. The order of the list, starting from the top, indicates which functions LISP started evaluating most recently. Thus the first entry in the list is *backtrace*, since at the point that it was being evaluated, it was the function that LISP had started evaluating most recently. However, we are not interested in *backtrace*, we are interested in the next function call on the list, because that is the function that LISP must have been evaluating when it encountered the error, and indeed, it turns out to be a call to *car*. The next line in the list indicates that this call appears in the function *second*, so we can rule out the call to *car* in *outer-pair* as the cause of the error.

At first it may be unclear which call to *car* in *(car (car z))* is the source of the problem, but it is the outer call to *car* which yielded the error. The error message informed us that the illegal argument was *a*. Since we are in the break loop, we can simply type the variable *z*, to see what its value is, and we see that it is *(a b c d)*, so the inner *(car z)* cannot be the source of the error.* In this case, the error was in the argument to the outer *car*, which is an atom. The function *second* is intended to return the second item in the list, but there is no way we can do that if we start by taking the *car* of the list. However, changing *(car (car z))* to *(car (cdr z))* solves the problem. Note that while the outer *car* caused the error, its origin was the argument calculated by the inner *car*.

Debugging Functional Errors

LISP provides the function *trace*, which is particularly useful for debugging functional errors. Let us consider an example to see how we can use it. Consider the function *main-clause* that accepts one argument, which is a list of embedded lists. This function is intended to return the first and last lists appended together. (If we assume that the argument represents a complex sentence, *main-clause* is intended to return a simpler sentence with just the beginning main subject and the ending verb phrase.) We might try to define *main-clause* as follows:

```
=> (defun main-clause (sentence)
        (append (car sentence) (last sentence)))
main-clause
=> (main-clause '((the mailman) (with gray hair) (drank some coffee)))
(the mailman (drank some coffee))
```

---

*In addition to evaluating variables in the break loop, you can simply type in any LISP expression and LISP will evaluate it. If you use a *setq* in the break loop to change the value of one of your variables, you will indeed change its value.

It may not be apparent at first, but there is a functional error here. The function was intended to return *(the mailman drank some coffee)*, but instead *drank some coffee* appears in an embedded list. Clearly, the call to *append* is returning an unexpected value. The question is why?

When a function call returns an unexpected value, some function in its definition is doing something other than what we intended it to do. For instance, we might suspect that the problem in the above definition is with *append*. It is extremely useful to find out what arguments a function such as *append* is receiving and what it is doing with these arguments. The function *trace* allows us to do that. Consider the following example:

```
= ) (trace append)
(append)
= ) (main-clause '((the mailman) (with gray hair) (drank some coffee)))
Entering: APPEND, Argument list: ((the mailman) ((drank some coffee)))
Exiting: APPEND, Value: (the mailman (drank some coffee))
(the mailman (drank some coffee))*
```

When we call *(trace append)*, we are asking LISP to **trace** calls to the function *append*. When a function is traced, each time a call to that function is evaluated, LISP prints two things on the screen: (1) a list of the arguments to the function; and (2) the value returned by the function. When we called *main-clause* after tracing *append*, we were able to see how *append* produced its result. The line labeled "entering" shows us a list of the argument values for *append*. There were two arguments with values *(the mailman)* and *((drank some coffee))*. The line labeled "exiting" shows us the value that was returned by *append*, which is the final value of the call to *main-clause*.

Notice that the second argument is not just the list *(drank some coffee)*, but the list *((drank some coffee))*. Perhaps we forgot that *last* returns a list of the last item. Seeing this problem, we can correct the definition so that *main-clause* will work correctly.

```
= ) (defun main-clause (sentence)
        (append (car sentence) (car (last sentence)))))
= ) (main-clause '((the mailman) (with gray hair) (drank some coffee)))
(the mailman drank some coffee)
```

Once you have traced a function, LISP will continue to show its arguments and results until you shut the tracing off with the function *untrace*. If you call *untrace* with an argument, e.g., *(untrace append)*, LISP will stop tracing that

---

*While all LISP implementations have a trace facility, the exact message they print out will vary.

function. If you provide no arguments, e.g., *(untrace)*, then LISP will discontinue tracing all the functions that you had previously asked it to trace. Calling *trace* with no arguments, e.g., *(trace)*, will return a list of arguments currently being traced.

Consider one more situation in which we might use *trace*. Suppose we had written code for the function *winner*, which determines the winner of a tic-tac-toe game (LISP Exercise 4.10). Suppose that when we called *winner* with a winning configuration we got *t* rather than *x* or *o*. The solution to this problem in the answer section employs six helping functions, but we might suspect the problem is in the function *check*, since that function checks a set of three squares to see if each holds the same letter. As a result, we could trace *check* to see what happens each time it is called in the course of executing *winner*. The interaction we would get is shown below.

```
= ) (trace check)
(check)
= ) (winner '((x o x) (nil x nil) (o o o)))
Entering: CHECK, Argument list: (x o x)
Exiting: CHECK, Value: nil

Entering: CHECK, Argument list: (nil x nil)
Exiting: CHECK, Value: nil

Entering: CHECK, Argument list: (o o o)
Exiting: CHECK, Value: t


t
```

The function *check* is called three times in the course of evaluating our call to *winner*. The first two calls to *check* are checking the first two nonwinning rows and the third call is checking the winning configuration of *os* in the bottom row. Here *check* returns *t* rather than *o*. In each of these three calls, *check* is being passed the correct arguments. Therefore the error must be in *check* (or its helping functions), causing it to return the wrong value.

This is the code for *check*:

```
(defun check (cell1 cell2 cell3)
      (or (check-help cell1 cell2 cell3 'o)
          (check-help cell1 cell2 cell3 'x)))
```

If we are uncertain about what *or* does, we could trace it, but let us assume we know what *or* does. In that case, we can see that *check* either returns a value returned by the helping function *check-help*, or else *nil*. So, if *check* is returning *t* instead of *o*, the error must involve the code for *check-help*. We could trace *check-help* at this point, but once again, it is probably more efficient to inspect the code directly. We can see that *check-help* is called directly with the arguments to *check* and a literal atom (either 'x or 'o), so it is clear what arguments are passed to *check-help*, and in fact these are the arguments we intended. As a result the error must be in the code for *check-help*.

Indeed, this error was actually produced by a buggy version of *check-help*. In contrast to the correct definition of *check-help* in the appendix, the buggy version of *check-help* is

```
(defun check-help (cell1 cell2 cell3 letter)
    (and (equal cell1 letter)
        (equal cell2 letter)
        (equal cell3 letter)))
```

To correct this code, we need to recognize that *and* returns the value of its last argument. If we want to return the letter rather than *t* when all three cells hold the same letter, we need to add a final argument, *letter*, to the *and*.

Tracing is a popular means of debugging complex code. This example shows how *trace* can be used to narrow down the portion of code that contains a bug. However, it also demonstrates that after the incorrect code has been narrowed down sufficiently, it may be more efficient to inspect the code itself for bugs, rather than continuing to *trace* additional functions.

LISP Exercises

Try the following problems. In each case, you should type the function definition into LISP and then call the functions as shown. Then, see if you can debug the functions.

4.11 The function *add-pairs* takes one argument, which is a list with three embedded lists. Each of the embedded lists has two elements. The function should find the embedded lists that consist of two numbers and return the sum of all the numbers in those embedded lists. For example:

```
= > (add-pairs '((4 5) (6 (a)) (1 2)))
12
= > (add-pairs '((c d) (e f) (g h)))
0
```

However, there are bugs in the code. Try to find them. Here is the code for *add-pairs* and its helping function.

```
(defun add-pairs (lis)
      (+ (add-one-pair (car lis))
         (add-one-pair (cadr lis))
         (add-one-pair (caddr lis))))

(defun add-one-pair (pair)
      (cond ((and (numberp (car pair)) (numberp (caddr pair)))
             (+ (car pair) (caddr pair)))
            (t nil)))
```

Hint: Assume that the basic logic of *add-pairs* is correct. That is, we want to call *add-one-pair* on each embedded list of *lis* and sum the results of those three function calls. In that case, what should *add-one-pair* return if a embedded list does not contain two numbers?

4.12 The function *check-class* takes three arguments. The first is a list, which contains a student's class schedule. The second and third arguments are atoms — the second argument represents a day of the week and the third argument represents a time of day. The function returns *t* if the student has a class that meets at the day and time specified by the second and third argument; otherwise the function returns *nil*. The following examples show how the function should work, but if you try them, you will find there are bugs in the code. Try to fix the code so that these examples work correctly.

```
=> (setq sched '((spr 86) (engl (m w f) 10) (math (m w f) 11) (phys (tu th) 9)))
((spr 86) (engl (m w f) 10) (math (m w f) 11) (phys (tu th) 9)))
=> (check-class sched 'm 10)
t
=> (check-class sched 'tu 10)
nil
```

Note that the schedule consists of exactly three classes. Here is the code:

```
(defun check-class (schedule day time)
      (or (and (member day (days (first-class schedule)))
               (equal time (hour (first-class schedule))))
          (and (member day (days (second-class schedule)))
               (equal time (hour (second-class schedule))))
          (and (member day (days (third-class schedule)))
               (equal time (hour (third-class schedule))))))

(defun days (class) (cadr class))

(defun hour (class) (caddr class))

(defun first-class (sch) (cdar sch))
```

(defun second-class (sch) (caadr sch))

(defun third-class (sch) (last sch))

In this chapter we have introduced some issues in good programming style and discussed some debugging techniques. These issues and techniques will become more and more important as you write longer programs both in the later chapters of this text and when you are writing programs on your own.

Summary of LISP Functions

abs This function accepts one numeric value and returns its absolute value.

Example: *(abs -5)* returns *5*.

car/cdr contractions A function call such as *(caadr lis)* is equivalent to *(car (car (cdr lis)))*, where there is one *car* for each a and one *cdr* for each d.

Example: *(cdaar '(((a b c)) (d e f)))*
returns *(b c)*.

mod This function accepts two numeric arguments and returns the remainder of dividing the first by the second.

Example: *(mod 23 5)* returns *3*.

sqrt This function accepts a single positive number as its argument and returns its square root.

Example: *(sqrt 25)* returns *5*.

trace This function accepts zero or more arguments that are function names and causes each function to be traced. If it is called with no arguments, it returns a list of all functions currently being traced. Do not quote the arguments to *trace*.

Example: *(trace square append)*
causes *square* and *append* to be traced.

untrace This function accepts zero or more arguments, which are function names and causes LISP to cease tracing each function. If called with zero arguments, it causes all functions currently being traced to be untraced. Do not quote arguments to *untrace*.

Example: *(untrace square append)* causes
square and *append* to be untraced.

Glossary   **break loop**   A LISP environment you enter in some LISPs when a syntactic
error is encountered. In the break loop you can inspect the state of LISP
at the point of the error.

bug   An error in the program that causes it to function incorrectly.

debugger   A LISP environment you enter in some LISPs when a syntactic
error is encountered; it helps you to debug an error.

debugging   The process of finding and eliminating bugs in a program.

functional error   A bug that does not result in a wrong error message, but
which causes our program to do something other than what we want
it to.

helping function   A function that performs part of the computation for a
higher-level function.

sub-function   A function that performs part of the computation for a higher-
level function.

syntactic error   A bug that results in an error message from LISP because we
have called a function with the wrong number of arguments, the wrong
type of argument, or because we are using an undefined function or
variable.

top-level function   A function that implements a program to solve a problem. A top-level function may call helping functions, but is not called by
higher-level functions.

tracing   A mode in which LISP prints out the arguments to a specified function and the value that the function returns each time the function is
called.

Input, Output, and Local Variables

In Chapter 4 you wrote a function that could determine whether one opponent or the other had won a game of tic-tac-toe. Suppose you now want to write a program that can actually play tic-tac-toe with a person. You know almost enough LISP to do that; indeed, by the end of this chapter you will be able to write a program to play tic-tac-toe (although you will be able to write more effective versions of the program after you have read future chapters). There is one remaining issue we need to address before we can write such a program: It must be possible for the program and the player to communicate their moves to each other while the game is played. That is, the program must be **interactive**; while it is running, the program needs to accept information from the keyboard and display information on the screen. In this chapter we will discuss **input/output** functions that allow programs to be interactive. In addition, we will discuss how to perform multiple actions and create local variables in the body of function definitions.

Input/Output Functions

As you know, when we call a function the value returned by any embedded function call does not appear on the screen. For example,

```
=> (setq row '(nil x x))
(nil x x)
=> (cdr row)
(x x)
=> (cons 'o (cdr row))
(o x x)
```

After setting the value of *row*, we called *cdr* on *row*, and of course, the tail of the list appeared on the screen. In the next line, the function call *(cdr x)* was embedded in a call to *cons*. As a result, the value of *(cdr x)* never appeared on the screen, since the value returned by embedded functions does not automatically appear. Only the value returned by the top-level function (in this case *cons*) automatically appears on the screen.

There are situations, however, in which it would be useful to have the results of embedded function calls appear on the screen. Our tic-tac-toe program is an example; each time the program computes a new move, we would like it to print the move on the screen. LISP provides several **output** functions that print information when they execute. One of the most useful of these is the function *print*.

Printing

The function *print* accepts one argument. It prints the value of its argument on the screen, and it returns the value of the argument.* Consider the following example:

```
=> (print (cdr row))
(x x)
(x x)
=> (cons 'o (print (cdr row)))
(x x)
(o x x)
```

In the first function call, *(cdr row)* evaluates to *(x x)*, and *print* simply prints that value on the screen. Then, since *print* is the top-level function, the value that it returns also appears on the screen. This distinction between printing a value

---

*In Common LISP, *print* returns the value of its argument, but this is not true in all LISP dialects. In some versions of LISP, *print* returns *nil*, while in other versions, it returns *t*.

and returning a value is important; they are not the same thing. The value returned by a function can serve as an argument of another function (if we embed one function inside another), but a value that is printed by *print* cannot be used by another function call, it is just something displayed on the screen.

The second example above illustrates a case where the value returned by *print* is used as an argument to another function — in this case, *cons*. The function *cons* takes the value returned by *print* and inserts *o* into that list. Thus the expression *(x x)* on the screen is the value printed by *print*, while the expression *(o x x)* is the value returned by *cons*.

The distinction between the value returned by a function and a printed value is an example of a very basic distinction in LISP: the distinction between values of functions and **side effects** of functions. Every function in LISP returns a value, but some functions perform additional actions, which are called side effects. Printing is a side effect of *print*. We have encountered two other operators in LISP that have side effects: *setq* and *defun*. The side effect of *setq* is to assign a value to a variable. The side effect of *defun* is to define a new function. While each of these three operators returns a value, we use them mainly because of the side effects they perform. Now let us look at a function whose side effect enables us to read a value from a terminal keyboard.

Reading

LISP provides several **input** functions that accept information typed by the user on the terminal keyboard. (The term **user** refers to the person interacting with a program.) The most useful of these functions is *read*. Let us consider an example function called *read-try*, which employs *read*. The function *read-try* accepts one argument and reads two inputs from the keyboard. The function adds together its argument and the first value it reads and then makes a list of that sum and the second value it reads.

```
(defun read-try (arg)
    (list (+ arg (read)) (read)))
```

As you can see, *read* is a function that does not accept any arguments. Each time *read* is called it monitors the keyboard, gets whatever LISP expression the user types (either an atom or a list) and returns that expression. Here is what happens when we call the function *read-try*:

```
= )(read-try 8)
14
pencils
(22 pencils)
```

When we call *read-try*, the first thing that is evaluated is *arg*, which evaluates to *8* in our example. Then the first call to *(read)* is evaluated. At that point the user is able to type a value on the keyboard. Ordinarily, if you type while a function is executing, nothing appears on the screen, which indicates that LISP is not able to accept any input (although the characters may still be stored in your computer's memory). But when *(read)* is called, LISP accepts input from the keyboard, and indeed, will not progress any further until you do type something. As you can see, in this example, the user types *14*, so the function call *(+ arg (read))* returns *22*. Then a second call to *read* is evaluated and returns the next value the user types, which is *pencils*. Finally, the function returns the list *(22 pencils)*.

Notice that when you type an input to *read*, it is not quoted. This is because *read* does not evaluate the input. Notice, also, that LISP does not print any prompt character on the screen when it is seeking input for a *read*. Since there is no indication to the user when a function requires input, the user must simply know when and what to type. Shortly, however, we will discuss how to print a prompt.

A final point: Each time you call *read*, how much does the function read from the keyboard? It reads exactly one atom or list and stops reading as soon as the atom is terminated or the list is balanced.*

LISP Exercises

5.1 Write a function called *read-aver-3* that does not take any arguments. The function gets three inputs and returns the average of those inputs (i.e., the sum of the inputs divided by three). For example,

= ⟩ *(read-aver-3)*
15
8
22
15

5.2 Write a function called *read-combine* that accepts one argument, which must be a list. The function should get an input that must also be a list,

---

*This feature varies from one LISP implementation to another. In some implementations *read* will wait for a carriage return, but only return the first atom or list.

and return a new version of the input list in which the first element has been replaced by the first element in the argument. For example,

```
= ⟩ (read-combine '(a b c))
(x y z)
(a y z)
```

Multiple Actions in a Function

As you will recall, the template for the function definitions we have discussed so far looks like this:

```
(defun ⟨function-name⟩ ⟨parameter-list⟩
    ⟨function-body⟩ )
```

The symbol ⟨function-body⟩ represents a single top-level function call. Of course, that function call may in turn have embedded function calls, so we can actually write complex functions based on this template. Now that we want to write functions that do input/output, we may want to do several function calls in succession, rather than embedding them into a single top-level function call. We can actually use *defun* to write a function that performs multiple actions. Thus our elaborated template for a function definition is

```
(defun ⟨function-name⟩ ⟨parameter-list⟩
    [⟨LISP expression1⟩
    ⟨LISP expression2⟩
        .
        .
    ⟨LISP expressioni⟩])
```

The following function, *print-sum*, is an example of a function that performs two actions sequentially. This function prints a list on the screen, then reads two numbers and prints their sum.

```
(defun print-sum ()
    (print '(type two numbers))
    (print (+ (read) (read))))
```

Note the empty parameter list following the function name in this example. Although this function does not accept any arguments, we cannot simply omit the parameter list; instead, we type the list with nothing in it. Here is an example of a call to this function:

```
=> (print-sum)
(type two numbers) 3 4
7
7
```

This function prints a prompt for the user, specifying that two inputs are required and specifying what the inputs should be. The user types both inputs on the same line, each followed by a space.* Then the function prints the sum of the numbers and returns the value of the final expression that was evaluated, which of course was the call to *print*. When *print-sum* is called as a top-level function it appears to be redundant to print the sum of the numbers instead of just computing it, since the value returned by the function appears on the screen. However, it is not redundant when *print-sum* is called as a helping function. In that case, the sum will only appear on the screen if we print it.

There is one subtle detail to appreciate about *print*. It issues a carriage return to the screen before printing its value and then it prints a space after its value. That is why the *7* did not appear on the same line as the *3* and the *4*. Thus *print* provides us with a convenient means of printing multiple outputs without having them bunched up on a single line. In a later section, we will describe other output functions that give us more control over the format of output on the screen.†

LISP Exercises

5.3 Write a function called *print-pal* that accepts two arguments, each of which must be a list. The function should print a palindrome of the first list, then print a palindrome of the second list. Finally, the function

---

*We could type a carriage return rather than a space after each input, in which case the format of the information on the screen would be somewhat different than in this example.

†While this is true of Common LISP, in some LISPs *print* issues a carriage return after printing the value. The manifestation of the distinction can be subtle, and you need to be prepared to experiment with your LISP. Franz LISP, a common dialect, issues no carriage return before or after printing the value. If you have such a dialect of LISP, you have to issue your own carriage returns by *(terpri)*, as discussed later in this chapter.

should print a palindrome of the list formed by merging the two arguments into one long list and return that final palindrome. For example,

```
=> (print-pal '(a b c) '(d e f))
(a b c c b a)
(d e f f e d)
(a b c d e f f e d c b a)
(a b c d e f f e d c b a)
```

5.4 Write a function called *read-check* that accepts one argument, which must be a list. The function should type the prompt *(type an expression)* and read an input from the user. The function should return *t* if the input is a member of the argument list, and return *nil* otherwise. For example,

```
=> (read-check '(a b c d))
(type an expression) b
t
```

Local Variables and *let*

When we write functions that perform multiple actions, we frequently need to store the results of one action for use in a subsequent action. We can store such results by means of local variables. For example, suppose we want a function that reads two inputs, prints their sum, and then prints their difference. We will need to use local variables to store the values that are read by the function so that we can compute their difference after computing their sum. The only local variables we have discussed are parameters, but since they are bound to arguments when the function is called, they are not useful for the purposes discussed here.* Instead, LISP provides the special form *let* to allow us to create additional local variables.

Consider the following function that reads two inputs, prints their sum, and then prints their difference. This function employs a *let*† to create two local variables, *hold1* and *hold2*.

---

*We can reset the value of parameters in a function definition, but if we do that we will no longer have access to the corresponding argument of the function. Hence, parameters are not generally useful for storing results in a function.

†Some older versions of LISP, such as Interlisp, do not have *let*, which is a relatively new LISP construct. In these LISPs you will have to use the older *prog* structure, which is discussed later in this chapter.

```
(defun sum-diff ()
    (let (hold1 hold2)
        (print '(type a number))
        (setq hold1 (read))
        (print '(type another number))
        (setq hold2 (read))
        (print '(the sum of the inputs is))
        (print (+ hold1 hold2))
        (print '(the difference of the inputs is))
        (print (- hold1 hold2)))))
```

This function performs multiple *read*s, *print*s, and *setq*s, but they are all embedded in a call to *let*. The first argument of the *let* is a **local-variable list**, which is similar to the parameter list in a *defun*. The local variable list in a *let* **declares** the local variables that will be used in the *let*. In the example above, *hold1* and *hold2* are the local variables. Unlike parameters, however, the local variables in a *let* are not bound to function arguments. Thus the local variables in a *let* are available for storing any results that are computed in the body of the *let*.

A *let* can have any number of additional arguments following the local-variable list. These additional arguments are LISP expressions that will be evaluated in sequence, just like multiple actions in a *defun*. And, like a *defun*, a *let* returns the value of its last argument. In our example, there are eight LISP expressions following the local-variable list. As you can see, when the *let* is evaluated, each of the local variables *hold1* and *hold2* is used to store a user input. That is, two calls to *read* are executed, and each time the input value is assigned to one of the local variables. Then the function prints the sum of the two numbers, followed by the difference of the two numbers. Finally, *let* returns the value of its last expression, *(print (- hold1 hold2))*. If we call the function *sum-diff*, this is what happens:

```
= > (sum-diff)
(type a number) 56
(type another number) 78
(the sum of the two numbers is)
134
(the difference of the two numbers is)
- 22
- 22
= > (+ hold1 5)
error: unbound variable: hold1
```

Recall that since *hold1* and *hold2* are local variables, they will no longer have any value once the evaluation of the *let* has terminated. Thus we obtain an error message in the example when we try using one of the variables after the function has been evaluated.

LISP Exercises

5.5 Write a function called *print-nums* that does not take any arguments. The function should print the prompt *(type two numbers)*, and then get two inputs from the keyboard. The function should print the second number it reads, followed by the first number, then print the sum of the two numbers and return that sum. For example,

```
=> (print-nums)
(type two numbers) 19 32
32
19
51
51
```

5.6 Write a function called *read-print* that accepts one argument, which can be any LISP expression. The function should go through the following steps:
   1. Type the prompt *(type an input)*.
   2. Read and print the input without storing it in a variable.
   3. Type the prompt *(type another input)*, and read and store the input.
   4. Finally, the function should print a list consisting of the argument to the function and the second input and return that list.
For example,

```
=> (read-print '(a b c))
(type an input) (j k)
(j k)
(type another input) x
((a b c) x)
((a b c) x)
```

Initializing Variables in a *let*

As we have seen, we can assign a value to local variables in a *let* with a call to *setq*, but *let* will also allow us to assign an initial value to a variable when we declare it in the local-variable list. In order to **initialize** a variable in the local-variable list, we replace the variable name with a list containing two elements: the variable name and the initial value for the variable. For example, consider a function called *rectangle* that accepts a list containing the length and width of a rectangle and prints the area, perimeter, and diagonal of the rectangle. Since we will need to use the two dimensions in three calculations, we will start by extracting them from the argument and assigning them to local variables. Here is how we can write the function:

```
(defun rectangle (dimensions)
    (let ((len (car dimensions)) (wid (cadr dimensions)))
        (print (list 'area (* len wid)))
        (print (list 'perimeter (* 2 (+ len wid))))
        (print (list 'diagonal (sqrt (+ (square len) (square wid)))))))
```

The local-variable list contains two elements, each of which is a list. Each of these sublists contains two elements: an atom, which serves as a local variable, and a function call. In each case, the function call is evaluated and the value is assigned to the variable.* An important point about *let* is that you cannot use one local variable in a *let* to initialize another local variable. For example, the following version of *rectangle* will not work, because it tries to use *len* and *wid* to initialize the variable *area*.

```
(defun rectangle (dimensions)
    (let ((len (car dimensions)) (wid (car dimensions))
            (area (* len wid)))
        (print (list 'area area))
        (print (list 'perimeter (* 2 (+ len wid))))
        (print (list 'diagonal (sqrt (+ (square len) (square wid)))))))
```

If you tried to call this function it would return the error message "unbound variable: len."

Given our examples, we can generate the following template for a *let*:

```
(let ([⟨variable⟩] . . .)
      [⟨LISP-expression1⟩
      ⟨LISP-expression2⟩
             .
             .
      ⟨LISP-expression⟩]
   )
```

---

*If a variable is not explicitly assigned an initial value in the local-variable list, most versions of LISP will assign it the value *nil* by default. However, it is not wise to count on this.

The symbol ⟨variable⟩ can take the form of an atom, which is a variable name, or a list of the form (⟨name⟩ ⟨initial-value⟩), in which ⟨name⟩ must be an atom and ⟨initial-value⟩ can be any LISP expression.

A New Function: *length*

Let us introduce another useful function before doing more exercises. The function *length* accepts a list as an argument and returns the number of elements in that list. Here is an example:

```
= ⟩ (length '(a (b c) (d (e f)) g))
4
```

LISP Exercises

5.7 Write a function called *longer-list* that accepts two arguments, each of which must be lists. The function returns the list that contains the most elements. If the lists contain the same number of elements, *longer-list* will return the word *equal*. For example,

```
(longer-list '(a) '(x y)) returns (x y).
(longer-list '(1 a) '(b (c d))) returns equal.
```

   In writing this function you should create two *let* local variables and initialize one variable to the length of the first list and the other variable to the length of the second list.

5.8 Write a function called *return-list* that does not take any arguments. This function reads one input from the user. If that input is an atom, *return-list* returns the atom in a list. If the input is already a list, *return-list* returns that list. If the argument is an empty list the function returns the empty list. For example,

```
= ⟩ (return-list)
cat
(cat)
= ⟩ (return-list)
(dog)
(dog)
```

   In writing this function you should create a *let* local variable and initialize it to the input that is read in.

Local and Global Variables

In Chapter 1 we discussed global variables, which are assigned values outside the context of any function we define. In this chapter, we have discussed how to create local variables to use in function definitions; but it is possible to use global variables as well. We can simply use a global variable inside the body of a function, much as we would a local variable. When a variable appears in a function definition that is not a parameter of the function and not in a local-variable list, LISP will treat it as a global variable.* Consider the following function definition:

```
= > (defun update-library (book)
       (setq library (cons book library)))
update-library
```

The variable *library* is a global variable, in contrast to *book*, which is a local variable. After we have assigned a value to *library*, we can call *update-library* as follows:

```
= > (setq 'library '(Dune Hamlet Oliver-Twist))
(Dune Hamlet Oliver-Twist)
```

```
= > (update-library 'Texas)
(Texas Dune Hamlet Oliver-Twist)
```

This function returns a new list in which the argument to the function has been inserted at the beginning of the global variable. Note that this function also changes the value of the global variable.

Global variables may be useful when you have several functions in a program that require the same value. If you assign a value to a global variable, you do not need to pass the value as an argument to each of the functions that use it. However, global variables should be used cautiously. The very nature of a global variable makes it difficult to track down the functions that use it and change its value. As a result, it can be difficult to debug functions that use global variables. When we pass values as arguments between functions, on the other hand, it is easy to see which functions change their value.

It is never appropriate to use a global variable to store values that are used only in a single function. Thus it is not appropriate to use global variables in place of the local variables we have declared in this chapter. If we do use global variables for this purpose we run the risk that we will inadvertently use the

---

*When a non-local variable appears in a helping function, some versions of LISP will check to see if the variable is local to a higher-level function, and if so, access its value rather than look for a global variable. If that search fails, then these versions of LISP check whether the variable is global. However, Common LISP only checks to see if the variable is global.

same global variable in different functions and as a result, may increase the difficulty of debugging our functions.*

Conditionally Exiting a Function: *prog* and *return*

Sometimes we need to define a function with multiple actions such that we can return from the function without performing all the actions. For example, consider the function *sum-diff* that we coded earlier. This function needs two non-numeric inputs from the user, but there is no way to prevent the user from inadvertently typing a non-number. As a result, it would be convenient to check each input after it is read and exit the function immediately without attempting to compute the sum and difference, if a non-numeric input is typed. LISP provides two special forms, *prog* and *return*, which when used together allow us to exit a function without performing all the actions. Consider the following version of *sum-diff*:

```
(defun sum-diff ()
    (prog (hold1 hold2)
        (print '(type a number))
        (setq hold1 (read))
        (and (not (numberp hold1)) (return nil))
        (print '(type another number))
        (setq hold2 (read))
        (and (not (numberp hold2)) (return nil))
        (print (+ hold1 hold2))
        (print (- hold1 hold2))))
```

As you can see, a *prog* is very much like a *let*. The first argument to a *prog* is a local-variable list. As in the case of a *let*, this list can contain either variable names or variable initializations.† The other arguments to a *prog* are LISP expressions that are evaluated in sequence.

Here are two sample interactions with *sum-diff*:

```
= ) (sum-diff)
(type a number) 38
(type another number) (12)
```

---

*If a local variable is declared in a parameter list or a local-variable list, LISP will treat it as a local variable, even if a global variable with the same name exists.

†In some LISP dialects, the local-variable list of a *prog* can contain only variable names and not initializations.

```
nil
=> (sum-diff)
(type a number) 38
(type another number) 12
50
26
nil
```

The function *sum-diff* tests each input as soon as the input is read to see if it is a number. If it is not, then the call *(return nil)* is evaluated. The special form *return* accepts one argument. When it is called in a *prog*, its argument is evaluated and the *prog* immediately returns the value of that argument, without evaluating any further expressions.* Thus if a non-number is typed, we exit the function without attempting illegal arithmetic operations. On the other hand, if the user types two numbers, then all of the expressions in the *prog* will be evaluated.

Notice that after printing the sum and difference of the inputs, the *prog* returned *nil*. A *prog* always returns *nil* unless a call to *return* is evaluated in the body of the *prog*. Thus while a *prog* is more useful than a *let* if we want to terminate execution of a function, *let* is more convenient to use whenever we want to evaluate every expression in the function and return the value of the last expression.

To summarize this section: The function *return* is important because it allows us to control which LISP expressions in the *prog* are executed, and it allows us to return a value other than *nil*.

Reusing and Updating Variables

Sometimes it will be necessary to store several values that are read or computed in a function. In some circumstances you will be able use the same variable to store different values instead of creating a different variable for each one. Of course, at any given time, each variable can have only one value, but you can use the same variable to store a new value when the old value is no longer needed.

Consider the following function that reads three values and prints the largest.

---

*Technically, *return* can be called with no arguments, in which case the *prog* will return *nil* by default.

```
(defun largest ()
    (let (newvalue max)
        (setq max (read))
        (setq newvalue (read))
        (and () newvalue max) (setq max newvalue))
        (setq newvalue (read))
        (and () newvalue max) (setq max newvalue))
        (print max)))
```

Notice that after the first two values are read, they are compared and the larger value is assigned to the variable *max*. At that point we no longer need the value that is bound to *newvalue*. So we can reuse that variable to get the third input. Note that if new value is greater than the value of *max*, we no longer need the old value of *max*, so we can just assign the value of *newvalue* to *max*.

LISP Exercises

5.9 Write a function called *right-triangle* that accepts two arguments, the hypotenuse and one other side of a right triangle. The function should check that the hypotenuse really is longer than the second side. If not, the function should return impossible. If the triangle is possible, then the function should compute the length of the third side. You can determine the length of the third side by using the equation

$$side3 = sqrt (hypotenuse^2 - side2^2).$$

The function should print a list of the lengths of the hypotenuse, second side, and third side, then print the sum of the three lengths and return *nil*. For example,

```
=) (right-triangle 13 5)
(13 5 12)
30
nil
```

5.10 Define a function called *mean3* that does not accept any arguments. The function should print the prompt *(Type three numbers)* and should employ a single local variable to sum three inputs from the user. Then the function should print the total of the three inputs, and on the next line print the average of the three inputs (the sum of the inputs divided by 3). Finally, the function should return the average. For example,

```
=) (mean3)
(Type three numbers) 234 768 33
1035
345
345
```

Literal Strings, *princ* and *terpri*

The *print* function allows us to print information on the screen conveniently, but it does not allow us much control over the format of the output. In this section we will discuss a data type and some output functions that give us more control.

Generally when you print information on the screen, you want to print more than one word — for example, we may want to print the prompt *type an input*. So far, you have learned how to achieve this by printing a literal list, like *(type an input)*. Of course, then the message appears on the screen in parentheses, which is all right, but it would be nicer if the parentheses were not there. LISP provides another data type, called a **literal string**, that allows us to print the phrases we want, without parentheses. A literal string is a sequence of characters surrounded by double quotes.* The following are examples of literal strings:

```
"type an input"
"28 Maple Avenue"
"Hi. What's your name?"
```

In many ways literal strings are similar to numbers. First, literal strings are atoms; for example, *(atom "type a number")* returns *t*. Like numbers, literal strings are not quoted (i.e., a literal string is not preceded by a single quote), because literal strings evaluate to themselves. Finally, although they are atoms, literal strings cannot be used as variables or function names. Literal strings can be used instead of lists to print a multiword message, and can even include punctuation that would be illegal inside an ordinary atom. For example, consider the following function:

---

*The character (") is called a "double quote," to distinguish it from the single quote (') you have already been using for literal atoms and lists.

```
=> (defun sphere ()
      (let (radius)
         (print "please type the radius of a sphere:")
         (setq radius (read))
         (print "the volume of the sphere is")
         (print (* (/ 4 3) 3.14 radius radius radius))))
sphere
=> (sphere)
"please type the radius of a sphere:" 5
"the volume of the sphere is"
523.33
523.33
```

When we employ literal strings, the output is improved somewhat, but there is still a flaw in the output from *sphere*: When you print a literal string with *print*, the quotation marks also appear. This is better than parentheses, but it would be nice to omit punctuation marks altogether. LISP provides a function, *princ*, that allows us to print strings without quotation marks.

Like *print*, the function *princ* prints the value of its argument on the terminal screen and returns that value. However, *princ* prints its argument differently than *print*. First, when printing a literal string, *princ* does not print the quotation marks. Second, *princ* only prints its argument, without providing any spaces or carriage returns. Thus *princ* allows more flexibility than *print*; if you want to print several outputs on one line, you can use *princ*.

It is important to remember that when you call *princ*, you will have to provide your own spaces and carriage returns. To create a space between outputs on a line, you can either print a literal string consisting of a single space (i.e., " "), or you can add an extra space to the beginning or end of a literal string you are already printing. In order to generate a carriage return, you can use the function *terpri*. This function does not accept any arguments. It outputs a carriage return and returns *nil*. The following function demonstrates the use of *princ* and *terpri*:

```
=> (defun greet (firstname lastname)
      (let (answer)
         (princ "Hello ")
         (princ firstname)
         (princ " ")
         (princ lastname)
         (terpri)
         (princ "May I call you ")
         (princ firstname)
         (princ "?")
         (print "please type yes or no:")
         (read)))
```

greet

=⟩ *(greet 'Jack 'Harrison)*
Hello Jack Harrison
May I call you Jack?
please type yes or no: *yes*
yes

Notice that in order to space the first line correctly, a trailing space was included after *Hello* and another was inserted between the first and last name. Similarly, a trailing space was included after *May I call you*. The final line of output was printed with *print* rather than *princ*. Since *print* issues a carriage return before printing its argument we did not call *terpri* after printing the question mark. We also did not need a trailing space after *please type yes or no:*, because *print* automatically prints a space after the value of its argument.

LISP Exercises

5.11 Write a function *greet1* that does not accept any arguments. The function should print

What is your name:

(without parentheses or quotes). The function should read the person's name (e.g., Fred), which the user should type on the same line beginning one space after the colon. Then the function should issue a carriage return and print:

Well, Fred, what is your favorite color:

The user should type a color (e.g., green) on the same line, one space after the colon. Then the function should issue a carriage return and print the following line, filling in whatever color the user types

What a coincidence, Fred! Green is my favorite color too.

5.12 Write a program, *tic-out*, which accepts one argument, a list of three lists describing a tic-tac-toe position. Each sublist corresponds to a row of the board and contains a combination of *x*s, *o*s, and *nil*s (which represent blanks). The function should print the board on the screen and return *nil*. In printing the board, each *nil* in the list should be replaced by an underline character __. For example,

```
=> (tic-out '((x o o)(o x o)(x nil x)))
xoo
oxo
x_x
nil
```

5.13 (Optional) Write a program called *play-tic-tac-toe* to play tic-tac-toe. You can use the functions *tic-out* and *winner* (LISP Exercise 4.10) as helping functions in your solution. This program will always let the user go first. When the program makes its move, it should simply select the next free square, picking the lowest numbered square in the sequence

```
2 6 4
7 1 8
5 9 3
```

Below is an example of its play.

```
=> (play-tic-tac-toe)
Do you want to be X or O: x
Enter the number of the row and then the column: 1 2
_x_


___

___


Now I'll make my move:
_x_
_o_
___


Enter the number of the row and then the column: 1 3
_xx
_o_
___


Now I'll make my move:
oxx
_o_
___


Enter the number of the row and then the column: 3 3
oxx
_o_
__x
```

Now I'll make my move:
oxx
_o_
o_x

Enter the number of the row and then the column: *2 3*
oxx
_ox
o_x

Congratulations! You have won.
nil

In this chapter we have learned how to write functions that create local variables and execute multiple actions, and how to write functions that can communicate with the user. In Chapter 6 we will build on these capabilities and learn how to write functions that will execute a series of expressions not just once, but repeatedly.

Summary of LISP Functions

length This function accepts a list as an argument and returns the number of elements in the list.

Example: *(length '(a b c))* returns 3.

let This special form can be used to create local variables. The first argument of a *let* is a local-variable list. Each element in this list is either a variable name or a list containing a variable name and its initial value. The other arguments in the *let* are LISP expressions that are evaluated in sequence. A *let* returns the value of its last argument.

Example:
(let (a)
    (setq a (read))
    (list (times a 4) (times a a)))

If the user types 10, this *let* returns (40 100).

princ This function takes one argument, prints the value of that argument on the terminal screen and returns that value. Unlike *print*, *princ* does not issue a carriage return nor print an extra space.

Example: *(print 'hi)* prints *hi* on the screen and returns *hi*.

print This function takes one argument and prints the value of that argument on the terminal screen. It issues a carriage return before printing the argument and prints a space after the argument. It also returns the value of its argument.

Example: *(print 'hi)* prints *hi* on the screen and returns *hi*.

prog This special form can be used to create local variables. The first argument of a *prog* is a local-variable list. Each element in this list is either a variable name or a list containing a variable name and its initial value. The other arguments in the *prog* are LISP expressions that are evaluated in sequence. A *prog* returns *nil* except when a call to *return* is evaluated in the *prog*. In that case, the *prog* returns the argument of the *return*.

Example:
```
(prog (a)
    (setq a (read))
    (and (not (numberp a)) (return 'non-number))
    (print (list (times a 4) (times a a))))
```
If the user types *10*, this *prog* prints *(40 100)* and returns *nil*. If the user types a non-number, such as *x*, this *prog* returns *non-number*.

read This function does not accept any arguments. It returns an input (a single atom or list) typed by the user.

Example: *(read)* will return the expression typed by the user.

return This special form can be used in the body of a *prog*. It takes one argument, and causes the *prog* to return the value of that argument without evaluating any further expressions.

Example: *(return 'non-number)* will return *non-number* as the value of the *prog* within which it is embedded.

terpri This function does not accept any arguments. It issues a carriage return and returns *nil*.

Example: *(terpri)*.

Glossary

declaring local variables   Creating local variables by including them in the local-variable list of a *let* or *prog*.

initializing a variable   Assigning an initial value to a variable, usually before entering the body of a special form, such as a *let* or *prog*.

interactive processing   processing in which a program communicates with the user by means of the terminal.

input functions   Functions that read inputs from the user.

output functions   Functions that print outputs.

literal string   A sequence of characters surrounded by double quotes. LISP treats the sequence of characters literally.

local-variable list   A list in a *let* or *prog* in which local variables are declared and optionally initialized.

side effects   Actions performed by operators other than returning a value. Operators with side effects include *defun*, *print*, *read*, and *setq*.

user   A person interacting with a program.

Loops: Numeric Iteration and Input-Controlled Iteration

6

In Chapter 5 you learned how to write functions that perform a sequence of actions. In this chapter you will learn how to use a programming structure to write functions that repeatedly perform a sequence of actions. These functions are called **iterative functions** or **loops**, because they cycle through a sequence of LISP expressions, evaluating them over and over until a specified condition is reached and the function terminates. You will learn how to write two types of iterative functions in this chapter: loops that decide when to terminate by counting how many times they execute, and loops that read inputs and terminate when a specified kind of input is typed in by the user.

Iteration: Making Programs Repeat Actions

Iteration is a powerful programming tool. In the functions you have written so far, you have had to specify every function call that you wanted to perform. For example, suppose you want a function that will read three inputs, add them together, and return the final sum. If you want to print a prompt before each input, you would have to write a function similar to *add-three*, shown here.

```
(defun add-three ()
  (let ((sum 0))
    (print "Type a number")
    (setq sum (+ sum (read)))
    (print "Type a number")
    (setq sum (+ sum (read)))
    (print "Type a number")
    (setq sum (+ sum (read))))))
```

This function includes three identical function calls that print the prompts, and another three identical function calls that read the three numbers and add them into the total. Clearly, this is not the ideal method for repeating actions. Suppose we want to write a function, *add-ten*, that reads ten numbers and prints their sum. We would have to include the lines

```
(print "Type a number")
(setq sum (+ sum (read)))
```

in the function ten times instead of three times. Think how much easier it would be if we could just include those lines in the code once, and then indicate to LISP how many times they should be evaluated. That is exactly what we can do by writing an iterative function. Common LISP provides a special form, *loop*, for performing iteration.

The *loop* Construct*

The special form *loop* can take any number of arguments, which LISP repeatedly evaluates in sequence until it is forced to exit. The template for a *loop* is

---

*The *loop* construct is especially useful to introduce iteration, but it is not a built-in form in all dialects of LISP. If your version of LISP is Franz LISP or MACLISP, you should try using the following code to define *loop* before starting the exercises:

```
(defmacro loop (&rest code)
  '(prog nil tag ,@code (go tag)))
```

This definition includes constructs not yet covered in this book, so it is not important for you to understand why this definition works. The symbol in front of the *prog* is a backquote. In Interlisp the following code provides a definition for *loop*.

```
(defineq (loop (nlambda code
  (prog nil tag (mapcar code 'eval)
    (go tag)))))
```

```
(loop ⟨expression1⟩
      ⟨expression2⟩
           .
           .
      ⟨expressionn⟩)
```

Each expression in the loop is evaluated in order from left to right (top to bottom in the diagram). After LISP evaluates the last expression in the *loop*, it jumps back to the first expression and starts evaluating the expressions in sequence again. LISP will continue cycling through the expressions in the *loop* until it evaluates an expression that forces it to exit. We will use the special form *return* to cause the *loop* to terminate.

Numeric Iteration: Keeping Count

One way to write an iterative function is to keep count of how many times the actions in the loop are executed, and then quit when they have been performed a specified number of times. This type of iteration is called **numeric iteration**, because the loop is controlled by counting to a particular number.

Functions for Counting

LISP provides two functions that are especially useful for counting by ones. The function *1+* (pronounced "one-plus") takes one argument, which must be a number, and adds 1 to it. So *(1+ num)* is equivalent to *(+ num 1)*. The function *1−* (pronounced "one-minus") also takes one number as an argument and subtracts 1 from it. Thus *(1− num)* is equivalent to *(− num 1)*.

Now let us write a function that performs numeric iteration. Suppose we need a function that will add up all the integers between 1 and some specified value — for example, all the integers between 1 and 5. We can write a function called *add-integers*, which does this addition. This function will take one argument, which must be a positive integer, and return the sum of all the numbers between 1 and that argument. For example, *(add-integers 5)* will add together *1, 2, 3, 4,* and *5* and return *15*. Below is the code for *add-integers*. (We have numbered each line in the function so that we can go through it step by step to explain how it works.)

```
(defun add-integers (last)                              [1]
    (let ((count 1) (total 1))                          [2] Initialize local variables
        (loop                                           [3] Begin loop structure
        (cond ((equal count last) (return total)))      [4] Perform exit test
        (setq count (1+ count))                         [5] Update counter
        (setq total (+ total count)))))                 [6] Update result*
```

1. As you can see, the function *add-integers* accepts one argument, which is assigned to the parameter *last*. The value of *last* determines how many times the expressions in the loop will be evaluated, as we see in line 4.

2. Two local variables, *count* and *total*, are declared and initialized in line 2. These variables must be initialized before entering the loop, because each time around the loop they are evaluated before they are assigned a new value.

   a. The variable *count* is the **counter** for the loop — that is, it counts how many times the actions in the body of the loop are executed. The counter is the **control variable** for the loop because it controls how many times the actions in the loop are performed. As you will see, each time around the loop, the value of *count* will be increased or **incremented** by *1*, and the loop will terminate when the test in line 4 finds that the value of *count* has reached the value of *last*. Since we want to generate each of the numbers between *1* and *last*, we will start *count* with an initial value of *1*.

   b. The variable *total* serves as a **result variable** in the loop. We use this variable to cumulate a value as we go around the loop. When we exit, we return the final value of this variable. In particular, *total* is used to cumulate the sum of the integers we generate; each time we increment the counter in the loop, we will add the resulting integer

---

*You may be using a LISP that does not have *loop* and does not allow you to define *loop* as in the previous footnote. In this case, you will have to resort to the older *prog* structure to get the same effect. The equivalent code for *add-integers* is

```
(defun add-integers (last)
    (prog (count total)
        (setq count 1)
        (setq total 1)
    loop (cond ((equal count last) (return total)))
        (setq count (1 + count))
        (setq total (+ total count))
        (go loop)))
```

This uses the same syntax as *prog* introduced in Chapter 5, with the addition of the ability to insert a tag — *loop* — and to specify that LISP jump back to this tag and repeat the actions; *(go loop)* does this. The mapping between the code in the text and this *prog* construct should be apparent.

to the running total stored in *total*. If we initialize *count* to *1*, then the cumulative sum of all the integers up to that point is 1, so *total* is also initialized to 1.

3. The entire body of the *let* consists of a call to *loop*. The expressions in the loop will be performed repeatedly until a call to *return* causes the loop to terminate. Let us consider what each expression in the loop accomplishes.

4. First, in line 4, we have the **exit test** for the loop. In numeric iteration, the exit test checks to see if the counter has reached a specified value or **limit** that is usually passed as an argument. If so, then *return* is called to terminate the loop and return a result. Thus in *add-integers*, when the counter has reached the value of the parameter *last*, we exit the loop and return the final value of *total*. If *count* and *last* are not yet equal, then the next expression in the loop will be evaluated.

5. If we do not exit the loop, then we need to **update** the variables. As you can see, in line 5, the function adds *1* to the control variable *count*. This variable was initialized to *1*, so the first time line 5 is evaluated, *count* will be assigned the value *2*. We will continue incrementing the counter each time we go around the loop, generating the integers *3, 4, . . .* until we reach the value of *last*.

6. After updating *count* to obtain the next integer in the sequence, we need to add that new number to the running sum in *total*. Thus in line 6, the new value of *count* is added to the current value of *total*, and *total* is reset to that value. The first time around the loop, *count* has been incremented to *2*, while *total* still has its initial value — *1*; so *total* is reset to the sum of those numbers — *3*. The next time we reach line 6, *result* will have the value *3*, while *count* will have been incremented from *2* to *3*, so *total* will be assigned the value of *(+ 3 3)*, which is the cumulative sum of the first three integers. Thus each time we jump back to the exit test, *total* will hold the sum of the integers we have generated so far.

7. After the final line in *loop* is executed, LISP jumps back to the first line in *loop* and continues evaluating expressions from there. If the value of *count* has reached the value of *last*, then the exit test in line 4 causes the value of *total* to be returned. Otherwise, we will go through the body of the loop again.

LISP Exercises

6.1 Write a function called *factorial* that accepts one argument, which must be a positive integer. This function computes the factorial of its argument. (The factorial of a number is the product of all the integers between 1 and the number multiplied together.) For example,

(factorial 5) returns *120*, which equals $1 \times 2 \times 3 \times 4 \times 5$.

The function should accept the argument *0* in addition to the positive integers. (The factorial of 0 is defined as 1.) The function *factorial* has a structure very similar to the example *add-integers*. Think carefully about the initial values of your local variables and how each should be updated.

The General Form of Numeric Iteration Functions

Let us consider another example of a numeric iteration function. Suppose we did not already have the built-in function *, and we wanted to write a function that performed integer multiplication. It is a fact of arithmetic that you can multiply two numbers, *x* and *y*, simply by adding *x* to itself *y* times. For example, you can multiply 3 and 6 by adding 3 to itself 6 times:

$$3 \times 6 = 3 + 3 + 3 + 3 + 3 + 3 = 18.$$

The function *int-multiply* uses numeric iteration to perform multiplication by repeated additions:

```
(defun int-multiply (x y)
      (let ((result 0) (count 0))
         (loop
            (cond ((equal count y) (return result)))
            (setq count (1+ count))
            (setq result (+ result x)))))
```

LISP Exercises

6.2 Answer the following questions about the function *int-multiply*.
   (a) Which variable is the control variable?
   (b) Which variable is the result variable?
   (c) Suppose we call *(int-multiply 4 6)*. What value of the control value will cause the function to exit the loop and return a value?
   (d) How is the value of *count* updated each time through the loop?
   (e) Suppose we call *(int-multiply 3 8)*. How is the value of *result* updated each time through the loop?

(f) Suppose we call *(int-multiply 5 0)*. How many times will the variables be updated inside the loop?

By comparing *add-integer* and *int-multiply*, we can lay out the general form of a numeric iteration function. The template for numeric iteration is

```
(defun ⟨function-name⟩ ⟨parameter-list⟩
    (let (⟨counter variable initialization⟩
          [⟨result variable initializations⟩])
        (loop
            (cond ⟨exit test of counter variable⟩ (return [⟨result⟩]))
                ⟨update the counter variable⟩
                ⟨other loop actions,
                    including updating result variables⟩)))
```

Planning Numeric Iteration

We can specify some general principles for initializing and updating variables. These principles assume that we are counting up in the loop and that the exit test employs the predicate *equal* to compare the counter to a "limit" parameter. In later sections we will discuss variations on these assumptions.

Initializing the Control Variable

Notice that in *add-integers* the counter is initialized to *1*, but in *int-multiply* it is initialized to *0*. In numeric iteration the counter should be set to the lowest value of the limit parameter that we want the function to be able to process. In *add-integers*, we want to add integers beginning with 1, so the counter was initialized to *1*, and a function call such as *(add-integers 0)* would not work. In the case of *int-multiply*, however, *0* was the lowest value we wanted the function to accept, so we initialized the counter in that function to *0*.

Initializing the Result Variable

Determining the initial value of a result variable is relatively easy when we recognize that we can exit the loop without ever updating the variables. A function will return a value without updating variables whenever it is called with an argument that is equal to the counter initialization. For example, if we call *(add-integers 1)* the exit test will immediately return *t*, and we will exit the loop. So we need to figure out the correct answer to be returned when the function is called with the initial value of the counter, and we need to assign that value to the result variable. Thus *(add-integers 1)* should return *1*, so the result variable is initialized to *1*.

Notice that we need to initialize our result variable to something we can build on as we go around the loop. If we are computing a numerical result, we need to initialize the result to a number; if we are building a list we need to initialize the result variable to a list.

Ordering the Loop Actions

One or more loop actions will always follow the exit test. Whenever the counter is employed to update the result variable, as in *add-integer*, it is necessary to update the counter first, so that the result update will employ the new counter value. If the result update does not employ the counter, as in *int-multiply*, it is not strictly necessary to update the counter first. It is still a good habit always to update the counter first, to ensure that it is updated first when necessary.

LISP Exercises

6.3 Write a function called *num-sum*, that takes one argument, which must be an integer greater than or equal to 0. The function should read a series of numbers from the user and return the sum of those numbers. The argument indicates how many numbers to input. If the argument is 0 the function should return *0* without reading any numbers. The function should print the prompt *Enter the next number:* before reading each number. For example,

```
=> (num-sum 3)
Enter the next number: 15
Enter the next number: 30
Enter the next number: 45
90
```

Computing Final Results

In all the examples and exercises so far, our functions have simply returned the value of a result variable. However, *return* can accept a function call as an argument, and it is often useful to return a result computed from the result variable. For example, suppose we wanted to write a function called *num-average* that reads a series of numbers and returns the average. In order to do that, we need to add up all the numbers, and then divide that total by the number of inputs. You can modify your code for *num-sum* to do this fairly easily; you need not change the body of your loop at all, just the value returned by the function. Suppose you called your result variable *total* and your control variable *count*. Instead of calling *(return total)* when you exit the loop, you can call *(return (/ total count))*, since *total* holds the sum of the numbers and *count* holds the total number of inputs.

LISP Exercises

6.4 Write a function called *nth-item* that takes two arguments — a positive integer and a list. The function should return the element of the list in the position specified by the integer. For example,

(nth-item 4 '(a b c d e f)) returns *d*.

If the integer exceeds the number of items in the list, the function should return *nil*.

Hint: Each time you go around the loop without exiting, you should reset the list parameter to discard the first item. Then when you exit the loop you can return whatever item is first.

Variations on Counting

So far, all the problems we have discussed have involved counting up by ones. In fact, it can also be useful to count down in an iterative function. Repeatedly subtracting a constant from a variable is called **decrementing** (as opposed to incrementing). As mentioned earlier, LISP provides a special function for counting down by ones called *1-*, e.g., *(1- 5)* returns *4*. Counting down is useful if you need to generate numbers in descending order. For example, the function *nasa-countdown* takes a starting number and then prints a countdown followed by the word *blast-off*.

```
(defun nasa-countdown (start)
  (let ((count start))
    (print start)
    (loop
       (cond ((equal count 0) (return 'blast-off)))
       (setq count (1- count))
       (print count))))
```

In other circumstances you may not want to count by ones at all. For example, if you were adding just the even numbers or just the odd numbers in a sequence, you could count by twos.

Variations on Exiting

So far, we have discussed numeric iteration as a method for executing a sequence of actions a specified number of times. We know the value of the stopping point for the iteration, so we know exactly how many times a loop will execute. For example, *(add-integers 4)* will go through the loop body three times, updating the variables, and exit the fourth time around.

Numeric iteration can also be useful in finding a value that is unknown to us. To do this, instead of exiting at a predetermined number, we exit the loop when the counter has reached a number with a particular property. For example, we might write a loop that starts counting at a given value and stops when it reaches the first perfect square (that is, the first number that is the square of an integer).

For this loop, instead of using *equal* in the exit test, we would need to write a predicate that we might call *is-square* to see whether the counter is a perfect square. (Such a predicate would not be difficult to write in LISP, although you have not yet learned some of the functions you would need.) No result variable is necessary in this loop — when the counter satisfies the exit test, the counter *is* the result we want to return. Note that since we cannot predict the value on which the loop will stop, we do not know how many times we will go around the loop.

These type of loops are called **find loops**, because they are used to find an item with a particular property. Using a find loop is the simplest form of searching — looking through a sequence of items for one or more items possessing a particular property. In later chapters you will learn how to look through lists and other types of data structures to find one or more items satisfying a particular property.

LISP Exercises

6.5 Write a function called *create-list* that accepts one argument, which must be a positive integer. This function returns a list of all integers between *1* and the value of the argument, in ascending order. For example,

(create-list 8) returns (1 2 3 4 5 6 7 8).

You should count *down* in this function, so that you can just insert each new number into the front of the result variable.

6.6 Write a function called *add-negs* that accepts one argument, which must be a negative number. This function returns the sum of all the numbers between *-1* and the argument. For example,

(add-negs − 5) returns − 15, which equals − 1 + − 2 + − 3 + − 4 + − 5.

6.7 Write a function called *next-prime* that accepts one argument, which must be an integer. This function returns the first prime number that is greater than or equal to the argument. (A prime number is a number divisible only by itself and by 1.) For example,

(next-prime 24) returns 29,

because 29 is the smallest prime number larger than 24.

You will need to define a predicate in this problem that accepts a number and determines if the number is prime. We can define such a function, which we will call *primep*, with numeric iteration. The function *primep* returns *t* if its argument is prime and *nil* otherwise.

```
(defun primep (n)
    (cond ((< n 4) t)
        (t (psearch n)))))

(defun psearch (num)
    (let ((count 2) (stop (sqrt num)))
        (loop
            (cond ((> count stop) (return t))
                ((zerop (mod num count)) (return nil)))
            (setq count (1+ count))))))
```

6.8 Write a function *add-threes* that accepts one argument, which must be a number greater than or equal to 0. The function returns the sum of all the multiples of 3 between 0 and the argument. For example,

(add-threes 13) returns 30, which equals 0 + 3 + 6 + 9 + 12.

You will need a more complex exit test than in previous iterative functions to deal with the fact that the argument may not be a multiple of 3 (as in the example).

Input-controlled Iteration: Repeating under User Control

In a function that employs numeric iteration, an argument usually specifies how often to go around the loop. In some circumstances, however, it is convenient to start a loop without specifying ahead of time how often to go around it. For example, you may have a long sequence of numbers to add up, and you may not know how many numbers there are. In such circumstances we can use an alternative form of iteration called **input-controlled iteration**. In this type of iteration, the function reads an input each time around the loop. It continues going around the loop until it reads a particular type of input or a specific value, at which point execution terminates.

Consider the function *print-pals*, which is an iterative version of the function *print-pal* from LISP Exercise 5.3. This function reads an input each time around the loop and prints out a palindrome of the input.

```
(defun print-pals ()
    (let (input)
        (loop
            (print "Type a list, or an atom to quit:")
            (setq input (read))
            (cond ((not (listp input)) (return 'done)))
            (print (append input (reverse input))))))
```

First, note that the overall structure of this loop is somewhat different than in numeric iteration. A counter is not used as the control variable. Instead, each time through the loop, an input is read and assigned to *input*. The value assigned to *input* is used to determine when to exit the loop.

Second, consider the variables in the function. We need to declare only one local variable, *input*, which stores items as they are read. No result variable is necessary because we print the result each time, and return the literal atom *done* when the loop is finished. Furthermore, there is no need to initialize the variable *input*, because the variable is assigned a value in the loop before it is evaluated.

The first step in the loop body is to prompt the user to type an item. This item is read and stored in the variable *input*. Then the exit test is performed to determine whether or not the input is a list. The variable *input* therefore is the control variable of the loop. Its value determines when to exit the loop. If the input is not a list, then we immediately exit the loop. If it is a list, the palindrome is printed, and we then go back to the beginning of the loop, to print another prompt and read another input. Here is an example interaction with *print-pals*:

```
= ) (print-pals)
Input a list, or an atom to quit: (dog cat horse)
(dog cat horse horse cat dog)
Input a list, or an atom to quit: (john albert brian)
(john albert brian brian albert john)
Input a list, or an atom to quit: carnegie
done
```

The value that will cause us to exit the loop is called the **sentinel value** or simply the sentinel. When a sentinel value is input, we usually want to terminate the loop immediately, without performing the other actions in the body. Therefore it is important to test the input immediately after it is read, before performing other loop actions.

A sentinel can be used to mark the end of a sequence of inputs, if you do not know in advance how many inputs will be processed. We can just start the loop, type an input each time around until we run out, and then enter the sentinel value. When we write the function, we simply have to choose a sentinel value that we know will not appear in the sequence of inputs we need to process. In *print-pals*, we decided we would only make palindromes of lists, so we set up the function to exit when we type a non-list.

Here is an example of an input-controlled loop in which a cumulative result variable is used.

```
(defun guess-key (secret-key)
    (let ((input) (count 1))
        (loop
            (print "Type a guess:")
            (setq input (read))
            (cond ((equal input secret-key) (return count)))
            (setq count (1 + count)))))
```

This loop gets inputs from a user until the user guesses the ''secret'' code that was passed as an argument to the function (a simple-minded game that could last a long time). Note several things about this function. Each time through the loop we are updating a result variable *count*. As suggested by its name, this variable actually is a counter; it is counting how many times we go around the loop. However, we are not performing numeric iteration in this function, because the counter is not the control variable. Notice that the counter is initialized. As is generally true of result variables, *count* is evaluated in the loop (on the right-hand side of a *setq*) before it is assigned a value, so it must be initialized. On the other hand, the control input variable is not initalized, because it is assigned a value in the loop before being evaluated.

Note also that the local variable list in this function differs from the lists in previous functions. In other cases, we have either had a list containing only variable-value pairs, e.g., *(let ((count 1) (total 1)) ...)* or a list containing just variable names *(let (input) ...)*. In this case, we need to initialize *count*, but we do not need to initialize *input*, so we use variable-value pairs and leave out the value for *input*. When a variable is listed without an initial value, it is assigned the value *nil*, so *(let ((input) (count 1)) ...)* is the same as *(let ((input nil) (count 1)) ...)*.

Here is the template for an input-controlled loop:

```
(defun ⟨function-name⟩ ⟨parameter-list⟩
    (let (⟨input variable initialization⟩
            [⟨result variable initializations⟩])
        (loop
            [⟨prompt⟩]
            ⟨input⟩
            (cond (⟨exit test on input⟩ (return [⟨results⟩])))
            ⟨loop actions⟩)))
```

The prompt to the user is optional. It is usually a good idea to prompt for input, particularly in a loop, so that the user knows the function is waiting for something to read.

LISP Exercises

6.9 Write a function called *read-square* that does not accept any arguments. The function should contain a loop that prints the prompt *Enter the next number:*, reads a number and prints the square of the number. The function should return the atom *done* when the user types something that is not a number. For example,

=⟩ *(read-square)*
Enter the next number: *5*

```
25
Enter the next number: -11
121
Enter the next number: x
done
```

6.10 Write a function called *read-sum* that does not accept any arguments. The function should read a series of numbers and return the sum of those numbers when the user types a non-number. The function should print the prompt *Enter the next number:* before reading each number. For example,

```
=> (read-sum)
Enter the next number: 15
Enter the next number: 30
Enter the next number: 45
Enter the next number: stop
90
```

The function *read-sum* is similar to the function *num-sum* that employs numeric iteration. Thus you will be able to compare directly the two types of iteration. There is one interesting difference between them. In input-controlled iteration you have to create a local variable to hold the input, since you need to test its value before using it. In numeric iteration, you do not necessarily have to create a local variable to hold the input.

6.11 Write a function called *running-list* that does not accept any arguments. The function should read a series of non-numeric inputs and return a list of the inputs in the order they were obtained when the user types a number. The function should print the prompt *Enter the next item for the list:* before reading each input and the function should print the list variable right after it is updated each time, so we can see the list developing. For example,

```
=> (running-list)
Enter the next item for the list: This
(This)
Enter the next item for the list: is
(This is)
Enter the next item for the list: a
(This is a)
Enter the next item for the list: list
(This is a list)
Enter the next item for the list: 1
(This is a list)
```

6.12 Write a function called *diff-quot* that accepts one argument, which must be a number. The function should contain a loop that performs the following steps:
1. Print the prompt *Type a number:*.
2. Read an input from the user.
3. Print the result of subtracting the input from the argument.
4. Print the result of dividing the argument by the input.

You should use only one *let* local variable in this function (to hold the inputs). When the user types something that is not a number, the function should return the atom *done*. For example,

```
=> (diff-quot 25)
Type a number: 5
20
5
Type a number: 10
15
2.5
Type a number: x
done
```

6.13 Write a function called *withdrawals* that accepts one argument, which must be a number. This argument represents a savings-account balance. The function should input a series of positive numbers from the user, which indicate withdrawals from the account, and should keep track of the total amount of money that has been withdrawn from the account. Before inputting each number, the function should print the prompt *Type the next withdrawal:*. When the user types *statement*, the function should return a list of the total amount withdrawn and the new balance. For example:

```
=> (withdrawals 1000)
Type the next withdrawal: 100
Type the next withdrawal: 200
Type the next withdrawal: statement
(300 700)
```

Hint: The new balance is the total amount withdrawn subtracted from the starting balance.

Numeric iteration is useful for processing a sequence of numbers, and input-controlled iteration can be used to process an undetermined number of inputs. Both types of iteration require an exit test to determine when to exit the loop, a control variable that contains the value used in the exit test, and updating actions to update the control and result variables. In later chapters, you will learn to use iteration to go through a list and process each item (Chapter 8), to use iteration to process other types of data structures (Chapter 11), and to write iterative functions using more advanced constructs (Chapter 10). Iteration is only one method of repeating actions, however. In the next chapter, you will learn about another method called recursion.

Summary of LISP Functions

1+   This function accepts one argument, which must be a number, and adds 1 to the argument.

Example: *(1+ 5)* returns 6.

1−   This function accepts one argument, which must be a number, and subtracts 1 from the argument.

Example: *(1 − 5)* returns 4.

loop   This special form can accept any number of arguments, each of which can be any LISP expression. The arguments are evaluated in sequence: when the final argument has been evaluated, LISP jumps to the first argument and continues the evaluation process. LISP continues cycling through the arguments until an operator such as *return* forces an exit.

Example:
```
(loop
     (cond ((equal count 10) (return result)))
     (setq count (1+ count))
     (setq result (+ count result)))
```
If *count* has been set to 1, this call to *loop* will return *55*.

Glossary

control variable   A variable that is updated each time around a loop; its value controls when the loop is exited.

counter   A variable that is used to count how many times we go around a loop.

decrementing a value   Decreasing the value of a variable repeatedly by a constant amount.

exit test   A test to determine whether to exit from a loop.

find loop   A numeric loop that searches for a number with a specified property.

incrementing a value   Increasing the value of a variable repeatedly, by a constant amount.

input-controlled iteration   Iteration controlled by inputs that the function reads.

iterative function   A function that performs actions repeatedly in a loop.

limit   A counter value that causes termination of a numeric loop.

loop   A structure in which the operations are performed repeatedly, until some condition for exiting is met.

numeric iteration   Iteration that is controlled by a counter.

result variable   A variable employed to cumulate a result in a loop.

sentinel value   An input value that causes termination of an input-controlled loop.

updating a variable   Resetting the value of a variable in a loop.

Introduction
to Recursion

In this chapter you will learn how to define **recursive functions**. A recursive function is a function that calls itself as a helping function. In other words, the function calls itself in its own definition. Such functions are useful because they can solve complex problems that require some operation to be carried out repeatedly. In this chapter we will discuss two basic types of recursion: **numeric recursion**, in which a sequence of numbers is processed, and a simple type of **list recursion**, in which the elements of a list are processed. We will discuss the general logic of recursion, show how a recursive function is carried out in LISP, and describe a way of planning recursive functions that should greatly help you in writing such functions.

Numeric Recursion

Suppose you wanted to write a function called *sumall* that will take any integer greater than or equal to zero and return the sum of all the integers between 0 and that number. For example, *(sumall 9)* would return *45*, because

$$9 + 8 + 7 + 6 + 5 + 4 + 3 + 2 + 1 + 0 = 45.$$

We wrote an iterative definition of this function when we defined *add-integers* in Chapter 6. In this chapter we will learn how to do the same thing with a recursive definition. A recursive function employs a much different control structure to perform the same task. (Later we will discuss how to decide whether to write an iterative or a recursive function to solve a problem.) A recursive function that adds the numbers between 0 and 9 employs the following observation:

> The sum of the integers between 0 and 9
> equals
> 9 plus the sum of all the integers between 0 and 8.

More generally, a recursive algorithm for this function is based on two facts:

1. For any integer *n* that is greater than 0,

> The sum of the integers between 0 and *n*
> equals
> *n* plus the sum of the integers between 0 and *n* − 1.

2. If *n* = 0,

> The sum of all the numbers between 0 and *n*
> simply equals 0.

These two facts can be translated directly into the following definition of *sumall*:

```
(defun sumall (n)
    (cond ((zerop n) 0)
        (t (+ n (sumall (1 - n))))))
```

As suggested above, this function checks whether the value of the parameter *n* is *0* or greater than *0*. If the value of *n* is *0*, the function simply returns *0*. Otherwise, the function calls itself as a helping function to compute the sum of all the numbers between 0 and *(1 − n)*, and adds the value of *n* to that sum.

Understanding How Recursive Functions Work

Let us consider a few calls to *sumall* to see how recursion works. Suppose we call *(sumall 0)*. The *zerop* test in the first *cond* case is satisfied, and the function returns *0*. This case is called a **terminating case**, because the function returns a value without calling itself recursively.

If we call *(sumall 1)* then the action in the second case, *(+ n (sumall (1 – n)))* is evaluated. This case is a **recursive case** because the function calls itself in computing a result. This call to + is evaluated like any other function call. First the two arguments *n* and *(sumall (1 – n))* are evaluated, and then the function + is applied to them. Since *n* has the value *1*, this expression is equivalent to *(+ 1 (sumall 0))*. We have already seen that *(sumall 0)* returns *0*, so this expression evaluates to *1*.

Finally, what if we call *(sumall 2)*? The recursive action will be evaluated. That action is equivalent to *(+ 2 (sumall 1))*, and we have just seen that *(sumall 1)* returns *1* (by first calling *(sumall 0)*), so this expression evaluates to *3*.

If we trace a call to *sumall*, we can see the function called recursively with progressively smaller arguments, until the recursion terminates upon reaching the terminating case. Recall from Chapter 4 that to trace a function, we type *(trace ⟨function-name⟩)*. Then, each time the function is called (whether at the top level or by another function) LISP prints a list of the arguments to the function, and each time the function exits, LISP prints the value that the function returns. Here is an example:

```
=> (trace sumall)
(sumall)

=> (sumall 3)
Entering: sumall, Argument list: (3)
   Entering: sumall, Argument list: (2)
     Entering: sumall, Argument list: (1)
       Entering: sumall, Argument list: (0)
       Exiting: sumall, Value: 0
     Exiting: sumall, Value: 1
   Exiting: sumall, Value: 3
Exiting: sumall, Value: 6
6
```

As you can see, *(sumall 3)* returns the correct answer, 6. Before *(sumall 3)* returned a result, however, it called *sumall* recursively with the argument 2. That call to *(sumall 2)* in turn called *(sumall 1)*, which called *(sumall 0)*. We can see that *(sumall 0)* returned the value *0*, without a further recursive call. After *(sumall 0)* returned a value, LISP could finish evaluating *(sumall 1)*, and that call returned *1*. Then LISP finished evaluating *(sumall 2)*, which returned *3*, and finally the top-level function call *(sumall 3)* was completed.

This sample call illustrates several important points about recursive functions:

1. *The terminating case is essential.* A terminating case keeps the function from calling itself recursively forever.* The terminating case returns a result, which provides the basis for computing the results of the recursive calls.
2. *Each time the function calls itself, we get closer to the terminating case.* You should note in the example that *sumall* was repeatedly called with smaller and smaller integers. This guarantees that at some point *sumall* will be called with *0*. Always make sure that the recursive call is leading to the terminating case.
3. *Tracing out the operations in recursion can be extremely complex.* It is very difficult to trace through a recursive function in your head. This is particularly true for functions that are more complicated than *sumall*. Thus we want to be able to write recursive functions without having to trace through sample calls.

How to Write Recursive Functions

In writing a recursive function, we need to plan the terminating cases and the recursive cases. Table 7.1 illustrates how this is done.

1. *Planning the terminating case(s).* In writing a recursive function, we need to decide when the function can return a value without calling itself recursively. A numeric recursive function processes a sequence of numbers, so it will need a terminating case that checks for the final number in the sequence.

    When a terminating case is evaluated, it should return the correct answer, given the current argument(s) to the function. For example, when we call *(sumall 0)*, the correct result is *0*, because that is the sum of the integers between 0 and 0, and that is what the terminating case returns.
2. *Planning the recursive case(s).* In a recursive case, we call the function recursively with a simpler argument and use that result to compute the answer for the current argument. Thus one thing we need to decide is how to generate the simpler argument. In numeric recursion, we need a new argument that is one step closer to the final value in the sequence,

---

*Actually, a computer has a limited capability to embed function calls, and LISP would return an error message when that limit was exceeded.

Table 7.1. Working out a recursive function for *sumall*

Step 1. Terminating case

   n = 0   *(sumall 0) = 0*

Step 2. Recursive case
   Recursive relation between *(sumall n)* and *(sumall (1 − n))*
   2a. Recursive Examples

(sumall n)	*(sumall (1 − n))*
(i) *(sumall 5) = 15*	*(sumall 4) = 10*
(ii) *(sumall 1)= 1*	*(sumall 0) = 0*

   2b. Characterizing Recursive Relation
   (sumall n) can be obtained from *(sumall (1 − n))* by adding *n*.

Final code
```
(defun sumall (n)
    (cond ((zerop n) 0)
        (t (+ n (sumall (1 − n)))))))
```

and we can typically generate that value by subtracting 1 from the current argument.

We also need to figure out how to use the value of the recursive call to compute a result for the current call. In planning this action, you should assume that the recursive call will return the correct answer for its argument. Then you need only to figure out how to combine the value of the current argument with the result of the recursive call to obtain the correct answer for the current argument. In the case of *sumall*, we can compute the correct answer for the current argument by adding that argument to the result of the recursive call.

The relation between the result of the recursive call and the correct answer for the current call is called the **recursive relation**. Sometimes it is fairly easy to figure out this relation, but when it is not, try going through the following steps:

a. Figure out the value of some sample function calls, and their corresponding recursive calls. In Table 7.1 we have shown some sample values of *(sumall n)* and *(sumall (1 − n))*.

b. Characterize what the relation is between the pairs of function calls. That will indicate how to use the result of the recursive call to compute the correct answer for the current argument. In Table 7.1, we can see that the value of *(sumall n)* is equal to the value of *(sumall (1 − n))* plus the value of *n*.

LISP Exercises

In these exercises try going through the steps we have just discussed to plan your recursive solution before actually writing any LISP code. After you have written each function, you should *trace* it to see how it works.

7.1 In Chapter 6, you defined an iterative function that computes the factorial of its argument. Now you should try to write a recursive version of this function. The function *fact* takes one argument *n*, which must be an integer that is greater than or equal to 0. The function returns the factorial of *n*, which is the result of multiplying
$n \times (n - 1) \times (n - 2) \ldots \times 1$.
For example,

(fact 3) returns 6, because $3 \times 2 \times 1 = 6$.

By definition, the factorial of 0 is 1.
Before doing this problem, work out the missing parts of the recursive table below for *fact*.

1. *Terminating Case*

   n = 0   *(fact 0)* = ?

2. *Recursive Case*
   Relation between *(fact n)* and *(fact (1 − n))*
   2a. Recursive Examples
   (fact n)   *(fact (1 − n))*

   (i) *(fact 5)* = ?   *(fact 4)* = ?
   (ii) *(fact 1)* = ?   *(fact 0)* = ?
   2b. Characterizing Recursive Relation
   (fact n) can be obtained from *(fact (1 − n))* by ?

7.2 Define the function *power*. It takes two numeric arguments *m* and *n* and computes the value of *m* raised to the power of *n*. For example,

(power 2 3) returns 8, because $2^3 = 2 \times 2 \times 2 = 8$.

By definition, any number to the power 0 is 1.
Again, first work out the recursive table for *power*.

1. *Terminating Case*

   n = 0   *(power 4 0)* = ?

2. *Recursive Case*
   Relation between *(power m n)* and *(power m (1 − n))*

2a. Recursive Examples
(power m n)   (power m (1 – n))
(i) (power 5 3) = ?   (power 5 2) = ?
(ii) (power 3 1) = ?   (power 3 0) = ?
2b. Characterizing Recursive Relation
(power m n) can be obtained from (power m (1 – n)) by ?

7.3 Define the function *listnums*. It takes a numeric argument *n* and returns a list of all numbers from 1 up to and including *n*. For example,

(listnums 3) returns (3 2 1).

You can assume that *listnums* of 0 is the empty list *nil*.
Again, work out the recursive table, but this time you make up the examples.

1. *Terminating Case*
    ?
2. *Recursive Case*
    2a. Recursive Examples

    (listnums n)   (listnums (1- n))

    (i)   ?   ?
    (ii) ?   ?

    2b. Characterizing Recursive Relation
    ?

Multiple Terminating and Recursive Cases in Numeric Recursion

Each of the functions you have coded so far has had a single terminating case and a single recursive case. Some recursive functions require more than one terminating or recursive case, however. Let us consider some examples.

Suppose we wanted a function that accepts two integers and returns the largest prime number between those two integers. The function *find-prime* does this:

```
(defun find-prime (num1 num2)
    (cond ((primep num2) num2)
          ((equal num1 num2) nil)
          (t (find-prime num1 (1 – num2)))))
```

This function assumes that the first argument will be the smaller of the two. It employs the helping function *primep* from LISP Exercise 6.7 that returns *t* if its argument is a prime number. As you can see, this function recurses on the second argument. That is, when the function is called recursively, the second argument is decremented. The first argument is included each time so that we will know when we reach the lower bound on our original sequence. Notice that the function has two terminating cases. First it tests whether the second argument is prime; if so, it returns that value. The second terminating case tests whether the first and second argument are equal. If so, then we have tested all the numbers in our original sequence without finding a prime number, so the function returns *nil*. Finally, if neither of these tests is satisfied, then the function is called recursively to check the next smaller number in the sequence.

This function demonstrates a general principle: If we are searching for a target in a sequence of values and we want to return an answer as soon as we find it, our recursive function will require two terminating cases; one that returns an answer if the target is found and one that returns a different answer if we exhaust the sequence without finding the target.

On the other hand, we will need more than one recursive case when we want to process all the values in a sequence, but we do not want to treat all the values identically. For example, consider the following function that lists all the prime numbers between 0 and the value of its argument:

```
(defun list-primes (arg)
    (cond ((zerop arg) nil)
          ((primep arg) (cons arg (list-primes (1 − arg))))
          (t (list-primes (1 − arg)))))
```

As you can see, this function has two recursive cases. The first of these cases tests whether its argument is prime. If so, it calls the function recursively to obtain a list of the remaining prime numbers in the sequence, and inserts the current argument into that list. However, if the current argument is not prime, then the action in the second recursive case is evaluated. In that case we do not want to include the current argument, so the function is called recursively to obtain a list of the other primes in the sequence, and the function just returns the value of that recursive call without inserting the current argument.

As suggested by the discussion in this section, we can generate the following template for recursive functions:

```
(defun ⟨function-name⟩ ⟨parameter-list⟩
      (cond ⟨terminating case⟩
         [⟨terminating case⟩
             .
             . ]
          ⟨recursive case⟩
         [⟨recursive case⟩
             .
             . ]))
```

The LISP Functions *oddp, evenp* and *round*

There are three more LISP functions you will need for upcoming LISP exercises. The LISP predicates, *oddp* and *evenp*, accept a single numeric argument and test whether the number is odd or even, respectively. The function *oddp* takes one argument, which must be a number, and returns *t* if the number is odd. Otherwise it returns *nil*. For example, *(oddp 3)* returns *t*. The complementary function *evenp* takes one argument, which must be a number, and returns *t* if it is even, otherwise it returns *nil*. For example, *(evenp 3)* returns *nil*. Finally, Common LISP provides a function called *round* which rounds a floating-point number to the nearest integer.* For example, *(round 31.2)* returns *31*.

LISP Exercises

7.4 Define the function *sortnums*. It takes one argument, which must be an integer, and returns a list of all the numbers between 0 and that integer. The list should be sorted, however, so that the odd numbers appear in the front, the even numbers appear at the end, and 0 appears in the middle. For example,

(sortnums 5) returns *(5 3 1 0 2 4)*.
(sortnums 0) returns *(0)*.

Again, first work out the recursive table.

---

*Many other LISP dialects contain a function called *fix*, which differs from *round* in that it converts a floating-point number to an integer by truncating it, rather than rounding it. That is, *(fix 31.8)* returns *31*, not *32*.

1. *Terminating Case*
    ?

2. *Recursive Cases*
    2a. Recursive Examples

(sortnums n)	(sortnums (1 - n))
(i) (sortnums 3) = ?	(sortnums 2) = ?
(ii) (sortnums 4) = ?	(sortnums 3) = ?

    2b. Characterizing Recursive Relation
    In the case of an odd number *n*, *(sortnums n)* is gotten from *(sortnums (1 − n))* by ?

    In the case of an even number *n*, *(sortnums n)* is gotten from *(sortnums (1 − n))* by ?

7.5 Define the function *primep* that takes a numeric argument *n*. The function *primep* returns *t* if *n* is a prime number, otherwise it returns *nil*. There are many ways to write *primep*, but for this exercise you should write a recursive helping function, called *check-divisions*. (The top-level function *primep* itself is not recursive, but *check-divisions* will be.) This helping function will take two arguments, *x* and *count*. When you call *check-divisions* in the top-level function *primep*, the first argument in the call to *check-divisions* should be the argument to *(primep n)*, and the second argument should be the square root of *n* rounded to the nearest integer. You can use the function *round* described earlier.

The helping function *check-divisions* will determine if *x* is a prime by checking to see if the remainder of *x* divided by *count* is 0 for any value of *count* between 1 and its starting value (the square root of *n*). If the remainder is 0 for any of those divisions, then we know that *n* is not prime. (The largest number that can evenly divide into a number is its square root, so we do not have to test any divisors larger than the square root.) For example,

(primep 5) = t, because (check-divisions 5 2) = nil.
(primep 15) = nil, because (check-divisions 15 3) = t.

Before you write *check-divisions*, work out its recursive table.

List Recursion

In Chapter 6 and this chapter we have introduced iterative and recursive control structures that process a sequence of numbers. In the remainder of this chapter and in Chapters 8, 9, and 10, we will discuss iterative and recursive structures that are controlled by lists. When we have information stored in a list structure, it is frequently necessary to process all the items in the list. To take a simple example, we might want to add together all the items in a list. As a result, it is useful to define functions that will continue processing items in a list until the list is exhausted. In the following sections, we will discuss a basic recursive control structure for processing lists, called **cdr recursion** or **list recursion**.

The logic and structure of *cdr* recursion are very similar to the logic and structure of numeric recursion. For example, suppose you want to write a function called *list-sum* that takes a list of numbers as its argument and returns the sum of all the numbers in the list. For example, *(list-sum '(5 2 10 3 7))* returns *27*, because 5 + 2 + 10 + 3 + 7 = 27.

A *cdr* recursive solution to this task is based on the following observations:

1. The sum of all the numbers in an empty list is 0.
2. For any nonempty list of numbers,
   The sum of all the numbers in the list
       equals
   the sum of the first number in the list
       plus
   the sum of all the numbers in the *cdr* of the list.

Here is a recursive definition of *list-sum* that is derived from these observations:

```
(defun list-sum (lis)
    (cond ((null lis) 0)
          (t (+ (car lis) (list-sum (cdr lis))))))
```

As in the case of *sumall*, this function has one terminating case and one recursive case. If the argument to *list-sum* is an empty list, then the terminating case returns *0*. If the argument is a nonempty list, the recursive case is evaluated. In the recursive case, the function (1) calls itself to obtain the sum of all the numbers in the tail of the argument, and (2) adds the first number in the argument to that sum.

Understanding How cdr Recursion Works

Let us consider a few calls to *list-sum*. First, if we call *(list-sum nil)*, then the *null* test is satisfied in the terminating case, and the function returns *0*. Suppose we call *(list-sum '(5))*. Then the recursive action is evaluated. In this example, the action *(+ (car lis) (list-sum (cdr lis)))* is equivalent to *(+ 5 (list-sum nil))*. Since *(list-sum nil)* returns *0*, this expression evaluates to 5. Finally, suppose we call *(list-sum '(3 5))*. Then the recursive action is equivalent to *(+ 3 (list-sum '(5))*. We have just seen that *(list-sum '(5))* returns 5, so this recursive action returns 8.

As in the case with the numeric example, we can see how list recursion works by tracing a sample call:

```
=> (trace list-sum)
(list-sum)

=> (list-sum '(2 5 3))
Entering: list-sum, Argument list: ((2 5 3))
   Entering: list-sum, Argument list: ((5 3))
      Entering: list-sum, Argument list: ((3))
         Entering: list-sum, Argument list: (nil)
         Exiting: list-sum, Value: 0
      Exiting: list-sum, Value: 3
   Exiting: list-sum, Value: 8
Exiting: list-sum, Value: 10
10
```

As you can see, each time *list-sum* is called with a nonempty list, the function calls itself recursively on the *cdr* of its argument before returning a value. Finally, *(list-sum nil)* is called and returns a value without executing a recursive call. That allows LISP to finish evaluating *(list-sum '(3))*, which returns 3. This in turn allows LISP to finish evaluating the call *(list-sum '(5 3))*, and then LISP can finish evaluating the top-level call *(list-sum '(2 5 3))*, which returns *10*.

How to Write *cdr* Recursive Functions

In writing *cdr* recursive functions, we again need to plan the terminating cases and the recursive cases. This is illustrated in Table 7.2.

1. *Planning the terminating case(s)*. In *cdr* recursion, if the argument is an empty list, then there are no more items to process and the function can return a value without calling itself recursively. Thus a *cdr* recursive function will have a terminating case that tests whether the argument is *nil*. (Of course, some functions will include additional terminating cases that test for other conditions.)

Table 7.2. Working out a recursive function for *list-sum*

Step 1. Terminating case

  (list-sum nil) = 0

Step 2. Recursive case
  Recursive relation between *(list-sum lis)* and *(list-sum (cdr lis))*
  2a. Recursive Examples

(list-sum lis)	*(list-sum (cdr lis))*
(i) *(list-sum '(3 5 2)) = 10*	*(list-sum) '(5 2)) = 7*
(ii) *(list-sum '(7)) = 7*	*(list-sum nil) = 0*

  2b. Characterizing Recursive Relation
    (list-sum lis) can be obtained from *(list-sum (cdr lis))* by adding *(car lis)* to it.

Final code

```
(defun list-sum (lis)
    (cond ((null lis) 0)
          (t (+ (car lis) (list-sum (cdr lis)))))))
```

2. *Planning the recursive case(s).* In a recursive case, we need to call the function on an argument that is one step closer to the terminating case. In *cdr* recursion, we can do this by calling the function recursively on the *cdr* of the list. Indeed, that is why this algorithm is called *cdr* recursion. As in the case of numeric recursion, we need to figure out how to use the result of the recursive call to obtain the correct result for the current call. In planning this recursive action, you should assume that the recursive call will return the correct answer for the tail of the list. Then you just need to decide how to combine the *car* of the list with that result. In the case of *list-sum*, since *(list-sum (cdr lis))* returns the sum of the numbers in the tail of *lis*, we simply need to add the *car* of *lis* to that sum. If the recursive relation between the result of the recursive call and the result of the current call is not readily apparent, it is a good idea to work out some examples, as shown in Table 7.2 for *list-sum*.

LISP Exercises

7.6 Define a function called *new-length*. Given any list, it returns the number of elements in that list. (You should count only the top-level elements, not elements within the embedded lists.) For example,

(new-length '(a (b c) d)) returns *3.*
(new-length nil) returns *0.*

You should fill in the recursive table for this problem just as in the earlier section on numeric recursion. The result should be a completed table similar to Table 7.2. It is also a good idea to *trace* this function after you have defined it, to see how it works.

1. *Terminating Case*
   (new-length nil) = ?
2a. Recursive Examples

(new-length lis)	*(new-length (cdr lis))*
(i) *(new-length '(a (b c) d))* = ?	*(new-length '((b c) d))* = ?
(ii) *(new-length '(j i h g e d))* = ?	*(new-length '(i h g e d))* = ?

2b. Characterizing Recursive Relation
   The value of *(new-length lis)* can be gotten from *(new-length (cdr lis))* by ?

Multiple Terminating and Recursive Cases in List Recursion

Our example function has one terminating case and one recursive case, but as we saw earlier, recursive functions may have more than one of either type of case. Recall the two observations we discussed earlier:

1. A function that searches for the first occurrence of a target item in a data structure (e.g., a list or a sequence of numbers) will require more than one terminating case, because there are two different ways the search can end:

   a.   The target is found, and no more items need to be checked.
   b.   The target has not been found and there are no more items to check.

2. A function that processes all the items in a data structure but treats some items differently than others will require multiple recursive cases.

LISP Exercises

7.7 Write a function called *negnums*. Given a list of numbers, *negnums* returns a new list that contains only the negative numbers. (Zero is non-negative.) For example,

(negnums '(−1 5 −6 0 2)) returns *(−1 −6)*.

Again, let us work out a table of examples, but it will be a little more complicated in this case.

1. *Terminating Case*
    (negnums nil) = ?
2a. Recursive Examples

(negnums lis)	*(negnums (cdr lis))*
(i) *(negnums '(−1 5 −6 0 2))* = ?	*(negnums '(5 −6 0 2))* = ?
(ii) *(negnums '(6 −1 5 −6 0 2))* = ?	*(negnums '(−1 5 −6 0 2))* = ?

2b. Characterizing Recursive Relation
    The value of *(negnums lis)* can be gotten from *(negnums (cdr lis))* by?

In the problems that follow, you should work out the table of recursive relations for yourself.

7.8 Define a function called *greaternum*. It takes two arguments — a list of numbers and a previous maximum number. The function *greaternum* returns a new maximum number by searching the list. It should return the first item in the list that is greater than the old maximum, instead of searching for the largest item in the list. If all the numbers in the list are smaller than the previous maximum, return the previous maximum since it is the greatest number. For example,

(greaternum '(3 2 10 15) 8) returns *10*.
(greaternum '(10 20 30) 234) returns *234*.

7.9 Define a function called *add1nums*. Given any list, it returns a new list of numbers containing all of the numbers in the original list increased by 1, and none of the non-numbers. For example,

(add1nums '(5 a 3 (a 17 c) 2)) returns *(6 4 3)*.

7.10 Define a function called *intersect*. Given two lists, it returns their intersection. The intersection of these two lists is the list of elements that are common to both lists. You may assume these lists have no repeated elements. For example, the intersection of the lists *(psych ai english)* and *(french ai algebra psych philos)* is *(psych ai)*.

7.11 Write a function called *carlist*. The function takes a list of lists, and returns the first element of each embedded list. For example,

(carlist '((a b c) (dog cat) (1 2 3))) returns *(a dog 1)*.

7.12 Write a function called *union* that calculates the union of two lists. The union of two lists is all the elements that are in either of the two lists. You may assume these lists have no repeated elements. But be careful not to duplicate elements in the union. For example,

(union '(a b c d) '(c d e)) returns *(a b c d e)*.

7.13 Write your own version of the LISP function *reverse*, called *my-reverse*. You should use recursion to return a list with the order of the elements reversed. For example,

(my-reverse '(dog cat (1 2 3) horse)) returns *(horse (1 2 3) cat dog)*.

7.14 (Optional) Ackerman's mathematical function is defined as follows:

$$A(0,m) = m + 1$$
$$A(n + 1,0) = A(n,1)$$
$$A(n + 1,m + 1) = A(n, A(n + 1,m))$$

Write a recursive function *ackerman* to calculate Ackerman's function. Ackerman's function generates a large number of function calls for even very small arguments. Unless you want to incur a very large computational expense and possibly cause an error message indicating too many embedded function calls, do not call it with an argument larger than 3.

7.15 (Optional) Write a recursive function called *rectangle* that prints out a rectangle of letters. It takes three arguments, the number of columns, the number of rows, and the letter to print. For example, *(rectangle 3 2 'b)* will print:

```
bbb
bbb
```

Hint: This will require coding a recursive helping function to print a single row of letters.

7.16 (Optional) Write a set of recursive functions that will print out a diamond of Xs with sides of length *n*. Thus *(diamond 4)* would print:

```
        X
       XXX
      XXXXX
     XXXXXXX
      XXXXX
       XXX
        X
```

Hint: One way to solve this problem is to write a function, *triangle-top*, which prints out the top triangle of expanding rows and another function, *triangle-bottom*, which prints out the bottom triangle of contracting rows.

7.17 (Optional) Write a function called *sort* that sorts a list of numbers into ascending order. For example,

(sort '(3 8 1 4)) returns (1 3 4 8).

Hint: One way to do this is to write a recursive helping function that inserts a number in the correct position into a list of numbers that is already sorted. Then, your top-level function can recursively go through the list, inserting the *car* into the sorted *cdr*.

7.18 (Optional) Write a function called *powerset* that accepts a list as its argument and returns the powerset of the list. The powerset of a list is a list of all possible lists that can be formed with elements of the original list, including the empty list. For example,

(powerset '(a b c)) returns ((a b c) (a b) (a c) (a) (b c) (b) (c) nil).

The order of the elements in the list returned by *powerset* is not important.

Hint: This will require coding a helping function that is list recursive.

In this chapter we have discussed basic recursion. We have seen that recursion is useful when we need to process each number in a sequence or each item in a list. In Chapter 6 we described an iterative control structure that can also be used to process numbers in a sequence, and in fact, the numeric iteration and numeric recursion control structures we have discussed can be used to accomplish the same tasks. In the next chapter we will discuss an iterative control structure that we can use to process lists. Since we can accomplish the same tasks with an iterative control structure as we can with recursion, we will discuss in Chapter 9 how to decide when to employ an iterative solution or a recursive solution for a task.

Summary of LISP Functions

evenp   This predicate accepts one argument, which must be a number. It returns *t* if the argument is even and returns *nil* if the argument is odd.

Example: *(evenp 24) returns t.*

oddp   This predicate accepts one argument, which must be a number. It returns *t* if the argument is odd and returns *nil* if it is even.

Example: *(oddp 24) returns nil.*

round   This function converts a floating-point number to the nearest integer.

Example: *(round 31.7) returns 32.*

Glossary

cdr recursion   A type of recursive control structure in which a function is called recursively on the *cdr* of a list.

numeric recursion   A type of recursive control structure in which a function is called recursively on the next number in a sequence.

list recursion   A type of recursive control structure in which a function is called recursively on the cdr of a list.

recursive case   A *cond* case in a recursive function in which the function calls itself.

recursive function   A function that calls itself.

recursive relation   The relation between the result of a recursive call to a function and the result of the next-higher-level call to the function.

terminating case   A *cond* case in a recursive function in which the function returns a result without calling itself recursively.

List Iteration

In Chapter 7 you learned how recursion can be used to go through a list and process the items. As mentioned in that chapter, we can also use list iteration to perform the same type of list processing task. **List iteration** is a form of iteration that is controlled by a list variable, rather than by a counter or by user input.

Iterating Over Lists

Suppose we need a function that accepts a list of numbers, and returns a new list in which each of the numbers has been doubled. For example, the function should accept a list such as *(5 15 10 20)* and return *(10 30 20 40)*. The following function demonstrates how that task can be accomplished using list iteration.*

```
(defun double-list (lis)
    (let ((newlist nil))
        (loop
            (cond ((null lis) (return newlist)))
            (setq newlist (append newlist (list (* 2 (car lis)))))
            (setq lis (cdr lis)))))
```

Like the iterative functions you coded in Chapter 6, this function uses a *loop* structure. Each time we go around the loop, the function processes another item in the loop. We double the first item of *lis* and insert it at the end of *newlist*, which holds our answer. Then we set *lis* to *(cdr lis)* to discard the item that is currently first. We continue going around the loop until there are no more items to be processed, which is detected by the stopping test *(null lis)*.

Planning List Iteration

In designing such an iterative function there are a series of things that you have to consider.

The Control Variable

In list iteration, the control variable is typically a parameter of the function, rather than a local variable created for the loop. In *double-list*, the control variable is the parameter *lis*, which originally holds the list of numbers that is passed to the function.

Initializing Result Variables

Result variables typically must be initialized, because inside the loop they are generally evaluated before they are assigned a new value. To determine the initial value for the result variable, we need to recognize that the loop actions will not be performed if the function is passed an empty list. Thus the result value should be initialized to the correct result for the function when it is called with an empty list. If the argument to *double-list* is *nil*, then the correct result is simply *nil*.

---

*Actually, it would be more efficient to use *(cons (* 2 (csarlis)) newlist)* to accumulate the items in reverse order and then just reverse *newlist* upon returning from the loop. However, the given code is used for clarity.

Table 8.1. Examples of variable updates in a list-iteration function

Function definition:
(defun double-list (lis)
    (let ((newlist nil))
        (loop
            (cond ((null lis) (return newlist)))
            (setq newlist (append newlist (list (2 (car lis)))))*
            (setq lis (cdr lis)))))

Function call: *(double-list '(5 15 10 20))*

	newlist	**lis**
Initial Value:	*()*	*(5 15 10 20)*
Iteration 1	*(10)*	*(15 10 20)*
Iteration 2	*(10 30)*	*(10 20)*
Iteration 3	*(10 30 20)*	*(20)*
Iteration 4	*(10 30 20 40)*	*()*
Value returned	*(10 30 20 40)*	

The Exit Test

In list iteration, we typically want to exit the loop when the control list is empty, because that means we have processed all the items. Thus a *null* test is typically employed. As we will see in a later section, search functions may require additional exit tests.

Updating Variables

In list iteration, the control variable must be updated at the bottom of the loop. This is because each time we update the control variable in the loop, we discard one item, but we must finish processing the item before we discard it. In the case of *double-list*, we process and discard the first item in *lis* each time through the loop, so in updating the control variable at the bottom of the loop, we simply set *lis* to *(cdr lis)*. This update is typical of list iterative functions, but we will encounter some functions in a later section that discard other elements besides the first one each time through the loop. Result variables are updated much as in numeric iteration or list iteration. Typically, we use the *car* of the control list to update result variables.

Table 8.1 displays what happens to the value of *lis* and *newlist* as we cycle through the loop in *double-list*. As you can see, *lis* gets shorter each time around until it is finally set to *nil* the fourth time we reach the bottom of the loop.

When we subsequently jump to the top of the loop, the exit test evaluates to *t*, so the function returns the final value of *newlist*.

Consider a second example of list iteration, the function *new-reverse*. This function performs the same operation as the LISP function *reverse*.

```
(defun new-reverse (lis)
    (let ((revlis nil))
        (loop
            (cond ((null lis) (return revlis)))
            (setq revlis (cons (car lis) revlis))
            (setq lis (cdr lis)))))
```

This function is very similar in form to *double-list*. The difference lies in the operation that is performed with the *car* of the control variable *lis*. Like *double-list*, each time through the loop, we process the *car* and reset the control variable to its *cdr*, until the control list is empty. The following template describes the general form for list-iteration functions:

```
(defun ⟨function-name⟩ ⟨parameter-list⟩
    (let [⟨local-variable-initializations⟩]
        (loop
            (cond (⟨exit test on control list⟩ (return [⟨result⟩])))
        [⟨loop actions,
            including updating result variables⟩]
        ⟨update the control list⟩)))
```

In the examples we have seen so far, the loop actions consist of updating a single result variable and the control variable, but in some functions there may be multiple result variables to update. For example, we might write a function that keeps a separate count of the numbers and the non-numeric atoms in a list. Other types of loop actions, such as printing or reading inputs, are also possible.

LISP Exercises

8.1 Define a function called *list-sum*. Given a list of numbers, *list-sum* returns the sum of those numbers. For example,

(list-sum '(5 10 -4 27)) returns *38*.
(list-sum '()) returns *0*.

8.2 Define a function called *list-car*. The function takes a list of embedded lists, and returns a new list, consisting of the first item of each embedded list. For example,

(list-car '((a b c) (train) (45 96))) returns *(a train 45)*.

Note: You may assume that each element of the main list is a list without checking it.

Using List Iteration to Search a List

In Chapter 7 we briefly introduced the topic of processing a list to find one or more items with a particular property. Such processing, called **search**, is of central importance in artificial-intelligence programming. In general terms, search is the process of determining whether an item exists in a data structure, and if so, where. In this section, we will describe how to use list iteration to locate one or more items in a list. In the chapters that follow, we will consider more-complex search techniques.

Suppose we want to know whether an expression with a certain property is an element of a list. The object of the search is called the **target**. For example, we might want to know if any vowel appears in a list. Alternatively, we might want to know how many times the letter *e* appears in the list, or we might want to remove every occurrence of *e* in a list. We can readily modify our basic list-iteration control structure to handle each of these tasks.

Self-Terminating Search

An important distinction among different types of search tasks concerns the stopping point. In some tasks we want to end the search as soon as the target is found. In other tasks we need to search the entire list. For example, we might want to know how many times a target appears. A search that stops as soon as the target is found is called a **self-terminating search**, while an **exhaustive search** always goes through the entire list.

The function *find-vowel* is an example of a self-terminating search. This function accepts one argument, a list, and returns the first vowel that appears in the list, or returns *nil* if no vowels are present.

```
(defun find-vowel (lis)
   (let ()
      (loop
         (cond ((null lis) (return nil))
               ((isa-vowel (car lis)) (return (car lis))))
         (setq lis (cdr lis)))))

(defun isa-vowel (letter)
   (member letter '(a e i o u y)))
```

Thus *(find-vowel '(56 x a g 8 e i))* returns *a*, while *(find-vowel '(k 9 (a) w 25))* fails to find a vowel and so returns *nil*. The structure of this function is similar to the list-iteration functions we have seen so far, with two differences. First, note that no results are accumulated; instead, if the *car* of the control variable is found to be a vowel, it is immediately returned as the result of the loop. Second, there are two exit tests, because in a self-terminating search function, there are two conditions under which we need to exit the loop; if the *car* of the list is a vowel, we want to exit the loop and return the vowel, while if the list is empty, there are no more elements to check and we have failed to find a vowel, so we want to return *nil*. Even though we plan to exit as soon as we find a vowel, it is still important to test if the list is empty. If this test were omitted and there were no vowels in the list the function would enter an **infinite loop**, where the stopping test will never be satisfied.

Exhaustive Search

In an exhaustive search, the search does not end as soon as a target is found. Instead, every element in the list is checked. This type of search algorithm can be used to count all items of a certain type or to save all occurrences of items with a particular property. For example, the exhaustive-search function *count-vowels* returns the total number of vowels in its control list.

```
(defun count-vowels (lis)
   (let ((num 0))
      (loop
         (cond ((null lis) (return num))
               ((isa-vowel (car lis)) (setq num (1+ num))))
         (setq lis (cdr lis)))))
```

Notice that in this function every item in the parameter list is processed; we do not exit the function until the parameter list is empty.

The function *sum-odd-even* performs a similar type of exhaustive conditional processing. It takes one parameter, a list of numbers, and returns a list consisting of two numbers: the sum of the odd numbers in the parameter list and the sum of the even numbers in that list.

```
(defun sum-odd-even (numlis)
    (let ((sumodd 0) (sumeven 0))
      (loop
        (cond ((null numlis) (return (list sumodd sumeven)))
              ((oddp (car numlis))
                  (setq sumodd (+ sumodd (car numlis))))
              (t (setq sumeven (+ sumeven (car numlis)))))
        (setq numlis (cdr numlis)))))
```

So, *(sum-odd-even '(85 100 4 217))* would return *(302 104)*. As in *count-vowels*, the loop continues until the control list (*numlis*) is empty, so again, every item is processed.

The major difference in the structure of the two functions is that *sum-odd-even* has an else case in the *cond* structure. In *count-vowels* (and *find-vowels*) we essentially skipped over nontarget items and had no record of anything about those items. In *sum-odd-even* we are not skipping over any items in the control list; every item is used to update one of the two result variables.

LISP Exercises

8.3 Define your own version of the function *member*, called *new-member*. It takes two arguments. The first argument can be an atom or a list and the second argument is a list. The function should check whether the first argument is a top-level element of the second argument. If so, it should return the tail of the second argument beginning with the (first) occurrence of the first argument. If not, it should return *nil*. For example,

(member 'harpo '(groucho chico harpo zeppo)) returns (harpo zeppo).
(member 'a '(x y (a) (b))) returns nil.

8.4 Define a function called *make-sublists*. Given a list, *make-sublists* returns a list containing two embedded lists. The first embedded list contains all the numbers of the original list (in the same order), and the second embedded list contains all the non-numbers of the original list (again in the same order). For example,

(make-sublists '(cat 34 (8 9) train 45)) returns ((34 45) (cat (8 9) train)).
(make-sublists '(a b c d)) returns (nil (a b c d)).

8.5 Define a function called *remove-first* that takes two arguments — a target item and a list. The function returns a new version of the list with the first occurrence of the target item removed. If the target does not appear in the list, then the function returns a copy of the original list. For example,

(remove-first 'c '(a b c d c)) returns *(a b d c).*

8.6 Define a function called *save-negs*. Given a list of numbers, it returns a list of all the negative numbers in the original list. You should be careful to return the negative numbers in the same order that they appear in the original list. For example,

(save-negs '(2 4 -3 1 -10)) returns *(-3 -10).*

Note: To make the problem simpler, you may assume the list will contain only numbers.

Using List Iteration to Sort a List

An important use of iteration is to **sort** a collection of items — in other words, to arrange them in order according to some criterion. There are many different sorting algorithms and no single algorithm or control structure is always best. Instead, different algorithms and control structures are useful under different circumstances. In this section we will discuss two list-sorting algorithms that we can readily implement with a list-iteration control structure.

Whenever we sort the elements in a list, we must do so along some dimension. Numbers can be sorted by size, for example, or lists could be sorted by length. One common type of sort is to place a list of atoms into alphabetical order. In order to sort atoms alphabetically we will need a predicate that can compare atoms on the basis of alphabetical order. The function *alphalessp* will do this in Franz LISP and MACLISP. This function takes two atoms and returns *t* if the first argument appears before the second in alphabetical order. For example,

```
=> (alphalessp 'couch 'sofa)
t
=> (alphalessp 'sofa 'couch)
nil
```

Interlisp provides a similar function called *alphorder*, but Common LISP does not provide a predicate that compares atoms alphabetically. However, Common LISP does provide a predicate, *string-lessp*, that compares two strings alphabetically.* If the first string comes before the second alphabetically, *string-lessp* returns a non-*nil* value — an integer that indicates the first position in which the two strings vary (counting from 0). If the second argument comes before the first alphabetically, *string-lessp* returns *nil*. For example,

```
=> (string-lessp "coat" "couch")
2
=> (string-lessp "couch" "coat")
nil
```

In the first call to *string-lessp* "coat" comes before "couch", and the function returns *2*, indicating that the first two letters in the two strings are identical, while the third letter varies. In the second call, "couch" follows "coat" in the alphabet, so the function returns *nil*.

Common LISP also provides a function, *string*, that we can use along with *string-lessp* to define *alphalessp*. The function *string* accepts one atom and returns a corresponding string. For example,

```
=> (string 'coat)
"coat"
=> (setq sofa 'couch)
couch
=> (string sofa)
"couch"
```

With the functions *string-lessp* and *string*, we can define the function *alphalessp* in Common LISP as follows:

```
=> (defun alphalessp (arg1 arg2)
        (and (string-lessp (string arg1) (string arg2)) t))
alphalessp
=> (alphalessp 'coat 'couch)
t
=> (alphalessp 'couch 'coat)
nil
```

Selection Sort

One straightforward method for sorting a list is called a **selection sort**. The idea is simple. In such a sort, we keep two lists, the elements sorted so far, and the elements yet to be sorted. Each time through the loop, we look through the list of unsorted items, and select the one that should come next in the sorted list.

---

*The functions *alphalessp* and *alphorder* also accept strings as arguments.

Then, we put that item at the end of the sorted list, and delete it from the unsorted list. This process continues until there are no more items left to sort. The following functions perform a selection sort using list iteration.

```
(defun selection-sort (lis (next))
    (let ((sortedlist nil))
        (loop
            (cond ((null lis) (return sortedlist)))
            (setq next (select-lowest lis))
            (setq sortedlist (append sortedlist (list next)))
            (setq lis (remove-first next lis)))))

(defun select-lowest (lis)
    (let ((lowest (car lis)))
        (setq lis (cdr lis))
        (loop
            (cond ((null lis) (return lowest))
                  ((alphalessp (car lis) lowest)
                      (setq lowest (car lis))))
            (setq lis (cdr lis)))))
```

Let us consider the helping function *select-lowest* first. In order to do a selection sort, we need to be able to find the item in the unsorted list that should come next in the sorted list. The function *select-lowest* accepts a list of atoms as its argument, and uses an exhaustive search to return the item in the list that comes first alphabetically. The local variable *lowest* is used to save whatever atom is lowest (first) alphabetically. The function initializes that variable to the first atom in the control list, and then the function discards that atom from the list before entering the loop. Inside the loop, each item in the control list is compared to the value of *lowest* with the predicate *alphalessp*. Each time an atom is found in the list that is alphabetically prior to the current value of *lowest*, *lowest* is reset to that new atom. When the control list is empty, *lowest* contains the atom that is lowest in the list, and that value is returned.

Now let us consider how that value is used in *selection-sort*. In that function, the parameter *lis* holds the unsorted list and serves as the control variable for the loop. The local variable *sortedlist* holds the list of sorted items. As you can see, that variable is initialized to *nil*. Each time through the loop, we call the helping function *select-lowest* to find the atom that is lowest in the remaining list of unsorted items, and we save that atom in the variable *next*. That atom is then inserted at the end of the sorted list stored in *sortedlist*, and finally it is removed from the unsorted control list *lis*. We cannot remove the atom from *lis* by simply *cdr*ing it as we do in most list-iteration functions, because the atom we just added to the sorted list is usually not going to be the first item

Table 8.2. Examples of variable updates in a selection-sort function

Function call: *(selection-sort '(z x a b a))*

	next	*sortedlist*	*lis*
Initial Value:	---	*()*	*(z x a b a)*
Iteration 1	*a*	*(a)*	*(z x b a)*
Iteration 2	*a*	*(a a)*	*(z x b)*
Iteration 3	*b*	*(a a b)*	*(z x)*
Iteration 4	*x*	*(a a b x)*	*(z)*
Iteration 5	*z*	*(a a b x z)*	*()*
Value Returned	*(a a b x z)*		

in the control list. Instead, we update the control variable by calling the function *remove-first* from LISP Exercise 8.5 to remove the first occurrence of *next* from the control list. Note that we do not want to remove all occurrences of that item if there is more than one, because we have only put one copy into the sorted list. After all the items have finally been sorted, the control list is empty, and the function returns *sortedlist*, which will be a sorted version of the original list. Table 8.2 gives an example run of *selection-sort*.

Insertion Sort

An alternative algorithm that can be used to sort lists is called an **insertion sort**. In this algorithm, we again pull items out of the new list one at a time and insert them into the sorted list. However, instead of searching the unsorted list to find the item that should go next into the sorted list, we simply pull off the front of the unsorted list each time around the loop. Of course, now we can no longer just add this item to the end of the sorted list. Instead, we need to scan through the sorted list to find the correct position in which to insert the item. We will define such an insertion-sort function in the next LISP Exercise.

LISP Exercise

8.7 Define a function called *insertion-sort* that performs an insertion sort of a list. Given a list of numbers, *insertion-sort* should return a new copy of the list in which the numbers have been sorted into numeric order from lowest to highest. For example,

(insertion-sort '(10 26 55 2 28 58)) returns *(2 10 26 28 55 58)*.

You should use list iteration to pull the items off the front of the original list, one at a time, and insert them into the correct position in the sorted list. To do this, you should define a helping function that inserts a new item into the appropriate position of a sorted list and returns the new list.

Another LISP Function: *remove*

LISP provides a function, *remove*, that is very similar to the function *remove-first* that you coded. The function *remove* accepts two arguments, the second of which must be a list, but this function removes all occurrences of the first argument in the list. Here are some sample calls:

Function call	Value returned
(remove 'a '(a b c a c b))	*(b c c b)*
(remove 'x '(a b c a c b))	*(a b c a c b)*

The next problems make use of this function in updating the control list.

LISP Exercises

8.8 Write a function called *duplicates* that accepts a list as an argument. The function should return a list of all the items that appear more than once in the list. For example,

(duplicates '(a b c a b a)) returns *(a b)*.
(duplicates '(a b c)) returns *nil*.

You should use the function *remove* to update the control variable each time around the loop.

8.9 Write a function called *list-intersect* that accepts two lists as arguments. It should return a list that is an intersection of the two lists. That is, it should return a list of all the elements that appear in both argument lists. Be careful not to duplicate elements in the intersection. For example,

(list-intersect '(a b a c b) '(a a b c d)) returns *(a b c)*.

The past two chapters have described recursive and iterative control structures that perform basic list-processing tasks. We have not yet discussed the efficiency of iteration and recursion. In fact, LISP can evaluate the iterative control structures we have discussed more quickly than the recursive structures, because LISP evaluates expressions in a loop faster than it evaluates a series of embedded function calls. In general, any function that can be coded recursively can be coded iteratively, and vice versa. So it may seem that there is never any reason to code a recursive solution to a problem, since it should be possible to code an iterative function that works faster. However, when we begin talking about more complex list-processing tasks in Chapter 9, we will see that there is a good reason to code some functions recursively. Sometimes the tasks we confront are so complex that it is not immediately apparent how to code them. In such situations, it may prove easier to code the function recursively, by using our general planning template for recursive functions to help us figure out the algorithm.

Summary of LISP Functions

alphalessp   This function accepts two atoms or strings and returns *t* if the first argument comes before the second alphabetically. Otherwise, the function returns *nil*.

Example: *(alphalessp 'a 'h)* returns *t*.

remove   This function takes two arguments, the second of which must be a list. It returns a new copy of the list with all occurrences of the first argument removed.

Example: *(remove '2 '(1 2 3 2 1))* returns *(1 3 1)*.

string   This function accepts an atom and returns a corresponding string.

Example: *(string 'a)* returns *''a''*.

string-lessp   This function accepts two strings and, if the first string comes before the second alphabetically, the function returns an integer indicating the first position in which the strings vary (counting from 0). Otherwise, the function returns *nil*.

Example: *(string-lessp "a" "h")* returns *0*.

Glossary

exhaustive search   Search in which all targets in the search set are found.

infinite loop   A loop that continues execution indefinitely because its exit test can never be satisfied.

insertion sort   A sorting algorithm that repeatedly pulls an item out of the original list, scans the sorted list, and inserts the item in its appropriate position.

list iteration   An iterative control structure controlled by a list variable.

search   Processing a data structure (often a list) in order to find one or more items of a particular type.

selection sort   A sorting algorithm that repeatedly looks for the item in the original list that is first (or last) in order, removes that item from the original list, and inserts it at the end (or beginning) of the ordered list.

self-terminating search   A search that terminates as soon as a target item is found.

sort   Arrange a group of items in order along some dimension.

target   An item or class of items possessing a particular property that is the object of a search.

Advanced Recursion

In Chapters 7 and 8 we discussed control structures that allow us to go through a list and process each element. For example, we described both iterative and recursive functions that accept a list of numbers and return the sum of the numbers. We also discussed how to do conditional processing of the items in a list, so we know how to write a function that can accept a list containing numbers, non-numeric atoms, and embedded lists, and return the sum of the numbers while skipping over the non-numeric elements. Suppose, however, that we wanted a function that would add up all the numbers that appear at any level within the embedded lists contained in a list. We could not perform this task with the basic control structures we have discussed so far. In this chapter we will discuss more sophisticated recursive functions that will allow us to perform this and similar complex tasks.

Advanced List Recursion

The list-recursion functions we discussed in Chapter 7 employ *cdr* recursion. These functions compute a result for a list by calling themselves recursively on the *cdr* of the list, and combining that result with the result for the *car* of the list. We are not restricted to this control structure, however; there are tasks that will require functions to call themselves recursively on different components of a list, and to combine the results of more than one recursive call. The function mentioned above that will sum numbers at any level in a list is one such function. Frequently, these tasks will be so complicated that, at first glance, it is not clear how to code them. Before discussing more complex problems, it may be helpful to recall the *cdr*-recursive control structure from Chapter 7. To refresh your memory, try solving the following exercises.

LISP Exercises

9.1 Define a *cdr* recursive function called *addto*. It takes two arguments: an atom — *elt* — and a list of lists — *lis*. The function *addto* adds *elt* to each list in *lis*. For example,

(addto 'a '((b c) (b) (c) nil)) returns *((a b c) (a b) (a c) (a))*.

9.2 Define an iterative version of *addto*.

An Advanced Recursion Technique

Not all problems that require us to process elements in a list can be solved as simply as *addto*. For example, consider a function called *powerset* that accepts one argument. The argument must be a list and we will assume that it does not have any repeated elements. The function returns a list of all the possible lists that can be formed from the elements of the argument, ignoring order, and without repeating elements. The list that *powerset* returns should include the empty set and the original list. For example,

> => *(powerset '(a b c))*
> ((a b c) (a b) (a c) (a) (b c) (b) (c) nil)

Think for a moment about how you could write this function. The function will be more complex than the basic *cdr* recursive functions we have discussed, because it will combine the results of two recursive calls. The planning framework for recursive functions that we discussed in Chapter 7 is useful for writing functions exactly when it is not clear how to proceed.

LISP Exercises

9.3 (a) Recursive case: We have seen what *powerset* returns for the list *(a b c)*. What should *powerset* return if we call it on the *cdr* of that list? That is, what does *(powerset '(b c))* return?

   (b) General form of the recursive case: What is the relation between the result of *(powerset '(a b c))* and *(powerset '(b c))*? That is, what do we have to do to the latter result, in order to generate the former result?

   (c) Terminating case: What should *powerset* return when called with the empty list as an argument?

   (d) After answering the above questions, try coding *powerset*.

9.4 (Optional) Write a function *permut*, which generates all of the permutations (orderings) of a list. You can assume that the list does not contain repeated elements. For example,

(permut '(a b c)) returns *((a b c) (a c b) (b a c) (b c a) (c a b) (c b a))*.

   Note a function of length n has n x $(n - 1)$x ... x 1 permutations. As in the case of *powerset*, it is helpful to work out the recursive relationship for *permut* in a table. The function *permut* will require two helping functions, one embedded within the other.

Using Recursion

Since iterative code is evaluated by LISP more quickly than recursive code, students often wonder when they should write recursive functions instead of iterative functions. As suggested in coding *powerset*, you should turn to recursive code when the problem seems too difficult to design an iterative solution. It is easier to solve a complex problem recursively than iteratively, because recursion reduces your task to the relatively simple tasks of deciding the recursive relationship and deciding the terminating case(s).

Of course, there is no need to restrict yourself to list recursion and numeric recursion. Many of the appropriate applications of recursion involve data structures other than integers and lists. Whenever you have a data structure that (1) can be broken down into simpler and simpler cases, and (2) has one or more simple cases that do not need to be broken down you have a candidate for recursion. The first characteristic allows you to try to write the solution for a complex structure in terms of the solution for a simpler structure — i.e., to find a recursive relationship to exploit. The second characteristic allows you to write terminating cases to stop the recursion. In the remainder of this chapter we will look at some other types of recursion that work on list structures.

car-cdr **Recursion**

Suppose we need a function that tells us if an expression appears at any level of embedding in a list. We can call the function *isin*, and it will take two arguments, which we will call *elt* and *lis*. If *elt* appears at any level of *lis* (i.e., as an element of *lis* or one of its embedded lists), then *isin* should return *t*, otherwise it should return *nil*. For example,

```
=> (isin 'b '(a ((b) c) d))
t
=> (isin 'e '(a ((b) c) d))
nil
```

The function *member* would not help in this case since it determines only if an element occurs at the top level of a list. For example, *member* would determine that *b* occurred in the list *(a b c d)*, but not in the list *(a ((b) c) d)*.

The function *isin* also could not be written using simple list recursion because we need to get inside of the embedded lists and inspect their structure. This means that we need to call the function recursively on the *car* of the list as well as the *cdr*. We refer to this technique as *car-cdr* recursion. The following is a recursive definition of *isin* that uses the *car-cdr* technique.

```
(defun isin (elt lis)
    (cond ((null lis) nil)
          ((equal elt (car lis)) t)
          ((atom (car lis)) (isin elt (cdr lis)))
          (t (or (isin elt (car lis))
                 (isin elt (cdr lis))))))
```

Let us consider what each case in this function accomplishes:

1. The first two cases are terminating cases.
   a. As in other functions we have written, the function checks if *lis* is empty. If it is, we can be assured that *elt* is not in *lis*, and the function returns *nil*.
   b. If *lis* is non-empty, then the function checks if the first element of *lis* is equal to *elt*. If it is, then we have found *elt* and the function returns *t*.

2. The third and fourth cases are recursive cases.
   a. If we get as far as the third case, we know the first element of *lis* is not equal to *elt*, but we do not know if that first element is itself a list that contains *elt*, so we do an *atom* test. If the first element is an atom, then all we need to do is check whether *elt* is in the tail of *lis*, which we do by calling *(isin (cdr lis))*.
   b. The final case is the key to *car-cdr* recursion. If we reach this case, we know that the first element of *lis* is a list, and *elt* may be either somewhere in the first element of *lis* or in the *cdr* of *lis*. So in this case we call *isin* recursively on both the *car* and the *cdr* of *lis*. If either (or both) of these recursive calls returns *t*, then the function *or* will return *t*.* So,

      if *lis* = *(((b) c) d)*,
      then *(isin (car lis))* = *(isin '((b) c))* = *t*,
      and *(isin (cdr lis))* = *(isin '(d))* = *nil*.
      Thus *(or (isin (car lis)) (isin (cdr lis)))* = *(or t nil)* = *t*.

Let us consider a second example of *car-cdr* recursion. The function *numbers* accepts one argument, which must be a list, and returns a list of all the numbers in the argument. For example, *(numbers '((a 1 (2)) b 3))* returns *(1 2 3)*.

```
(defun numbers (lis)
  (cond ((null lis) nil)
        ((numberp (car lis)) (cons (car lis) (numbers (cdr lis))))
        ((atom (car lis)) (numbers (cdr lis)))
        (t (append (numbers (car lis)) (numbers (cdr lis))))))
```

In this function there are four *cond* cases, as in *isin*, but there are three recursive cases and only one terminating case. Whenever we find a number in

---

*There is an alternative way to code *car-cdr* recursion, which is illustrated by the following version of *isin*.

```
(defun isin (elt lis)
  (cond ((null lis) nil)
        ((atom lis) (equal elt lis))
        (t (or (isin elt (car lis))
               (isin elt (cdr lis))))))
```

In this code, whenever *lis* is a nonempty list, *isin* always calls itself recursively on both the *car* and the *cdr*. The two arguments are directly compared only when *lis* is itself an atom. This version of *isin* is more elegant than the definition in the main text, which "peeks" at the *car* of *lis* and does not call itself recursively on the *car* when it is an atom. Unfortunately, there are cases in which we want to avoid calling the function with an atom because such a call cannot be well defined, so the version in the text is more generally useful. The function *skeleton*, which you will code in LISP Exercise 9.8 is an example of such a function.

this function, we do not want to terminate processing of the list. Instead, we want to find all the numbers in the rest of the list and include the current number in the final result. Again, we can summarize what is taking place in each conditional case:

1. If *lis* is empty then there are no numbers in *lis*, and therefore the function returns an empty list.
2. If the first element of *lis* is a number, then we want it in the result. Assuming that *(numbers (cdr lis))* will return all the numbers in the *cdr* of *lis*, we can simply insert the first item of *lis* into the result of *(numbers (cdr lis))*.
3. If the first element is an atom (and not a number) then we do not want it in the result. We still call *(numbers (cdr lis))* to find the numbers in the tail of *lis*, but we will not *cons* the first item into the result of *(numbers (cdr lis))*.
4. In the last case, the first element of *lis* is a list. We can assume that *(numbers (car lis))* will return a list of all numbers in the *car* of *lis*, and that *(numbers (cdr lis))* will return a list of all numbers in the *cdr* of *lis*. Since we want to return a single list with all the numbers, we *append* the results of these two function calls.

In general, for *car-cdr* recursive functions, you should try to follow these guidelines:

1. *Planning the terminating case(s)*. As with all recursive functions, you should determine the terminating cases of the function. These are the cases in which we can return a value without calling the function recursively. There are two different types of terminating cases:
   a. If the list is empty, we need to return a value without calling the function recursively.
   b. We can have a terminating case if the *car* of the list is an atom. Specifically, if our function performs a self-terminating search, and the *car* of the list matches the target, we can return a value without calling the function recursively.
2. *Planning the cdr-recursive case(s)*. These are cases in which the *car* of the list is an atom (so you do not need to call the function recursively on the *car*), and you need the result of the function called on the *cdr* of the list. Again, there are two general types of *cdr*-recursive cases:
   a. In some cases, you simply need to return the results of the function called recursively on the *cdr* of the list, without combining it in any way with the *car* of the list. For example, in *numbers*, when the *car* of the list is a non-numeric atom, the function simply returns the value of *(numbers (cdr lis))*.

b. In other cases, the results of the *cdr*-recursive call have to be combined with a value that is derived from the *car* of the list. Again, in the case of *numbers*, if the *car* of the list is a number, the function *cons*es that number into the result of the recursive call.

3. *Planning the car-cdr recursive case*. Finally, you will need a case in which the function calls itself recursively on both the *car* of the list and the *cdr* of the list when the *car* is itself a list. This will usually be the last case in the *cond*. You will need to determine how you can combine the two results to obtain the correct result for the whole list. If it is not clear how to combine the results at first, work through an example or two. If you take a list and write down the correct answer for the *car* of the list, the correct answer for the *cdr*, and the correct answer for the whole list, it should be apparent how to combine the first two results to generate the overall result.

LISP Exercises

9.5 Define a function called *countatoms* that accepts one argument, which must be a list. This function returns the number of atoms contained at any level of embedding in the list. For example,

(countatoms '((a) (b (c)) (d))) returns *4*.
(countatoms nil) returns *0*.

9.6 Define a function called *delete-in*, which accepts two arguments, an atom and a list. The function deletes the atom from all levels of the list. For example,

(delete-in 'a '(a b (d (c a)) a d)) returns *(b (d (c)) d)*.
(delete-in 'x nil) returns *nil*.

9.7 Define a function called *flatten* that takes one argument, which must be a list. This function returns a single-level list containing all the atoms that appear at any level in the original list. For example,

(flatten '((a (b)) (c d) (((e))))) returns *(a b c d e)*.
(flatten nil) returns *nil*.

9.8 Define a function called *skeleton*, which removes all the non-*nil* atoms from a list. For example,

(skeleton '((a (b)) (c d) (((e))))) returns ((())()((()))
(skeleton nil) returns nil.

   Note: because *() = nil*, most dialects of LISP will print *((())()((())))* as *((nil) nil ((nil))).*

Formal Structure Recursion

The *car-cdr* recursive functions we have written to process embedded lists have assumed that there are no restrictions on the structure of the lists (other than the general rules of LISP). In some tasks, however, we will be processing lists that were created according to a set of rules that restrict their form. For example, consider the following lists that represent mathematical expressions:

*(4 * 3 * (7 − (6 / 2)))*
*((3 * 2) + (4 * 3) + (5 + 4))*

We can see that there are some constraints on the form of these lists; for example, every other element in each list (or embedded list) is a mathematical operator. When there are constraints such as this on the structure of a list, we may be able to write functions that take advantage of those constraints. Recursive functions that make assumptions about the form of the lists they process perform **formal structure recursion**.

   Here is a set of rules we can use to generate mathematical expressions such as the two above.

   A list represents a legal mathematical expression if

1. It contains a single number, or
2. If it contains more than one element and

   a.   There are an odd number of elements
   b.   Every other element in the list, beginning with the second, is one of the arithmetic operators, +, −, *, /.
   c.   If the operator is − or /, the list must contain exactly three elements (the operator and two arguments). If the operator is + or *, the list can have any odd number of elements (greater than 1), but every operator in the list must be the same.

  d. Each element in the list, other than the operators, is either
  i. A number
  ii. Another list that follows these constraints — i.e, another legal mathematical expression.*

A definition that refers to itself, as this definition of mathematical expressions does in 2dii is called a **recursive definition**. Structures that are generated with such definitions are called **recursive structures**. A recursive structure will contain substructures that have the same form as the structure itself. In the case of our mathematical expressions, the embedded lists of a list will obey the same rules as the list. That is, every component of a list will be a legal mathematical expression, including any embedded lists.

When structures are defined recursively, we can take advantage of that recursive structure to define recursive functions to process them. For example, the function *arith* accepts a mathematical expression as an argument, performs the arithmetic represented in the list, and returns the resulting value.

```
(defun arith (expr)
   (cond ((numberp expr) expr)
        ((equal (cadr expr) ' – ) ( – (arith (car expr))
                                       (arith (caddr expr))))
        ((equal (cadr expr) '/) (/ (arith (car expr))
                                   (arith caddr expr))))
        ((equal (cadr expr) ' + ) ( + (arith (car expr))
                                      (arith-help (cddr expr))))
        ((equal (cadr expr) '*) (* (arith (car expr))
                                   (arith-help (cddr expr)))))))

(defun arith-help (expr)
   (cond ((null (cdr expr)) (arith (car expr)))
        (t (arith expr))))
```

Since we know the structure of these mathematical expressions, we can take advantage of that knowledge in writing the functions. Note that the terminating case does not check for an empty list. Provided the function is called with an argument that satisfies the recursive definition given early, the function does not have to deal with an empty list. On the other hand, if the argument of the function is a number, then we can just return the number. If the second element is not a number, then it must be a list, the second element in the list must be an arithmetic operator and the *car* of the list must be a legal

---

*This is a somewhat more restrictive notion of a mathematical expression than is typically used in mathematics. However, we are using it here to make the example simpler because it avoids issues of precedence of operators.

expression. If the operator is − or /, then there can only be three elements in the list, so the third element in the list must also be a legal expression. Thus if the operator is − or /, we call *arith* on *(car exp)* and *(caddr exp)* and combine the two results with the appropriate arithmetic operation.

Note that if the operator is + or * we do not call *arith* with *(caddr exp)*, but rather, call a helping function on *(cddr exp)*. This is to process expressions with more than two terms added or multiplied. Let us consider what happens if we call *arith* on the list *(4 * 7 * 3)*. This expression is processed in the last case of *arith*. The function *arith* would be called recursively to evaluate *4* and *arith-help* would be called to process the list

   *(7 * 3)*

Since this is not a list of a single element, *arith-help* will call *arith* to evaluate this expression. Again, *arith-help* will be called, but now with the list

   (3)

Since this is a list of one element there are no further multiplications and *arith* is called to evaluate the *car* of this list, which is just *3*.

This example shows a case of recursion in which there is an intervening function. That is, *arith* calls *arith-help*, which then calls *arith* recursively. There are many ways that recursion can be used, and the point of this chapter is to get you to develop the inventiveness required to design new uses for recursion.

LISP Exercise

9.9 Define a function called *logic* that accepts one argument, which is a list that represents a logical expression. These expressions are constructed from two basic elements, *t* and *nil*, which stand for true and false. These can be combined by three logical operators:

1. − (which represents "not")
2. V (which represents "or")
3. & (which represents "and")

The following rules govern the structure of the arguments to *logic*.
   An expression is a legal logical expression if

1. It is an atom, which is either *t* or *nil*.
2. It is a list containing two elements; the first element must be the operator − and the second element can be any logical expression.

3. It is a list with an odd number of elements (greater than 1); every other element starting with the second must be either the operator *V* or the operator & and the other elements can be any logical expression.

The function should go through the list applying the logical operators and return the final value of the expression, which will be either *t* or *nil*. For example,

(logic '(((- t) V t V (nil & (- nil))) & t & (- (t V nil))))
     returns *nil*.

Binary Search

In this section you will be asked to write a function that performs **binary search**, a technique that makes it possible to search through a large body of data in a very efficient manner. Suppose you had 1 million numbers stored in a list and you wanted to determine if a particular number had been stored. If your target number is not in the list, you would have to check all 1 million numbers to find that out. (If your target is in the list, you will have to check anywhere from 1 to 1,000,000 numbers to find it, and on the average you would have to check 500,000.) Clearly, even a fast computer will take a relatively long time to do this. However, if we employ a binary search technique to search the numbers, we can find the number (or find out it is not there) after checking no more than 20 numbers.

Binary Trees

The trick to binary search is to store data in a constrained manner. Specifically, such data is stored in a structure called a **binary tree** that can best be presented with a diagram like Figure 9.1. That figure represents an abstract structure called a **tree**. Each circled number is referred to as a **node** in the tree. The top-most node is usually referred to as the **root** node, and the nodes at the bottom that have no other nodes beneath them are referred to as **leaves**. (This tree is upside down compared to the trees we see in nature.) A **subtree** of the tree consists of any node in the tree along with all the nodes below it. For example, one subtree of our tree consists of the node 12, along with the three nodes 6, 15, and 7, which are below 12. Finally, notice an important feature of this tree: each node has no more than two nodes below it. That is why it is called a binary tree.

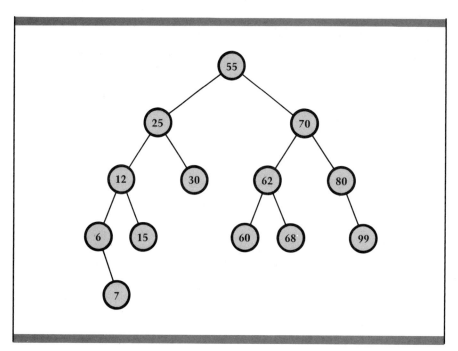

Figure 9.1
A Binary Tree

The nodes in this tree have been set up so it will be easy to search. Specifically, the number at each node is greater than each of the numbers in the subtree that is below it and to the left (for instance, 70 is greater than 62, 60, or 68). On the other hand, each node is smaller than all the nodes in the subtree that is below it and to the right (for instance, 70 is smaller than 80 and 99).

Now, suppose we need to find out if an item we are searching for, usually called a **key**, occurs in a binary tree. For example, suppose we want to know if the number 62 appears in the tree in Figure 9.1. First, we would compare the value of the key 62 to the value of the root node 55. If they are equal, we would immediately know that the key appears in the tree. However, the value of the key is, in fact, greater than the value of the root, so we do not know if the key is in the tree, but we do know that the key cannot appear anywhere in the subtree to the left. All the numbers in that subtree are smaller than the root, so they must be smaller than the key. Instead, we will search the subtree to the right. To do that we treat the node that is immediately below and to the right — 70 — as the root node of the subtree. When we compare the value of the key 62 to the the node 70, we find out the key is smaller. Thus if the key is in the tree it must be to the left of the node 70. When we repeat the process and compare the key to the node below and to the left of the node containing 70, we find their values are equal, so we terminate the search, having found the key in the tree.

Suppose we had been searching for 63 instead. We would have followed the same path, past the node containing 62 to the node containing 68. Since 63 is less than 68 we would have tried to examine the node below and to the left of 68, but there is no such node. As a result, we terminate the search, knowing that 63 cannot be anywhere in the tree, even though we have examined only four nodes.

So far this tree structure is just circles and lines on a piece of paper. We need to be able to represent it in LISP structures if we are going to code a function that performs a binary search. A tree is an abstract structure that we have to encode in a LISP structure. There are many possible ways to represent tree structures by a list.* Let us start by representing each node and its two immediate **descendants** (the two nodes directly below it) as a list. Thus we could use the list *(70 62 80)* to represent the fact that 62 and 80 are below 70. We can extend this idea to produce a recursive definition of a tree.

1. Every tree is represented by a list with three elements.
2. The first element must be a node (a number, in this case).
3. The second and third elements represent the descendants of the node on the left and right respectively. These elements can be
   a. a tree,
   b. *nil*, (if there are no descendants on that side)

This definition would give rise to the following representation of our tree:

(55 (25 (12 (6 nil (7 nil nil)) (15 nil nil)) (30 nil nil))
    (70 (62 (60 nil nil) (68 nil nil)) (80 nil (99 nil nil))))

Now we can write a recursive function that will search through this list structure and tell us if a particular number appears. See if you can write the function by doing the LISP exercise below. Notice that it is very difficult to look at this tree and see its structure. Thus you will probably find it helpful to refer to the figure as you design your algorithm. Then you can translate your algorithm into LISP code that processes the list.

---

*In Chapter 11 we will introduce another type of LISP structure, called a property, that is particularly useful for representing trees. We will discuss trees and search more fully in Chapter 14.

LISP Exercise

9.10 Define a function called *binary-search* that takes two arguments, a key and a recursively defined list that represents a binary tree. The function should return *t* if the key appears in the tree. Otherwise, it should return *nil*.

Association Lists

The recursive representation of a binary tree is extremely hard for a person to read. It is also hard to add nodes to the tree by hand; we would need to define a fairly complex function to add or delete nodes. Instead of using a recursively defined list, we can use another special kind of list, called an **association list**, or **A-list**, to represent the tree. The only structural constraint on an A-list is that every element must be a list. Beyond that, an A-list is defined by how we process it. In the case of our example, each embedded list in the list will contain three numbers. The first number will refer to a node, the second number will be the left descendant of the node, and the third number will be the right descendant of the node. As in the case of our recursive representation of the tree, we will use *nil* in the second or third position if there is no descendant on the corresponding side of the node. Thus the tree in the diagram would be represented in A-list form as:

tree = *((55 25 70) (25 12 30) (12 6 15) (6 nil 7) (7 nil nil)*
(15 nil nil) (30 nil nil) (70 62 80) (62 60 68)
(60 nil nil) (68 nil nil) (80 nil 99)(99 nil nil))

Notice that this tree is less overwhelming for a person to look at, and it is relatively easy to add or delete a node by hand, or even to insert subtrees in the tree.

Now the question arises: How do we access the nodes of this A-list? We need to introduce the function *assoc* to process our list as an A-list. The function *assoc* takes two arguments. The first argument can be any legal LISP expression, but the second must be an A-list. The function *assoc* compares its first argument to the *car* of each embedded list in the A-list and returns the first embedded list whose *car* is identical to that first argument. Here are some examples.

=⟩ *(assoc 'animals '((minerals iron lead copper)*
(animals dog cat mouse)
(vegetables carrot turnip squash)))

(animals dog cat mouse)
= 〉 *(assoc 12 '((25 20 45) (20 12 23) (12 10 nil) (45 nil nil)*
(12 10 nil) (23 nil nil) (10 nil nil)))
(12 10 nil)

The second call to *assoc* gives a hint about how we can use that function to search through our tree. When we call *assoc* with a node number and our A-list that represents the tree, the function returns the immediate descendants of the node. That is, when we call *(assoc 12 tree)*, *assoc* returns the embedded list in *tree* whose first element is *12*. Because of the way we set up the tree, the second item in that list is the node below and to the left of *12*, and the third number is the node below and to the right of *12*.

Now that we have converted our binary search tree into an A-list and we have discussed how to use *assoc* to find a node in the tree and to find the two nodes immediately below that node, you are in position to define a recursive version of the search function using an association list to encode the tree.

LISP Exercises

9.11 Define a function called *bsearch*. It takes three arguments, *key, root,* and *tree*. The variables *key* and *root* are numbers and *tree* is an A-list. The function *bsearch* should search through *tree* starting at *root* to determine if *key* is anywhere in *tree*.

9.12 (Optional) As a final challenging exercise in recursion, try to write a function *genset* that accepts one argument, which must be a list, and determines whether the list is a generalized set. A list is a set if and only if it has no repeated elements. Thus *(a b c)* is a set, while *(a b c b)* is not. A generalized set can have subsets as elements, but all of these subsets must be generalized sets, i.e., have no repeated elements. For example,

(genset '((a (b (c))) (b (c)))) returns *t.*
(genset '((a (b (c)) ((c) b)))) returns *nil.*
(genset '((a (b (c) (d (e)))) ((b ((e) d) (c))) a b))) returns *t.*
(genset '((a (b (c) (d (e)))) ((b ((e) d) (c) a b))) returns *nil.*
(genset '((a (b (c) (d (e)))) ((b ((e) d) (c)) a))) returns *nil.*

To define *genset* you will have to define a number of helping functions.

In this chapter we have described a variety of complex tasks that required us to process the items in a list and we have presented a few advanced recursive techniques to accomplish those tasks. In fact, we have suggested that recursion is most useful in performing such complex tasks because it provides us a framework for planning functions that are at first hard to conceptualize. We have examined a number of advanced recursive techniques for *car-cdr* recursion, formal structure recursion, and binary search. These examples show that the control structure of a recursive function depends heavily on the format of the data structures that it processes. In Chapter 10 we will complete our discussion of control structures by considering advanced iterative constructs. In that chapter we will be discussing a special form *do* and a function *mapcar* that LISP provides to write more concise iterative functions.

Summary of LISP Functions

assoc   This function takes two arguments. The first can be any LISP expression and the second must be a list of embedded lists. This returns the first embedded list of the second argument whose *car* is identical to the first argument.

Example: *(assoc 'c '((a b) (c d) (e f)))* returns *(c d)*.

Glossary

association list   A list whose elements are all embedded lists. Such a list (also called an A-list) is set up to be searched with the function *assoc*.

binary search   Search through a binary tree.

binary tree   A tree structure in which every node has two or fewer immediate descendants.

car-cdr recursion   Recursion in which a function calls itself on both the *car* and the *cdr* of an argument list.

descendant   Any node that appears below a particular node in a tree.

formal structure recursion   Recursion that employs knowledge of the recursive definition of an argument list in calling itself recursively on components of the list.

key   An item for which we search.

leaf   A node in a tree with no descendants (no nodes below it).

node   A component of a network structure. A point where links in the network meet, often represented as a circle.

recursive definition   A definition that refers to itself as part of the definition.

recursive structure   A structure satisfying a recursive definition.

root   The node in a tree with no ancestors (no nodes above it).

subtree   Any node of a tree, along with all its descendants.

tree   An abstract structure that can be represented as a network of nodes and links. In a tree, each node has only one parent node (i.e., only one node immediately above it in the network)

Advanced Iterative Constructs: *do* and *mapcar*

In this chapter you will learn about two operators, *do* and *mapcar*, that can be used in place of a *let-loop* combination for coding iterative functions. We introduced iteration with *let* and *loop* in Chapters 6 and 8 because those operators make it easy to see how an iterative function is evaluated step by step. Both *do* and *mapcar* employ a more concise structure for coding iteration.

A More Concise Iterative Structure: *do*

The special form *do* incorporates features of *let* and *loop*, and can be used to accomplish numeric, list, or input-controlled iteration. Let us start by considering list iteration. Suppose we need a function we can call *list-abs* that accepts a list of numbers and returns a list of the absolute value of each element.

We can code the function as follows with *let* and *loop*:

```
(defun list-abs (lis)
   (let ((newlist nil))
      (loop
         (cond ((null lis) (return (reverse newlist))))
         (setq newlist (cons (abs (car lis)) newlist))
         (setq lis (cdr lis)))))
```

As you can see, the function *cdr*s through the control list, *lis*, each time taking the *car* and inserting the absolute value of that element into the result variable *newlist*. The function reverses the result list when returning it so that it is in the appropriate order.

We can write the same function with a *do* as follows:

```
(defun list-abs (lis)
   (do ((oldlist lis (cdr oldlist))                              [1a]
        (newlist nil (cons (abs (car oldlist)) newlist)))        [1b]
       ((null oldlist) (reverse newlist))))                      [2]
```

This definition is a more concise version of the control structure in the first definition. The template for a *do* looks like this:

```
(do ( ⟨var-update-list1⟩
      [⟨var-update-list2⟩ ... ])
    ( ⟨exit-test⟩ ⟨return-value⟩ )
  )
```

The first part of the *do* is a list of variable-update lists. Each of these lists contains three elements: the name of a local variable, its initial value, and a specification of how to update the variable on each pass through the loop. Let us look at the two variable updates in lines 1a and 1b of the definition of *list-abs* above and then the exit test in line 2.

[1a] In the above example, the first variable update list is *(oldlist lis (cdr oldlist))*, which creates the variable *oldlist* and initializes it to the value of the parameter *lis*. The third element in this list indicates that each time through the loop *oldlist* will be reset to *(cdr oldlist)*. In a *let*, variables can be initialized without using *setq*, but *setq*s are needed in a *loop* to update those variables. In a *do*, both the initial and updated value are simply listed without an explicit *setq*. The format of a *do* allows us to update variables more concisely than in a *let*, but we cannot update a parameter like *lis* within this format. As a result, we create the local variable *oldlist* to use as a control variable instead of the parameter. While *oldlist* initially has the same value as *lis*, it is important to reset *oldlist* to the *cdr* of *oldlist* rather than the *cdr* of *lis*, because *oldlist* is updated each time through the loop and *lis* is not.

[1b] The second variable-update list creates the variable *newlist*. This result variable is initialized to *nil* and is updated as it is in the *let-loop* version. On each pass through the loop, we reset *newlist* by taking the absolute value of the first item in the control list (*oldlist*) and inserting it into the previous value of *newlist*.

[2] The second argument to our *do* is a list that contains the exit test and return value for the loop: *((null oldlist) (reverse newlist))*. The form of this list is exactly that of a *cond* case. The first item is the exit test. When this test is non-*nil*, the loop will terminate and return the value of the second item in the list. In *list-abs*, the loop will terminate when the control list *oldlist* is *nil*, and will return the result variable *newlist* after reversing it. Note that unlike a *loop*, the function *return* is not needed — the return value is automatically returned as the value of the *do*.

Like a *loop*, all the updates in the *do* are performed in each iteration until the exit test is satisfied, at which point the loop terminates and a value is returned. However, there is one very important difference between the flow of control of *do*s and that of *loop*s. In a *do*, all the initialization and updates can be thought of as **executing in parallel**. That is, it does not matter in what order you place your variable-update lists, because on each pass through the loop all update values are computed, and *then* the variables are reset to their updated values. Thus any reference to a variable in an update refers to the value of that variable from the previous pass through the loop. The initializations are like the initializations of a *let* — you cannot create a variable in one initialization and then use it in another initialization, again because these initializations are done in parallel. The flow of control in a *do* is summarized in Figure 10.1.

Consider the function *list-abs* called on the list *(4 − 7 − 3 5)*. The first time through the loop, *oldlist* is given the value of the parameter *lis*, which is *(4 − 7 − 3 5)*, and *newlist* starts out as *nil*. Then the exit test fails, so the updates are performed. First, we compute the two updated values. The expression *(cdr oldlist)* returns *(− 7 − 3 5)*, while *(cons (abs (car oldlist)))* is equivalent to *(cons (abs 4) nil)*, which returns *(4)*. Only after both these updates have been computed are the variables actually assigned their new values. The control variable *oldlist* gets the value *(− 7 − 3 5)* and *newlist* gets the value *(4)*. Note that we used the *car* and the *cdr* of the same *oldlist*, because we did not reset the variable *oldlist* until after we computed all the updates. Compare this parallel updating with the processing in *loop*s, in which we must be careful to place the update of the control list after the update of the results variable, to avoid *cdr*ing the list before we use its *car*. Since the variables in a *do* are not assigned their updated value until all the updates have been computed, both updates use the same value of *oldlist* (without changing *oldlist*) and the order of the updates has no effect. Table 10.1 summarizes the values of *oldlist* and *newlist* as the *do* executes.

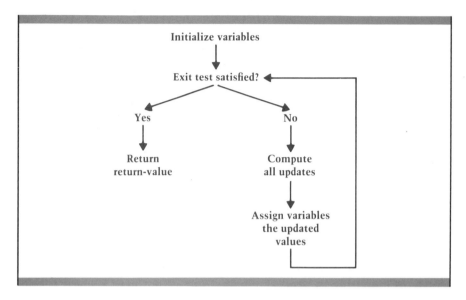

Figure 10.1
Flow of Control
in dos

Table 10.1. Examples of variable updates in a *do*

Function definition:

```
(defun list-abs lis)
    (do ((oldlist lis (cdr oldlist))
        (newlist nil (cons (abs (car oldlist)) newlist)))
        ((null oldlist) (reverse newlist))))
```

Function call:

```
(list-abs '(4 − 7 − 3 5))
                        oldlist        newlist
            (4 − 7 − 3 5)       ()
                (− 7 − 3 5)       (4)
                    (− 3 5)       (7 4)
                        (5)       (3 7 4)
                        ()       (5 3 7 4)
                exit = )       return (reverse (5 3 7 4)) = (4 7 3 5)
```

LISP Exercises

10.1 Define a function called *new-reverse* that performs the same operation as the LISP function *reverse* — i.e., it takes a list and returns a new list with the elements in the opposite order. For example,

(new-reverse '(apple orange lemon banana)) returns
    (banana lemon orange apple).

10.2 Define a function called *list-avg* that has one parameter, a list of numbers. The function should return the average of all the numbers in the list. You may assume the list contains only numbers. For example,

(list-avg '(10 20 5 5)) returns *10*.

Using *do* for Numeric Iteration

Now let us consider some examples of numeric iteration. We will want to discuss the use of *do* for two types of loops; those in which the counter is not employed in updating result variables and those in which the counter is employed to update result variables.

Numeric Iteration with Independent Updates

Recall the function *int-multiply* from Chapter 6, which uses repeated addition to perform multiplication. Below is its definition using *do*.

```
(defun int-multiply (x y)
    (do ((result 0 (+ result x))
         (count 0 (1+ count)))
        ((equal count y) result)))
```

In this function, each time through the loop the product is updated by adding the value of the first parameter to the previous product. Note that in this function the updates of the variables are independent. That is, the result variable is not updated using the counter, and of course the counter is not updated using the result variable (it is simply incremented by 1). Functions such as *int-multiply* with independent updates can be written easily using a *do*.

Numeric Iteration with Nonindependent Updates

In some cases, the parallel nature of *do* updates requires a different update than the one we would use in a *loop*. The parallel *do* updates are fine for list iteration as in our definition of *list-abs*, because we can update the control list by *cdr*ing the previous value of the control list, and use the *car* of the previous value of the control list to update the result variable. Thus both updates use the previous value of the control variable.

We come to a different situation in numeric iteration, however. If the variable updates are independent, it does not matter that they are performed in parallel. However, if the counter is used to update result variables, we need a different update than in a *loop*. Recall that when we perform nonindependent updates in a *loop* we first update the counter, and then use that new value to compute the new value of the result variable. In a *do*, the parallel updates present a problem, because any reference to the counter in the result update will get the old value of the counter instead of the new value, and our loop will be out of synch. To solve this problem, when the updates are nonindependent, you need to compute the next value of the counter in the update of the result variable. The definition of *factorial* below illustrates this.

```
(defun factorial (n)
   (do ((count 0 (1+ count))
        (product 1 (* product (1+ count))))
       ((equal count n) product)))
```

Note that the update of the result variable *product* multiplies *product* by *(1 + count)* instead of by *count*, since we need to get the next value of the counter, rather than the previous value.

LISP Exercises

10.3 Define a function called *expon* that has two arguments. The first argument is a base and the second is an exponent. The function *expon* returns the base raised to the power of the exponent (which is the base multiplied by itself "exponent" times). For example,

(expon 3 5) returns 243, which is 3 × 3 × 3 × 3 × 3.

This function should work with 0 or any positive number as an exponent. (Any number raised to the power 0 is defined as 1.)

10.4 Write a new version of the function *create-list* from LISP Exercise 6.5 using do. The function should take one argument, *n*, and return a list of the numbers from 1 to *n*. Your resulting list should have the numbers in ascending order from left to right.

10.5 Rewrite the function *next-prime* from LISP Exercise 6.7 using *do*. The function takes one parameter and returns the first prime number that is greater than or equal to the value of the parameter. For example,

(next-prime 24) returns *29*.

Use the predicate *primep* described in Exercise 6.7, which takes one argument and returns *t* if the argument is prime and *nil* otherwise.

10.6 Use a *do* to write an iterative version of the recursive function *sumall* described in Chapter 7. The function *sumall* should take one argument and return the sum of all the numbers from 0 to that number. For example,

(sumall 5) returns 15, which is 0 + 1 + 2 + 3 + 4 + 5.

Conditional Updates in *dos*

In the examples we have discussed so far, the variables are updated in the same fashion on each pass through the loop. However, suppose we want to check something about the data and make our update contingent upon that property of the data. For example, suppose we wanted to go through a list of numbers and save all of the numbers larger than 100. The following function accomplishes this with a *do*:

```
(defun save-large (lis)
     (do ((oldlist lis (cdr oldlist))
          (result nil (cond ((> (car oldlist) 100)
                                  (cons (car oldlist) result))
                            (t result))))
         ((null oldlist) (reverse result))))
```

In this function, we use a *cond* to code a conditional update. If the next element in the control list is larger than 100, then *result* is set to the list created by inserting that element into the old value of *result*. If the next element is not larger than 100, then *result* is reset to its previous value — i.e., it does not change. Thus we can use conditional updates to use differentially an item contingent on some property. For example, we can save only those items having a certain property, add an item to one of two separate lists, and so on.

It is important to remember that unlike the conditional updates you wrote in Chapter 8, you need an explicit *cond* case to leave the result variable unchanged. In a *loop*, you could simply have the following *cond* with one case:

```
(cond ((> (car oldlist) 100)
        (setq result (cons (car oldlist) result))))
```

If the test in this case fails then the update action is not performed; the *cond* just returns *nil* and the value of *result* is not changed. However, if we included only this case in the *do* version of this function, then the result variable would not be correctly updated. In a *do*, each variable is reset to the value of its update every time through the loop. If we had only one case that tested for values greater than 100 in our update of *result*, then when a number less than or equal to 100 was tested, the *cond* would return *nil*, and *result* would be reset to *nil*, wiping out any previous values that had been accumulated. Thus a second *cond* case is necessary to set *result* to *result*; that is, to assign the variable the value it already had.

LISP Exercises

10.7 Define a function called *save-atoms* that goes through a list and returns a list of all the elements of the argument list that are atoms. You should be careful to save the atoms in the same order that they appear in the original list. For example,

(save-atoms '(x y (a b) z (c))) returns *(x y z)*.

10.8 Define a function called *sortnums* that takes one argument, a list containing numbers. The function should take the original list and return a new list with two embedded lists — the first contains the negative numbers and the second contains the positive numbers, and any zeros that appear. You should make sure you keep the negative and positive numbers in the order in which you find them in the original list. For example,

(sortnums '(3 − 3 0 − 7 1)) returns *((− 3 − 7) (3 0 1))*.

Actions in the *do* Body

Each time we have coded a *do* so far, we have given it two arguments, a list of variable updates and an exit test. Many of the functions you will write will have that structure. However, a *do* can actually take any number of arguments following the exit test. These arguments are additional actions to be performed in the body of the loop. Each time through the loop, if the exit test is not satisfied, then these additional arguments are evaluated in order before the variables are updated.

Thus the template for a *do* is

```
(do ( ⟨variable-update1⟩
    [⟨variable-update2⟩ ... ])
    ( ⟨exit-test⟩ ⟨return-value⟩ )
    [⟨loop-action1⟩
      ⟨loop-action2⟩
        .
        .                ]
  )
```

Additional actions are necessary if you want to produce some side effects, such as printing to the screen. Suppose, for example, that you wanted to rewrite the function *nasa-countdown* from Chapter 6 using a *do*. Recall that this function prints each digit from the value of its argument down to 0 and then returns *blastoff*. For example,

```
(nasa-countdown 3)
3
2
1
0
blast-off
```

This definition of *nasa-countdown* uses a *print* statement in the body of the loop to accomplish the task.

```
(defun nasa-countdown (n)
    (do ((count n (1- count)))
        (((< count 0) 'blastoff)
        (print count))))
```

Another reason for including additional actions in the *do* is to allow for more than one exit test. For example, suppose you want a function that adds a list of numbers, but prints the error message *"non-number in list"* and returns *0* if it encounters a non-number. The function *check-add* uses a *cond* in the *do* body to check each element, returning from the *do* if a non-number is found.

```
(defun check-add (lis)
    (do ((temp lis (cdr temp))
         (sum 0 (+ sum (car temp))))
        ((null temp) sum)
        (cond ((not (numberp (car temp)))
               (princ "non-number in list")
               (return 0)))))
```

LISP Exercises

10.9 Write a function called *rectangle* that takes two arguments, *m* and *n*, and produces a rectangle consisting of *m* rows of *n* columns consisting of the letter *x*. For example,

```
=> (rectangle 3 4)
xxxx
xxxx
xxxx
nil
```

10.10 Write a function called *printout* that will take a list of words and print them out, one by one, on the same line. Whenever it sees the atom *ret*, it will start printing on the next line. For example,

```
=> (printout '(Hi there ret What is your name? ret My name is John))
Hi there
What is your name?
My name is John
nil
```

A Mapping Function: mapcar

In addition to *loop* and *do*, a third function, *mapcar*, can be used to code iterative functions. To see how *mapcar* can be used, suppose we need a function we will call *list-add-one* that adds 1 to each number in a list and returns the resulting values in a new list. The following three functions accomplish this task with a *loop*, a *do*, and a *mapcar*.

```
(defun list-add-one (lis)
    (let ((newlist nil))
        (loop
            (cond ((null lis) (return newlist)))
            (setq newlist (append newlist (list (1 + (car lis)))))
            (setq lis (cdr lis)))))

(defun list-add-one (lis)
    (do ((oldlis lis (cdr oldlis))
            (newlis nil (append newlis (list (1 + (car oldllis))))))
        ((null oldlis) newlis)))

(defun list-add-one (lis)
    (mapcar '1 + lis))
```

So, *(list-add-one '(2 0 5 9))* returns *(3 1 6 10)*, regardless of which of these three ways it is coded.

As you can see, *mapcar* takes two arguments. The first argument is the name of a function and the second argument is a list.* When a *mapcar* executes, the function designated by the first argument is applied to every item in the second argument in succession, and the result is put into a new list. Then *mapcar* returns that list of results.

Although we have frequently used a function call as an argument to another function, this is the first case in which an actual function *name* is used as an argument to another function. The function name is quoted in the code because we want it to be treated literally.

The function *mapcar* is just one of several **mapping functions** that are available in LISP. These functions "map" a function over a list; that is, they apply the function to each item in the list. One advantage of using a function such as *mapcar* is immediately apparent: The code for the function is much shorter than it would be with a *loop* or even a *do*. Furthermore, the code is easier to understand — it says simply to take each element of *lis*, and add one to it, and return a list of the results.†

It is important to determine which types of iteration can use *mapcar*. First, we can use *mapcar* only when iterating on a list. If our iteration is controlled by a counter (numeric iteration) or input (input iteration) we will have to use a *do*, because a function can only be mapped over a list, not over a sequence of numbers or inputs to be read in. Second, we can use *mapcar* only when the output from our function is also a list. For example, if you wanted to count up all negative numbers in a list, you could not simply use *mapcar*, because

---

*In Interlisp the order of these two arguments is reversed.

†You will learn about another mapping function in Chapter 13.

mapcar can only return a list of the results of a function call involving each element of the original list.

LISP Exercises

10.11 Define a function called *list-decrement* with one parameter that holds a list of numbers. This function subtracts 1 from each element in the parameter list, and returns a list of the resulting numbers (in the same order). For example,

(list-decrement '(75 3 109 − 24)) returns *(74 2 108 − 25)*.

10.12 Define a function called *embed-lists* that has one parameter, which is a list. The function returns a new list in which each item of the original list has been embedded in a list. For example,

(embed-lists '(a (b) cat)) returns *((a) ((b)) (cat))*

Mapping over Multiple Lists

In the preceding example and exercises we mapped functions that accept one argument; but it is possible to map functions that take more arguments. To map a multiple-argument function, you have to provide a separate list for each argument. Then *mapcar* will apply the function to the successive elements of each list.* For example, suppose we wanted to add together the corresponding elements of two lists and return a list of the resulting values. The following function performs that task:

```
=) (defun addlists (lis1 lis2)
        (mapcar '+ lis1 lis2))
addlists
=) (addlists '(1 2 3) '(4 5 6))
(5 7 9)
```

---

*If the lists are of different lengths, *mapcar* will apply the function to successive elements until the shortest list is exhausted. Thus the list that is returned will be the same length as the shortest list being mapped over.

In this example, the function + is applied in succession to the values *1* and *4, 2* and *5*, and finally *3* and *6*, with the results of each calculation being saved in a list.

LISP Exercise

10.13 Define a function called *pair-up*, which takes two lists of names and returns a new list, in which the corresponding names have been placed in embedded lists. For example,

(pair-up '(john bob sam) '(mary alice karen)) returns
((john mary) (bob alice) (sam karen)).

---

lambda **Expressions**

In the preceding examples we have mapped only built-in LISP functions. In many cases though, we will need to define the function we want to map. In fact, sometimes it will be necessary to define a function for mapping that we would not define in other circumstances. For example, suppose we want a function that multiplies each number in a list by the constant −*1* (to reverse the sign). Ordinarily to multiply a value by −*1* we would just call *, as in (* x −*1*). But if we try something such as *(mapcar '* lis* −*1*)* to multiply every element in a list by −1, we will get an error message, because −*1* is not a list. We can instead define a new function that takes one argument and multiplies it by −*1*. For example,

```
(defun list-invert (lis)
    (mapcar 'timesneg1 lis))

(defun timesneg1 (x)
    (* x −1))
```

A similar problem arises if we need to map an embedded set of function calls. For example, suppose we want to add 1 to each item in a list and then take the square root of the resulting values. There is no way to code both the *1+* and *sqrt* functions in the same *mapcar* expression. Instead, we will have to define a function to accomplish the task:

```
(defun list-sqrt-add1 (lis)
   (mapcar 'sqrt-add1 lis))
```

```
(defun sqrt-add1 (x)
   (sqrt (1+ x)))
```

Note, however, that *timesneg1* and *sqrt-add1* do not really meet our criteria for coding a helping function. They are not very complex and they are not deeply nested in a function definition. Defining a function such as *timesneg1*, if anything, makes the code harder to read than just calling *, and *list-sqrt-add1* is not a function that is likely to be generally useful. Nevertheless, we need to define a function if we are to use a *mapcar* here. We can use *lambda* expressions in these circumstances.

A *lambda* expression serves very much the same purpose as a helping function — both allow you to define a function. However, there are two important differences: A *lambda* expression allows you actually to define a function within another function and the function defined in a *lambda* expression does not have a name. Thus you can use it to define a temporary function that you will need only in the body of the *mapcar*. Consider the following examples:

```
(defun list-invert (lis)
   (mapcar '(lambda (x) (* x −1)) lis))
```

```
(defun list-sqrt-add1 (lis)
   (mapcar '(lambda (x) (sqrt (1+ x))) lis))
```

In each of these functions the first argument to the *mapcar* is a *lambda* expression. Moreover, the form of each *lambda* expression is almost identical to the helping function it replaced. The *defun* and function name are replaced by *lambda*, but otherwise, each *lambda* expression has a parameter list and a function body just as the corresponding helping function does. However, the entire *lambda* expression appears in the middle of another function definition (i.e., the definition of *list-invert* or *list-sqrt-add1*). Moreover, the function defined within each *lambda* expression does not have a unique name. As a result, there is no way to call either of these *lambda* expressions from any function except from the one in which it is embedded.

So, a *lambda* function allows us to define a function with no name and has the following template:

(*lambda* (parameters...) ⟨function-body⟩)

Remember that when you use a *lambda* expression as the first argument of a *mapcar*, it must be quoted just as an actual function name would be quoted.

Suppose we wanted to define a function that would insert an element into each embedded list of a list. The following definition using *mapcar* would accomplish this task.

```
(defun insert (elem lis)
        (mapcar #'(lambda (x) (cons elem x)) lis))
```

The peculiar feature to note about this definition is that we have preceded the *lambda* expression by #' rather than simply '. This symbol is an abbreviation for a special form called *function* and, among the major LISP dialects, is required only in Common LISP. The reason for its use is that the parameter *elem* of the function *insert* appears in the *lambda* definition. If the *lambda* expression were simply quoted, Common LISP would treat this as a global variable and generate an error. By using the *function* symbol, #', we make Common LISP treat variables like *elem* inside the *lambda* expression as local variables from the definition of *insert*. In other implementations of LISP you can simply use the single quote.

LISP Exercises

10.14 Define a function called *add-to-lis* that has two parameters. The first parameter holds a number and the second parameter holds a list of numbers. This function returns a list of sums that is created by adding the value of the first parameter to each number in the second parameter. For example,

(add-to-lis 45 '(2 98 − 38)) returns (47 143 7).

10.15 The covariance of two lists, X and Y, of the same length, is defined as:

$$\frac{\Sigma X_i Y_i / \text{n} - (\Sigma X_i / n)(\Sigma Y_i / n)}{n - 1},$$

where

X_i is the i th element of list X,
Y_i is the i th element of list Y, and
n is the number of items in each list.

Write a function to compute the covariance of X and Y. *Hint*: You can use *mapcar* to get the crossproduct of X and Y, which is a list of $X_i Y_i$.

This chapter concludes our discussion of basic control structures, although we will make use of these control structures in the following chapters. In Chapter 11 we will introduce two more data structures, and in Chapters 12 and 13 we will take a closer look at how lists are represented in LISP and how functions are evaluated. In Chapters 14–16 we will apply what we have learned about LISP to three major topics in artificial intelligence.

Summary of LISP Functions

do   This special form allows us to code iteration concisely. Its first argument is a list of variable updates. Its second argument is an exit test, and it optionally ends with a list of actions to perform each time through the loop. The variable updates are lists consisting of the variable name, its initial value, and the code for updating it. The updates are performed in parallel.

Example definition of *factorial*:

```
(defun factorial (n)
    (do ((count n (1 – count))
        (product 1 (* product count)))
        ((zerop count) product)))
```

lambda   This special form allows you to define a nameless function within another function. A *lambda* expression consists of a list of parameters for the defined function, plus a body.

Example: *(lambda (x) (* x –1))*
defines a function that changes the sign of a numerical argument.

Note: the *lambda* expression must be quoted when it appears in a function definition. In Common LISP it must be preceded by #' if it uses local variables from the function definition in which it appears.

mapcar   This special form applies a function to a list of arguments and returns a list of resulting values.

Example: *(mapcar '+ 1 '(1 4 2))*
returns (2 5 3).

Glossary

parallel execution   Actions that occur simultaneously.
variable update   An element in the local variable list of a *do*. A variable update declares a variable, and specifies its initial value and its update.
mapping function   A function that applies a function to elements of a list.

More-Complex Data Structures: Property Lists and Arrays

In this chapter we will discuss some useful methods for storing data to be processed by a program. In Chapter 1 you learned one method for storing information — assigning a value to a variable. The fact that we have made extensive use of variables throughout this book indicates the importance of storing information for subsequent processing. Variables are too limited for some situations, however, because a variable can have only one value. If we need to store large amounts of information, then we would have to choose between two unappealing options: (1) keeping track of lots of variables and (2) using just a few variables to store long, complex lists that can be difficult to process. For example, in Chapter 9 we used a single variable to store a binary-tree structure, and wound up storing a complicated list. LISP provides other alternatives for storing data that allow us to store large amounts of data without employing long lists or multiple variables. In this chapter we will describe two LISP constructs — property lists and arrays — that allow you to associate large amounts of information with an atom, but unlike simple variables, allow you to store and access that information conveniently.

Property Lists: Associating Property Values with an Atom

Atoms are special in LISP. As we have seen, atoms can serve as variables; that is, we can assign a value to an atom. Let us consider an example. Suppose we want to store four pieces of information about someone named Mary: her age (28), her sex (female), the names of her children (Bill, Susan, and Alice), and her occupation (lawyer). We can use the atom *mary* to store this information, and since an atom can have only one value (at a time), we could put all the information into a list and assign that list to *mary*. For example:

> =) *(setq mary '((age 28) (sex female)*
> *(children (Bill Susan Alice)) (occupation lawyer)))*

This list is an A-list, or association list, first introduced in Chapter 9. In this A-list, each embedded list can be said to describe a characteristic or a property of Mary. The first element in each list corresponds to the name of a property (e.g., age or occupation), and we can think of the second item in each list as Mary's value for that property. To find Mary's age, we could then type *(cadr (assoc 'age mary))*, which would return *28*.

Assigning Properties to an Atom

LISP provides an alternate mechanism for storing such information. It not only allows atoms to serve as variables, it also allows an atom to have a **property list**. A property list is very similar to the A-list we have just discussed; it is a set of **properties** that are associated with the atom. Each property is designated by a **property name** — for example, *age* or *children* — and a **property value** — for example, *28* or *(Bill Susan Alice)*. Thus while a variable can have only a single value, we can associate any number of other values with an atom by assigning each one a property name.

It is useful to have a function *putprop* for assigning properties to atoms. In some Common LISP implementations *putprop* is not defined. You can define it for yourself as follows:

> *(defun putprop (atom value property)*
> *(setf (get atom property) value))*

We shall see more about *setf* and why this particular definition works later on in this chapter.*

---

*In Interlisp there exists a function called *putprop*, but its arguments are in the order atom, property, value.

The function *putprop* takes three arguments, the atom that is being assigned a property, the property value, and the property name. We can assign to *mary* the four properties that we discussed earlier by calling *putprop* four times:

```
= ) (putprop 'mary 28 'age)
28
= ) (putprop 'mary 'female 'sex)
female
= ) (putprop 'mary '(bill susan alice) 'children)
(bill susan alice)
= ) (putprop 'mary 'lawyer 'occupation)
lawyer
```

The effect of each *putprop* is to attach a property and its value to the atom so that it can later be retrieved. The template for a *putprop* is

> (*putprop* ⟨atom⟩ ⟨property-value⟩ ⟨property-name⟩)

As in the case of variables, only non-numeric atoms can be assigned properties. Each property name must be a non-numeric atom,* but the property value can be any LISP expression.

Accessing Values of Properties

Of course, after we have assigned a property to an atom it will be useful only if we can access or "retrieve" the property. We can retrieve a variable value simply by referring to the atom without a quote; but to retrieve a property value we need to use the function *get*.† As you might guess, *get* takes two arguments — the name of an atom and a property name — and returns the corresponding property value for that atom. For example,

```
= ) (get 'mary 'age)
28
= ) (get 'mary 'children)
(bill susan alice)
```

---

*Some LISP dialects allow numbers to be used as property names, but for the sake of clarity it is usually desirable to use non-numeric atoms for property names.
†In Interlisp get is called *getprop*.

The template for *get* is

> (*get* ⟨atom⟩ ⟨property-name⟩)

There is an important difference between retrieving the value of an atom and retrieving the value of a property of an atom. Consider the following examples:

```
=> mary
error: unbound variable: mary
=> (get 'mary 'hobbies)
nil
```

In this example, we have not assigned a value to *mary*, nor have we assigned the property *hobbies* to *mary*. If we try to retrieve a variable value when none has been assigned, we get an error message. However, if we attempt to retrieve a property that has not been assigned to an atom, we do not get an error message; instead, *get* returns *nil*.

Updating Property Values

Just as you can reset the value of a variable, you can change the value of a property with a *putprop*. For example, if Mary has a birthday, the following function call will update her age:

```
=> (putprop 'mary 29 'age)
```

Then, if you retrieve Mary's age, you find that *28* has been replaced by *29* as the value for that property:

```
=> (get 'mary 'age)
29
```

It is important to remember that although an atom can have more than one property, each property has only one value (just as a variable can have only one value). When you call *putprop* to update a property, the new value replaces the old value; it is not combined in some fashion with the previous value.

Frequently, you will want to update a property value by using the current value of the property — for example, we may need to update Mary's age without knowing her current age. We can combine calls to *get* and *putprop* to do this as follows:

```
=> (putprop 'mary (1+ (get 'mary 'age)) 'age)
```

Note that the second argument of this *putprop* is the function call *(1+ (get 'mary 'age))*, which does what we want: it retrieves the current value of Mary's age and adds one to it. Since Mary's age was 28, *(putprop 'mary (1+ (get 'mary 'age)) 'age)* is equivalent to *(putprop 'mary 29 'age)*.

A property can be removed entirely from an atom with the function *remprop*. The template for *remprop* is

```
(remprop ⟨atom⟩ ⟨property-name⟩)
```

This function removes the property designated by the second argument from the atom designated by the first argument. After using *remprop*, attempts to retrieve that property for the atom will return *nil*, just as if the property had never been assigned to the atom.

Properties in a Data Base

Properties can be very useful in storing data in an organized way. For example, suppose you had a data base of information about musical recordings. We could store many kinds of information associated with the name of each recording. For example:

```
(putprop 'born-to-run '(bruce springsteen) 'artist)
(putprop 'born-to-run t 'gold-record)
(putprop 'born-to-run 'columbia 'label)
```

To design an organized data base, you would decide on the properties you wanted to encode, and then write storage functions that would perform *putprop*s to store the appropriate values, and retrieval functions that would return the appropriate information. For example, you might want to write a function that would go through a list of recordings and return the names of all those that went gold. To do this you could just go down the list of recording names, getting the *gold-record* property of each one. You would want to save (in a list) the name of each recording whose *gold-record* property value is *t*. All our example calls to *putprop*, *get*, and *remprop* have been in isolation, but these functions can, of course, be used in function definitions, just like any other LISP function.

Lisp Exercises

11.1 Write a function called *buy*, which takes two arguments, an item and a store. If the store has the item, then return the address of the store. Otherwise, return *nil*. You can find out whether the store has the item by checking the *goods* property of the store which holds a list of items the store sells. You can find the address of the store on the *address* property of the store. For example, assume we assign the list (clothes appliances toys) to the goods property of Smiths and assign the value (Pittsburgh PA) to the address property of Smiths. Then

(buy 'toys 'Smiths) returns (Pittsburgh Pa)
(buy 'food 'Smiths) returns nil

11.2 Write a function called *add-data*, which takes three arguments — a person's first name, his or her age, and his or her sex. The function should record the age and sex of the person on the *age* and *sex* properties respectively.

11.3 Write a function called *childp*, which takes two arguments — the names of two people. The function returns *t* if the first person is a child of the second person, otherwise it returns *nil*. You can check whether one person is a child of the other by looking at the *children* property of the person. Assume that the value of the children property is a list. For example, if we assign the list *(bob mary chris)* to the *children* property of *alice*, then

(childp 'bob 'alice) returns t
(childp 'alice 'bob) returns nil

11.4 Write a function called *add-child*, which takes three arguments — a child, a mother, and a father. You should record the child's birth by placing the mother and father under the *mother* and *father* properties of the child, respectively. Also, you should add the child to the end of the list of children for the mother and for the father, kept for each parent on the *children* property.

11.5 Define a function called *list-props*, with one parameter that holds a list of names such as *(mary bill ted patty)*. Each name in the list has two properties associated with it — *age* and *sex*. For each name in the list, this function creates a list consisting of the name and the value of the age and sex properties for the name — for example, *(mary 20 f)* and *(bill 19 m)*. The function returns a list of these lists (in the same order that the names appeared in the parameter list). For example,

(list-props '(mary bill)) returns ((mary 20 f) (bill 19 m))

11.6 Define a function called *listsort*, which takes one parameter — a list. The function takes the original list and returns a new list with embedded lists — the first embedded list is the minors and the second is the adults. Each adult will have a value of *t* for the *adult* property; for minors that property will be *nil*. Your embedded lists should have the elements in the order you found them. For example, if *john* and *mary* are adults and *ted* is a minor, then

(listsort '(john ted mary)) returns *((ted)(john mary))*.

Creating New Atoms

When we are dealing with large data bases there are occasions when we would like our programs to be able to create new atoms in a systematic manner for the purpose of storing information. For example, if we are dealing with a large data base of people, some of those people may have the same name, and so we cannot simply use their names to store information. LISP provides methods for creating unique atoms that can prevent us from accidently reassigning values to the same atom. The method we recommend for starting out involves creating the following useful helping function called *newatom*:

```
(defun newatom (stem)
    (prog1 (intern (string (gensym stem))))))
```

This definition uses some of the advanced features of Common LISP that we will not discuss, but the function it creates is quite straightforward. The function *newatom** takes one argument called a stem — which must be an atom, and returns a unique atom by attaching a numerical suffix to that stem. For example,

```
= ) (newatom 'person)
person0001
= ) (newatom 'person)
person0002
```

---

*InterLISP has the function *gensym* which behaves just like *newatom*. Here is the definition of *newatom* for Franz Lisp or MacLisp:
```
(defun newatom (stem)
    (intern (gensym stem)))
```

Every time we call *newatom* with the same stem, it returns an atom with a different numerical suffix, so each atom we generate will be different. So, if we want to add information about a new person to a large data base, we can create a new atom from a stem such as *person* and associate information with that atom. If we enter two people into the data base in this fashion, we can be assured that they will be assigned to unique atoms:

```
=> (newatom 'person)
person0003
=> (putprop 'person0003 'Fred 'name)
Fred
=> (putprop 'person0003 17 'age)
17
=> (newatom 'person)
person0004
=> (putprop 'person0004 'Fred 'name)
Fred
=> (putprop 'person0004 32 'age)
32
```

The function *newatom* is particularly useful for creating new atoms inside a function. Suppose we want to write a function to add new persons to a data base. If the function calls *newatom* each time it encodes information about a new person, we can be sure that each person will be represented by a unique atom. For example, the function *encode-person* stores the name, age, and sex of a person.

```
(defun encode-person (nameval ageval sexval)
    (let ((node (newatom 'person)))
         (putprop node nameval 'name)
         (putprop node ageval 'age)
         (putprop node sexval 'sex)
         node))
```

This function first creates a new atom, and assigns that atom to the local variable *node*. Then the three properties *name*, *age*, and *sex* are attached to the new atom. Notice that in this function, we must assign the value of *(newatom 'person)* to a local variable and use the local variable in each call to *putprop*. If we called *newatom* in each *putprop*, we would attach each property to a different atom!

Lisp Exercises

11.7 In Chapter 9 we discussed representation of binary trees by an A-list. Reread that section if necessary, and write a function called *encode-tree* that converts an A-list representation of a binary tree into a property list representation. Thus where formerly we represented a node with value *55*, a lesser descendant with value *25*, and greater descendant with value *70* by the list *(55 25 70)*, we will now create a node such as *node0001* with three properties, *value*, *greater*, and *lesser*. The *value* property holds the value of the node, in this case, *55*. The *lesser* property holds the name of the descendant that is less than this node; in this case it might be *node0002* (which itself will have a *value* property of *25*). Similarly, the *greater* property holds the name of the descendant that is greater than this node. The function *encode-tree* should take two arguments — the root value on the A-list and the A-list itself. The function will be recursive and return the root atom in the tree.

11.8 Using the property-list representation created in Exercise 11.7, rewrite the function *binary-search* from Exercise 9.10. The new definition will take two arguments — a root atom and a key.

Arrays: Storing Easily Accessible Data

Let us consider a somewhat different problem in data storage. Suppose you have 50 numbers that you want to store so that they can be processed. It is not feasible to create 50 different variables to hold those numbers (nor is it feasible or particularly appropriate to create properties to store the 50 values). Instead, a reasonable solution is to put the 50 numbers into a list and to assign that list to a variable. It is then relatively easy to process these numbers in some ways. For example, in Chapter 8, you coded a list-iteration function that added up all the numbers in a list.

One thing that is relatively difficult to do is to access an arbitrary element in the list. For example, suppose you needed to get only the 8th, 19th, and 34th numbers. You would have to *cdr* through the list, keeping track until you got the right elements. Even more cumbersome would be the task of replacing a given element. Suppose you wanted to change only the 19th element in the list. Again, you would have to go through the list, storing up all the elements until the 18th one, append the new 19th element onto the end, and then append that list with the rest of the original beginning at the 20th element.

Fortunately, this type of list manipulation is not necessary. LISP provides another type of data structure, **arrays**, that can be useful for storing large sets of data. An array can be thought of as a collection of variables or **cells**, each having the same name, but with different numbers to distinguish them. Each cell in the array can store a value, if we need to store 50 numbers we can create an array with 50 cells. The function LISP *make-array* can be used to create an array of a given size.*

The function *make-array* takes one argument — a list — which specifies the number of cells in the array. The following function call creates an array called *data* with 10 cells:

```
=> (setq data (make-array '(10)))
#(nil nil nil nil nil nil nil nil nil nil)
```

The function *make-array* creates an array in memory. In order to make reference to the array subsequently, we assign it to an atom with a call to *setq*. The strange response printed when we created the array *data* is actually a representation of the empty array. Note that there are 10 *nil*s in a list, preceded by the symbol #. This sequence represents an array with 10 cells, each of which contains *nil*. The symbol # indicates that this object, which would otherwise appear to be a list, is actually an array.

It is useful to think of the atom *data* as the *name* of the array. Unlike variables so far, the value of *data* is neither a list nor an atom. Instead, the value of *data* is actually the array created by *make-array*.

Accessing Cells of an Array

The function *aref* allows us to retrieve values from an array. This function takes two arguments, the name of the array and the **index**, or number, of one of the cells, and returns the value stored in that cell. Since LISP filled the cells in our array *data* when we created it, we can already retrieve values from it with *aref*. Of course, LISP assigned *nil* to each cell, so that is all we will find:

```
=> (aref data 2)
nil
```

---

*The particular functions needed to create and access arrays varies among the LISP dialects. If your implementation is not Common LISP, check the syntax for creating arrays. Golden Common LISP supports only one-dimensional arrays and has a special syntax. However, the basic techniques for writing functions that use arrays are the same in different dialects.

This function call accesses cell number 2 of the array *data*. The template for *aref* is

> (*aref* ⟨array-name⟩ ⟨index⟩)

There are two important points to note about calls to *aref*. The first argument should be an unquoted array name. When that atom is evaluated it yields the array structure on which *aref* will act. Second, when LISP creates an array it begins numbering cells with the digit 0. Thus the second argument ⟨index⟩ must be an expression that evaluates to an integer between 0 and one less than the total number of cells in the array. For example, the array *data* has 10 cells numbered 0 through 9; if we tried to call (*aref data 10*), we would get an error message.

Entering Data into an Array

Now let us put some data into our array. To assign a value to an array cell we need to use the function *setf*. For example, the following function call would assign the value *dog* to cell 2 in the array *data*:

```
= ⟩ (setf (aref data 2) 'dog)
dog
```

This is a surprising function call. The second argument seems sensible enough. It is the element *dog* that we want to place into the array. But the first argument does not seem to be a specification of the array cell in which to store *dog*. Instead, according to our discussion in the last section, the expression (*aref data 2*) will return the value that is currently stored in the second cell. However, *setf* does not evaluate its first argument in this way. Instead, the reference to *aref* indicates to *setf* that an array cell is being updated, and the other two elements in the list indicate the array and the cell. Thus *setf* places the value of its second argument *dog* into cell number 2 of *data*. The template for using *setf* to store items in an array is

> (*setf* (*aref* ⟨array-name⟩ ⟨index⟩) ⟨value⟩)

As in the discussion of *aref* in the preceding section, ⟨array-name⟩ should be an unquoted array name, and ⟨index⟩ should be an expression that evalutes to the number of one of the cells in the array. Again, since cells are numbered beginning with 0, the maximum acceptable value for *index* is one less than the total number of cells in the array.

Here are some function calls that create an array called *testdata*, with five cells, and fill it with data:

```
=> (setq testdata (make-array '(5)))
#(nil nil nil nil nil)
=> (setf (aref testdata 0) 18)
18
=> (setf (aref testdata 2) '(a b))
(a b)
=> (setf (aref testdata 4) 0)
0
=> (setf (aref testdata 1) 'dog)
dog
=> (setf (aref testdata 3) -4)
-4
```

After these function calls are evaluated, the cells in the array would have the following values:

testdata	cell:	0	1	2	3	4
	value:	18	dog	(a b)	-4	0

Note that we can assign values to the cells in any order. We assigned a value to cell 4, for instance, before assigning values to cells 1 or 3.

We can retrieve values from this array as follows:

```
=> (aref testdata 0)
18
=> (cons (aref testdata 1) (list (aref testdata 4) (aref testdata 2)))
(dog 0 (a b))
=> (aref testdata (aref testdata 4))
18
```

Writing Functions That Process Arrays

Since each cell in an array is referenced by number, we can readily write functions that access cells to retrieve and/or store values. If we need a function that accesses every cell in an array, for example, we can employ numeric iteration to generate each of the cell numbers one after another. Consider the function *array-list* that takes two arguments — an array name and the length of the array — and returns a list of all the values in the array:

```
(defun array-list (arrayname len)
    (do ((index 0 (1+ index))
         (result nil (append result (list (aref arrayname index)))))
        ((equal index len) result)))
```

We can call this function with the array *testdata* as follows:

```
=> (array-list testdata 5)
(18 dog (a b) -4 0)
```

Note that when we call this function, the array name *testdata* is not quoted. Thus the value of the atom, which is an array, and not the array name, is assigned to the parameter *arrayname*.

This function has two local variables — *index*, which is used to generate cell numbers systematically, and *result*, which stores the list of cell values. Note that *index* is initialized to the number of the first cell in the array, and *result* is initialized to *nil*. On each loop through the code we increment the index and insert the value of the current cell into the result. Recall that these updates are done in parallel, so the new value of *index* will always be one greater than the index of the cell added to the result. When the value of the index equals the length of the array, it is one larger than the last cell of the array. For instance, the last cell of *testdata* is 4, while the length of *testdata* (counting cell 0) is 5. Thus when the index equals the length we have processed all the cells and can return the result.

Lisp Exercises

11.9 Define a function called *arraysum* that has one parameter — the length of an array called *data*. The function should go through *data* and return the sum of all the numbers in the array. You may assume the array contains only numbers. For example, if the numbers 9, −11, 4, 0, and 18 are stored in *data*, then

(arraysum 4) returns *20;*

11.10 Define a function called *array-switch* that takes two arguments — the name of an array and the length of the array (the number of cells). The function should go through all the elements in the array and replace each element with its additive inverse. For example, if a cell contains a *4*, replace that item with *−4* in the cell. When the loop is finished, it should return *done*. You may assume that the array contains only numbers.

11.11 Define a function called *array-search* that takes two arguments, the name of an array and the length of the array. The function should go through all the elements in the array and return a list of all the elements that are winners (in order). An element is a winner if its *score* property equals *won*.

11.12 Define a function called *count-runs* that goes through an array called *stats* and returns the total number of runs scored by a baseball team. Each element in the array is the name of a player. The number of runs scored by each player is associated with the player's name on the property *runs*. So *count-runs* should sum the value of the property *runs* across the elements in the array *stats*. The function takes one argument, which indicates the number of names in the array.

11.13 Define a function called *sort-by-sex* that takes two arguments — the name of an array and the length of the array. The function should go through all the elements in the array and return a list of two lists — a list of females and a list of males. You can tell whether an item is male or female by checking the *sex* property of the item. For example,

(sort-by-sex 'apple 6) might return *((john paul george) (yoko linda patti)).*

Multiple Dimensions in Arrays

The arrays we have discussed so far are called one-dimensional arrays or **vectors**, because each cell in these arrays is specified by a single number, and it is easy to think of the cells as being in a single row, or dimension. These arrays are actually only one type of array that you can use. It is possible in LISP, as in other computer languages, to create arrays with more than one dimension. For example, the function call *(setq table (make-array '(10 15)))* creates a two-dimensional array. There are a total of 150 cells in this array. Each cell in this array is specified by two numbers, for example, *(aref table 0 0)* or *(aref table 4 12)*. In the case of two-dimensional arrays, it is easy to think of one index as specifying a row and the other as specifying a column. Two-dimensional arrays are often referred to as **matrices**. Interestingly, when you create an array with multiple dimensions, the array marker (#) also indicates the number of dimensions. For example,

```
= ) (setq tic-tac-toe (make-array '(3 3)))
#2a((nil nil nil) (nil nil nil) (nil nil nil))
```

LISP Exercise

11.14 Write a function, *matrix-add*, that takes two two-dimensional arrays and computes their sums. The function takes four arguments: the names of the two arrays, the number of rows, and the number of columns. It should create a new array of the same dimensions and fill each cell of that array with the sum of the corresponding cells from the original arrays. It should return the new array.

Setf: A General Structure Modifier

We have looked at two of the most common types of data structures besides lists (property lists and arrays) and have found that *setf* is used to enter elements for both (recall that *putprop* was defined with *setf*). In fact, *setf* is a general structure modifier in Common LISP. The first argument to *setf* specifies how to access the structure at the "location" where the data will go. It employs the operator that is usually employed to retrieve data from the structure. Thus to modify a property you specify the property-access function (*get*) in the first argument, and to modify a cell in an array, you specify the array-access function (*aref*). The second argument can be any LISP expression, whose value will be assigned to the location specified by the first argument. For example,

```
= ) (setf (get 'mary 'occupation) 'lawyer)
lawyer
= ) (get 'mary 'occupation)
lawyer
= ) (setf (aref data 15) '(mary bill))
(mary bill)
= ) (aref data 15)
(mary bill)
```

In this chapter we have discussed two mechanisms LISP provides for storing large bodies of data, properties, and arrays. In Chapters 14–16, we will see that properties in particular are useful in artificial intelligence applications. Before discussing AI applications, however, we will look more closely at the representation of lists in Chapter 12 and at the evaluation process in Chapter 13.

Summary of LISP Functions

aref   This function takes an array name followed by as many numbers as there are dimensions. This function returns the value of the cell indexed by these numbers.

Example: *(aref data 2)* might return *(a b)*.

get   This function takes two arguments — an atom and a property — and returns the value of the property.

Example: *(get 'mary 'sex)* returns the value stored under the *sex* property of *mary*.

make-array   This function takes one argument that is a list of numbers. It creates an array with as many dimensions as there are numbers and the length of each dimension is the value of that number. The initial values of the cells of the array are all *nil*. The function returns a representation of that array.

Example: *(make-array '(5))* returns *#(nil nil nil nil nil)*.

newatom   This function (which must be defined) takes one argument, a stem, which must be an atom. It returns a new atom consisting of the stem and an integer.

Example: *(newatom 'dog)* might return *dog0001*.

putprop   This function (which must be defined in terms of *setf* for Common LISP) accepts three arguments — an atom, a value, and a property — and puts the property-value pair on the property list of the atom.

Example: *(putprop 'mary 'female 'sex)* puts *female* as the value of the *sex* property for Mary.

remprop   This function takes two arguments — an atom and a property — and removes the property-value pair from the property list for that atom.

Example: *(remprop 'mary 'age)* will remove the *age* property for *mary*.

setf   This operator takes two arguments — an access function and a value — and puts the value at the location accessed by the access function.

Example: *(setf (aref data 2) 'Tom)* puts *Tom* into cell 2 of the array *data*.

Glossary   **array**   A dimensional data structure of cells for storing large sets of data.
cell   A particular storage location in an array.
index   A number used to access a particular cell in an array.
matrix   A two-dimensional array.
property list   A list of properties and values stored with an atom.
property name   The name of a property of an atom, such as *sex* or *age*.
property value   The value of a property of an atom, such as *male* or *29*.
vector   A one-dimensional array.

List Structure and Destructive Functions

As we mentioned in Chapter 1, lists are the key to symbolic processing in LISP. So far we have discussed lists without inquiring seriously about how they are implemented. In this chapter we will explore the implementation of list processing in order to understand certain properties of our programs and to utilize certain advanced list-processing functions.

We can think of computer memory as a collection of locations in which data is stored. Each of these locations has an **address**, which is a number that functions like a street address. That is, we can refer to a location by its address when we want to access the information stored there. In this chapter we will discuss how two data types — lists and atoms — are stored in memory. Each atom, such as *dog* or *33*, is stored in a single location in memory. If we depict memory locations as rectangles, then we can portray atoms in memory like this:

```
 dog            33
```

A list is represented by a collection of memory locations. Each atom in the list is stored in a memory location as we just discussed, and these locations are linked together by a special storage element in LISP called a *cons* cell.

cons Cells

A **cons cell** is a memory location that is set up to hold two values. We can represent a *cons* cell as a rectangle that is divided in half, as in the figure below, and we will refer to each half of the *cons* cell as a **slot**.

Each slot in a *cons* cell can hold one of two things, the address of another memory location, or *nil*. An address that is stored in *cons* cells is referred to as a **pointer**, because it "points" to another location in memory. That location, in turn, can either hold an atom or another *cons* cell. In the following diagram we have depicted the simplest possible *cons* cell structure: a single *cons* cell with pointers to two atoms.

When a *cons* cell slot contains a pointer to an atom, we will frequently simplify the diagram, by just inserting the atom into the slot as shown:

If we ask LISP to print the expression that corresponds to this structure, we would see

(a . b),

which is referred to as a **dotted pair**. You may have seen such a thing in an error produced by one of your LISP programs. You can create this dotted pair by the following operation

```
=> (cons 'a 'b)
(a . b)
```

More generally, *cons*ing two atoms together will create a dotted pair. Such data structures are not intrinsically errors and can be useful because they are represented more efficiently in some versions of LISP than the corresponding list of two elements. Such dotted pairs are also handy because the *cdr* of a dotted pair is an atom rather than a list, but they must be used with caution, since other functions may return unexpected results when given a dotted pair.

Encoding Lists in *cons* Cells

As we mentioned earlier, LISP also uses *cons* cells to represent lists in memory. A list containing a single atom is represented in a single *cons* cell as shown:

Note that this structure is very similar to a dotted pair. Just as our dotted pair was created by *cons*ing a and b, our list can be created by *cons*ing a and *nil*. Thus a list containing a single element is really a dotted pair in which the second slot holds *nil*. The *nil* just marks the end of the list though, and is not treated as an element in the list. As a result, we often represent the *nil* as a slash through the cell.

You can see from these examples why these cells are called *cons* cells; each time we call *cons*, LISP creates a new *cons* cell to represent the resulting structure.

Lists with more than one element are represented in memory by a chain of *cons* cells. For example, the list *(a b)* is represented as shown:

As you can see, the left-hand slot of the first *cons* cell points to the first item in the list, but the right-hand slot points to a second *cons* cell. The left-hand slot of the second *cons* cell points to the next item in the list, and since there are no more elements, the right-hand slot of that cell points to *nil*. More generally, the memory representation of a list contains one *cons* cell for each item in the list. The left-hand slot in each cell points to the corresponding element and the right-hand slot points to the next cell, or to *nil* in the case of the last element. Thus the list *(a b c d)* is represented as shown:

So far our example lists have contained only atoms. Let us consider one more example, which contains an embedded list. The following diagram portrays the *cons*-cell structure for the list *(a (b c) d)*.

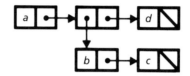

Each element in this list is again represented by a *cons* cell. The first of these cells points to the atom *a*, the second points to the embedded list *(b c)* and the third points to the atom *d*. Since the second item is an embedded list, it is also represented by a chain of *cons* cells. The first cell in this embedded list points to *b* and the second cell points to *c*.

cons Cell Structure and Simple List Functions

To clarify further the structure of lists, let us consider the actions of some simple list functions. The functions *car* and *cdr* do not add any *cons* cells to memory. Instead, when we call *car* or *cdr* on a list, they each access one of the pointers in the first *cons* cell of the list. Thus *car* returns the structure to which the left-hand slot points, while *cdr* returns the structure to which the right-hand slot points. If you refer to the memory representation of the list *(a b c d)* above, you can see why the *car* of the list is *a* and the *cdr* is *(b c d)*. Also, if you refer to the representation of the list *(a)*, you can see why the *cdr* of a single-element list is *nil*.

In contrast to *car* and *cdr*, both *cons* and *list* add *cons* cells to memory. As stated earlier, when we call *cons*, LISP always creates one new *cons* cell. We have seen the *cons* cell that is created when we call *cons* to form a dotted pair or a single-element list, but let us consider the more general case of inserting an item into a nonempty list. For example, suppose we type

    (cons 'x '(a b c d))

LISP will evaluate the two arguments, which have the following structures in memory:

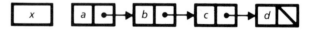

Then LISP goes through these steps:

1. Create a new *cons* cell;
2. Insert a pointer to the first argument, *x*, in the left slot of the new cell;
3. Insert a pointer to the second argument, *(a b c d)*, in the right slot of the new cell.

These actions create the following structure:

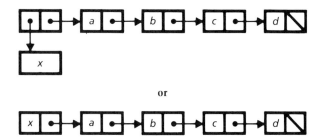

or

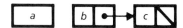

When we call *list*, LISP creates a new *cons* cell for each element in the new list. For example, suppose we type

(list 'a '(b c))

LISP evaluates the two arguments and obtains the following memory structures:

Then LISP goes through the following process:

1. Create a new *cons* cell for every argument in the function call (every element in the new list);
2. Insert a pointer to the corresponding memory structure in the left slot of each new *cons* cell;
3. Insert a pointer to the next *cons* cell in the list in the right slot of each new *cons* cell.

This process yields the following structure:

LISP Exercises

12.1 Try generating the *cons* cell representation of the following lists:
a) (hi there)
b) (hi (i am here) (where are you))
c) (down (we (go)))

12.2 Write out the list that corresponds to each of the following *cons*-cell structures:
a)   b)

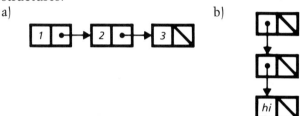

12.3 (Optional) Write a program, *display-cons*, that accepts three arguments — a list followed by two numbers. The function should print the *cons*-cell representation of the list on the screen and return *nil*. (The other two arguments are explained below.)
Consider the following examples:

```
=> (display-cons '(a (b c) d) 25 4)
[a|*]--[*|*]--[d|\]
        |
       [b|*]--[c|\]
nil

=> (display-cons '((a (b (c (d e f g))) h) i j k
   ((( l m n)))) 70 10)

              [*|*]--[i|*]--[j|*]--[k|*]--[*|\]
              |                            |
             [a|*]--[*|*]--[h|\]          [*|\]
                    |                      |
                   [b|*]--[*|\]           [*|\]
                          |                |
                         [c|*]--[*|\] [1 |*]--[m|*]--[n|\]
                                |
                               [d|*]--[e|*]--[f|*]--[g|\]

nil
```

To simplify the task, you should assume that every atom in the list will be a single character. Your function can print a diagram only a row at a time, and it is very difficult to generate the components of the diagram in that order. So, as you generate symbols for the diagram, you should enter each one into a two-dimensional array. Then you can generate them in whatever order you want, and when you are done you can print the array row by row. The second and third arguments to the function are the horizontal and vertical dimensions of the array that is required to store the *cons* cell structure. With certain complex lists, your function will run into a problem with overwriting the structure it is creating. For example, if we call

(display-cons '((a b c) (d e f)) 30 3)

the symbols that represent the *cons*-cell structure for the second embedded list will overwrite the symbols for the first embedded list in the array. As a result, the following diagram will appear on the screen.

```
[*|*]--[*|\]
 |      |
[a|*]--[d|*]--[e|*]--[f|\]
nil
```

It is very difficult to avoid overwriting symbols in the array when the diagram is crowded and you should not feel compelled to write a program that avoids the problem.

Referencing Lists: Variables and Literal Lists

Whenever we need to refer to a list such as *(big brown dog)* repeatedly, we can either assign that list to a variable and use the variable to reference the list, or we can repeatedly type the literal list. These two forms of reference have different consequences in computer memory. That difference has not been relevant to the topics we have discussed so far, but it becomes important later in this chapter.

Let us look at what happens when we assign a value to a variable. For example, suppose we assign a list to the variable *phrase* as follows:

(setq phrase '(big brown dog))

Variables are atoms, of course, and we can think of them as having pointers to their value. We will use a curved line to represent variable pointers, in order to distinguish them from *cons*-cell pointers. Thus the call to *setq* in our example would yield the following structure:

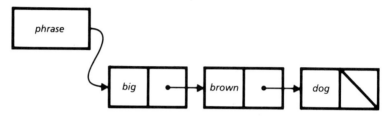

Whenever we use the variable name to refer to a list, LISP accesses the list structure that we created. For example, consider the following expression:

(setq newphrase (cons 'The phrase))

The resulting representation would be:

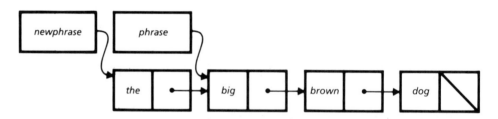

Notice that the variable *phrase* still points to the beginning cell in the list *(big brown dog)*. The *cons* operation has not changed the structure of that list. Instead, it has built a larger structure that includes the original one. The new variable *newphrase* points to the first cell of the new structure. Thus our two variables evaluate as follows:

=)*newphrase*
(The big brown dog)

=)*phrase*
(big brown dog)

So, when we assign a list to a variable, and refer to that variable, we always obtain the same list structure. The same is not true when we type literal lists. Every time we type a literal list, LISP creates a new list structure in memory. If we type the same literal list twice, LISP creates two equivalent structures in memory. Thus if we type the following two expressions,

=)*(setq phrase '(big brown dog))*
(big brown dog)

=)*(setq adj-noun '(big brown dog))*
(big brown dog)

the resulting memory representation would be

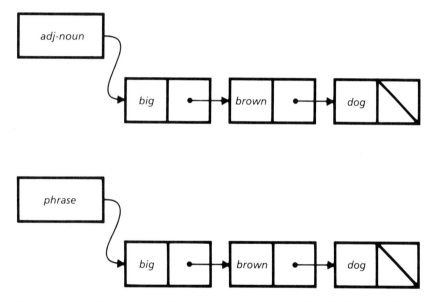

Since we can have multiple copies of the same list, LISP provides predicates that allow us to determine whether variables point to the same list structure or to different copies of the same list.

Identity versus Equivalence: *equal* and *eql*

In Chapter 3 we discussed the predicate *equal*, which returns *t* if its arguments have the same value. When those arguments are lists, *equal* returns *t* as long as those lists have the same elements, whether or not they are actually the same list structure in memory.

```
=> (setq lis1 '(a b))
(a b)
=> (setq lis2 '(a b))
(a b)
=> (setq lis3 lis1)
(a b)
=> (equal lis1 lis2)
t
=> (equal lis1 lis3)
t
```

In this example, *lis1* and *lis3* point to the same list structure, but *lis2* points to a different list structure. Nevertheless, *equal* treats them all as equal. LISP provides another predicate, *eql*, that also tests for equivalence, but *eql* only returns *t* if its arguments all point to the same memory structure.* Thus

```
=> (eql lis1 lis2)
nil
=> (eql lis1 lis3)
t
```

The representation of atoms is somewhat different from that of lists, since LISP does not make multiple copies of atoms.† If we type the same literal atom more than once, LISP accesses a single representation, rather than making multiple copies. Thus

```
=>(setq hold 'abc)
abc

=>(setq keep 'abc)
abc

=>(eql hold keep)
t
```

---

*In some versions of LISP *eql* is not defined, but *eq* performs the same function. In Common LISP *eq* is defined but does something slightly different.

†This is literally true in most versions of LISP, but Common LISP sometimes makes copies of atoms. We can ignore this property of Common LISP when we use *eql*, though, because *eql* only distinguishes among copies of lists, not atoms. That is, when we perform an *eql* on atoms, it will return *t* if the atoms have the same value, even if they are in different memory locations. In Common LISP the function *eq* only returns *t* if its arguments are all in the same memory location, regardless of whether they are atoms or lists.

LISP Exercises

12.4 Define a function *testsource* that takes two arguments, which must be lists. The function should determine if the two lists have identical structures, if the tails of the lists alone have identical structures, or if the two lists have the same value. The function should return *same-list*, *same-tail*, or *same-value* in these three cases, respectively, and return *different* otherwise.

12.5 Define a function *equal** in terms of *eql*. The function *equal** should be identical in behavior to *equal*.

12.6 Define a function *copy1* that accepts one argument, which must be a list, and returns a copy of the list. In making the copy the function should create a new *cons* cell for each top-level element, but the remaining cells in the structure should be the same as in the original list.

12.7 Define a function *copy2* that accepts one argument, which must be a list, and returns a copy of a list structure such that at all levels nothing is *eql* except the atoms.

Nondestructive Functions

All the list functions we have discussed so far are known as **nondestructive functions**, because they do not change the structure of their arguments. Another way to characterize nondestructive functions is that they do not change existing pointers. For example, we saw in an earlier section that *cons* and *list* do not change any pointers in their arguments; instead they create new *cons* cells and new pointers in order to embed the original arguments in larger list structures. Thus the components of the new list structure are identical to the original arguments (rather than being copies of the original arguments).

There are other nondestructive functions that behave slightly differently. These functions return lists that contain copies of the original arguments, rather than the original arguments themselves. An example of this type of function is *append*. In order for *append* to function nondestructively, it must make a copy of its arguments (except the last one). Recall that the right slot of the final *cons* cell in a list is set to *nil*. One way to append two lists would be to replace the *nil* in the first list with a pointer to the first *cons* cell of the second list; but this would be a destructive operation, since it changes the structure of the first list. Thus any variable that was pointing to the first list prior to the *append* operation, would no longer evaluate to the first list; rather it would evaluate to the whole new list. As a result, *append* makes a copy of its arguments, and replaces the *nil* in the copies with pointers to the appropriate *cons* cell.

Consider the following sequence of actions:

```
=>(setq first '(jan feb))          [1]
(jan feb)
=>(setq second '(mar apr))         [2]
(mar apr)
=>(setq both (append first second))   [3]
(jan feb mar apr)
```

The diagram below illustrates what happens when these three expressions are evaluated. The solid lines represent the structures that exist after the first two actions are performed and the dotted lines depict the structure that results from the third action.

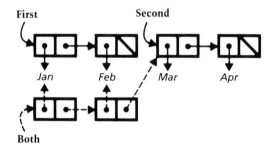

As you can see, *append* creates a new copy of all the *cons* cells for its first argument. Thus, whereas *cons* creates a single new *cons* cell, *append* creates a new *cons* cell for each element in all its arguments except the final argument.

LISP Exercise

12.8 The function *append* can be defined by a series of *cons* operations.
(a) Define a new version of *append*, called *append2*, in terms of *cons*. The function should accept two arguments, which must be lists. (b) Use your function *append 2* to define a function called *append3*, which appends three arguments.

Destructive Functions: *nconc, rplaca,* and *rplacd*

LISP provides some functions that do change existing pointers in the course of building new structures. These functions are called **destructive functions**, because once a pointer has been changed, the original structure has been destroyed. The function *nconc* is one example. It behaves just as *append* does except that *nconc* actually changes LISP pointers. Consider the following sequence of actions:

```
=> (setq lis1 '(a b c))          [1]
(a b c)
=> (setq lis2 '(d e f))          [2]
(d e f)
=> (setq lis3 (append lis1 lis2))  [3]
(a b c d e f)
=> (setq lis4 (nconc lis1 lis2))   [4]
(a b c d e f)
```

Below, we illustrate the results of these operations.

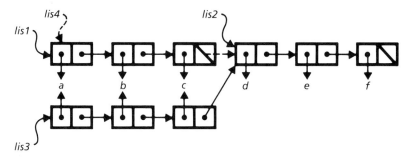

The top row of six *cons* cells portrays the structure of the original two lists, *lis1* and *lis2*. When *lis3* is constructed with *append*, the three *cons* cells in the first list are copied and connected by pointers. The new copy of the third cell, though, has a pointer to the first *cons* cell of the second list instead of holding *nil*. The solid lines in the figure represent the structure created by the first three LISP actions above. Finally, when *lis4* is constructed with *nconc*, no *cons* cells are copied. Instead, the *nil* in the final *cons* cell of *lis1* is replaced by a pointer to the first *cons* cell in *lis2*, as indicated by the dashed line. The dashed lines illustrate the changes introduced by the fourth LISP action above. As a result, the list *(a b c)* no longer exists, and *lis1* has the same value as *lis4* *(a b c d e f)*.

Two other functions that change the structure of their arguments are *rplaca* and *rplacd*. The name *rplaca* is short for "replace the *car*." This function takes two arguments, the first of which must be a list, and replaces the *car* of its first argument with the second argument. That is, the pointer in the left slot of the first *cons* cell of the list is changed so that it points to the second argument.

Similarly, *rplacd* is short for "replace the *cdr*." It also takes two arguments, the first of which must be a list, and replaces the pointer to the *cdr* of the first argument with a pointer to the second argument.* As an example, suppose we create the following lists:

```
=> (setq lis1 '(a b c))          [1]
(a b c)
=> (setq lis2 '(a b c))          [2]
(a b c)
```

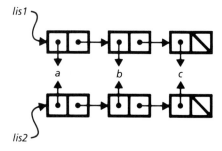

Now consider how these structures can be modified by *rplaca* and *rplacd*:

```
=> (rplaca 'lis1 'd)             [3]
(d b c)
=> (rplacd 'lis2 '(e f))         [4]
(a e f)
```

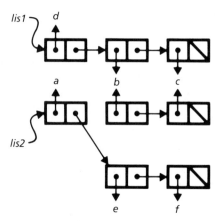

---

*If the second argument is an atom rather than a list, *rplacd* will return a dotted structure.

The figure above illustrates the changes created by these two destructive operations. When *rplaca* is called in line 3, the pointer to *a* in the first cell of *lis1* is replaced by a pointer to the atom *d*. When *rplacd* is called in line 4, the pointer from the first cell to the second cell in *lis2* is replaced by a pointer to the new structure that represents the list *(e f)*. Note that although we did not explicitly reset the value of *lis1*, it now has the value *(d b c)* and although we did not explicitly change the value of *lis2* it now has the value *(a e f)*.

These replacement functions can be used to go in and change any component of a list. For example, consider the function *replace-item* that takes three arguments, the first of which must be a list. This function destructively replaces the first occurrence of the second argument in the list with the third argument.

```
(defun replace-item (lis old new)
   (rplaca (member old lis) new))
```

This function finds the tail of *lis* beginning with the first occurrence of the second argument, and replaces the *car* of that tail with the third argument. Of course, by changing this tail of *lis* this function also changes the value of *lis*.

When to Use Destructive Functions

Destructive functions are useful because they save space in memory. Saving space can be very important when you are dealing with long lists. As we saw earlier, when you *append* lists as many *cons* cells are created as are required to represent all the arguments except the last. On the other hand, *nconc* does not add any new *cons* cells. Similarly, *rplaca* and *rplacd* do not add *cons* cells to memory, while nondestructive versions would. However, destructive functions can have unexpected side effects. For example, consider the example of *nconc* above. Line 4 of that example changed the value of *lis1*. The original list structure that was assigned to *lis1* no longer existed in memory after line 4 was evaluated, and *lis1* acquired the same value as *lis4*.

There is another kind of side effect that can have disastrous consequences. Consider the following example:

```
=> (setq var1 '(one two three))
(one two three)
=> (setq var2 var1)
(one two three)
=> (setq var2 (nconc var1 var2))
(one two three one two three one two three one two three ...
```

Below we illustrate the list structure that is created.

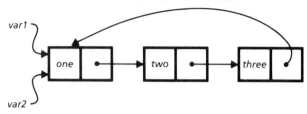

We have created a circular list. When we try to print this list, LISP tries to print *(one two three one two three...* forever. If we tried to search this list we could enter an infinite loop.

Such side effects make working with destructive functions dangerous and many experienced LISP programmers simply do not use them. However, if you are cautious these functions can be useful when you are writing large programs. Computer memory has a finite number of locations and when they are used up, LISP must **garbage collect**. That is, LISP must find locations that have been used, but whose contents are no longer needed. Such garbage collection can occur frequently with large programs and can add substantially to computation time.

LISP Exercises

12.9 Define a function *replace-all* that accepts three arguments. The first two arguments can be any LISP expressions, but the third argument must be a list. This function returns a new version of the third argument in which all occurrences of the first argument have been replaced by the second argument. This function should work destructively; that is, it should replace a value by replacing a pointer in a *cons* cell, and should not create any new *cons* cells. For example,

(replace-all 'b 'c '(a b c b)) returns (a c c c).

12.10 Define a function *splice-out* that accepts two arguments. The first argument can be any LISP expression, but the second argument must be a list. The function returns a new copy of the list in which all occurrences of the first argument have been destructively deleted. (Again, this function should not create any new *cons* cells.) For example,

(splice-out 'a '(a b c a b c a)) returns (b c b c).

12.11 Define a function *insert* that accepts two arguments, a number and a list of numbers. The numbers appear in the list in ascending order, and the function should return a new copy of the list in which the first argument has been placed in its appropriate position in the sequence. The function should work destructively; the new list should incorporate the old structures from the original list along with just one new *cons* cell to represent the number that is being added. For example,

(insert 3 '(1 2 4 5)) returns (1 2 3 4 5).

12.12 Define a function *sorter*, that accepts one argument, which must be a list of numbers, and returns a sorted version of the list in which the numbers have been placed in ascending order. Again, the function should work destructively; it should not create any new *cons* cells, but should sort the original list by changing pointers in the existing *cons* cells. For example,

(sorter '(5 3 4 1 2)) returns (1 2 3 4 5).

In this chapter we have looked more closely at the structure of lists in LISP, and have described some destructive functions that LISP provides. These functions are powerful, and are efficient because they save room in memory. However, they must be used cautiously, since they can have unintended side effects. In Chapter 13 we will take a closer look at another fundamental component of LISP — the evaluation process — and discuss some additional powerful and useful operators provided by LISP.

Summary of LISP Functions

eql   This function takes two arguments and returns *t* if its arguments both point to the same structure in memory.

Example: *(eql '(a b) '(a b))* returns *nil*.

nconc   This function is a destructive version of *append*. It takes two or more arguments, each of which must be lists, and merges them into a single list.

Example: *(nconc '(a b) '(c d))* returns (a b c d).

rplaca   This function accepts two arguments, the first of which must be a list. It destructively replaces the first element in the list with the second argument to the function.

Example: *(rplaca '(a b c) 'x)* returns *(x b c)*.

rplacd   This function accepts two arguments, the first of which must be a list. It destructively replaces the *cdr* of the list with the second argument to the function.

Example: *(rplacd '(a b c) '(x y z))* returns *(a x y z)*.

Glossary

address   A number that designates a location in memory.

***cons* cell**   A structure that LISP uses to represent lists in memory. A *cons* cell has two slots, each of which contains a pointer to a location in memory.

destructive functions   A function that creates new structures in memory by changing existing pointers, thereby destroying existing list structures.

dotted pair   A structure such as *(a . b)*, which is created when the second slot of a *cons* cell points to a non-*nil* atom rather than a list.

garbage collection   A process by which LISP reclaims *cons* cells that are no longer being used, so that they can be used to build new structures.

nondestructive functions   A function that does not destroy existing list structures in building new structures. It makes copies of existing structures, when necessary, to avoid destroying them.

pointer   An address stored in memory (e.g., in a *cons* cell slot). We can access the address and use it to access the location specified by the pointer; so the stored address is said to "point" to the location it designates.

slot   A component of a *cons* cell; each *cons* cell has two slots that hold pointers to other locations in memory.

Evaluation and Macros

13

In this chapter we will discuss the evaluation process in more detail and introduce some operators and special characters provided by LISP, which give us more control over the evaluation process. One reason we want more control over evaluation is so we can write programs that construct and evaluate function calls when they execute. We will discuss several operators provided by LISP that allow us to write code that will in turn create and execute function calls. Many of the techniques for controlling evaluation that we discuss in this chapter will prove useful in the final chapter of the book, which is devoted to writing a single large program called a production system.

The LISP Evaluation Process

Before introducing any new operators, let us review what we already know about the evaluation process. Table 13.1 summarizes the rules of evaluation that were introduced in Chapter 1.

Table 13.1. LISP evaluation

	Unquoted	Quoted
Atom	If a number or special atom, LISP returns that atom; otherwise, LISP interprets the atom as a variable, and returns its value.	LISP returns the atom.
List	LISP interprets the list as a function call. LISP evaluates each argument, and then applies the function to the evaluated arguments.	LISP returns the list.

As indicated in the upper left-hand cell of the table, LISP interprets an unquoted atom as a variable and returns its value.* The lower left-hand cell, on the other hand, indicates that LISP treats an unquoted list as a function call. In this case, LISP checks that the *car* of the list is a defined function and then treats each element in the *cdr* of the list as an expression that must be evaluated before the function is applied to them. If one of these arguments is itself an unquoted list, then LISP treats it, in turn, as a function call. Thus function evaluation is a recursive process; if we wrote a function to emulate the evaluation of LISP expressions, it would call itself recursively on each of the arguments in a function call.

The other evaluation rule from Chapter 1 is denoted in the right-hand column of the table. When an atom or list is quoted, LISP treats it literally rather than as a variable or function call. A quote mark is a special symbol that provides us some control over the evaluation process and in this chapter we will encounter some other special symbols that have a similar purpose. The symbol ' is really LISP shorthand for the special form *quote*; that is, the expression *'x* is equivalent to the expression *(quote x)*. Of course, since you know what ' does, you know what *quote* does; it takes a single argument and returns that argument without evaluating it.

Forcing an Extra Evaluation: The Function *eval*

LISP provides a function *eval* that accepts one argument and forces an extra evaluation of the argument. That is, when *eval* is called, LISP begins by evalu-

---

*We can think of numbers and the atoms *t* and *nil* as exceptions to this rule, or alternatively, as atoms that evaluate to themselves when unquoted.

ating its argument just as in the case of other functions. Then the resulting value is simply evaluated again when *eval* is applied to it.

This description may seem perplexing; let us consider an example:

```
=> (eval '(car '(a b c)))
a
```

In evaluating this function call, the first thing LISP does is evaluate the argument *'(car '(a b c))*. This expression is equivalent to *(quote (car '(a b c)))*, which evaluates to the list *(car '(a b c))*. Then when LISP applies *eval* to this resulting list, the list is simply evaluated. The list *(car '(a b c))* is not quoted, so LISP treats it as a function call that returns a. Thus the call to *eval* returns a. To further illustrate *eval*, consider the following examples:

```
=> (setq b 'dog)              [1]
dog
=> (eval '(car (cdr '(a b c))))   [2]
b
=> (eval (car (cdr '(a b c))))    [3]
dog
=> (eval (list '+ 2 3))          [4]
5
```

Line 2 is similar to the example we just saw. The argument evaluates to *(car (cdr '(a b c)))*, so *eval* returns b. In contrast, the argument to *eval* in line 3 is not quoted, so LISP treats the argument as a function call, which evaluates to b. Then *eval* causes LISP to evaluate the unquoted atom b, so *eval* returns the value of b, which is *dog*. Line 4 demonstrates the real usefulness of *eval*. In this call the argument to *eval* is unquoted, so LISP treats it as a function call, which evaluates to the list *(+ 2 3)*. Then *eval* causes LISP to evaluate the list *(+ 2 3)*, and since the list is not quoted LISP applies the function + to the arguments *2* and *3* and *eval* returns 5. Thus we have called the function *list* to create another function call. Of course, we've been able to write function calls like *(list '+ 2 3)* ever since Chapter 1, but we have only been able to treat the resulting expression *(+ 2 3)* as data, that is, as a literal list. Now we can use *eval* to treat the result of one function call as another function call. Thus we have an important new capability; we can write programs that can create and evaluate function calls as they are executing.

LISP Exercise

13.1 Try to predict what LISP will return in these cases:

(a) = ⟩ *(setq a 'dog)*
     ?

(b) = ⟩ *(setq b '(list 'a 'b))*
     ?

(c) = ⟩ *(setq dog 'b)*
     ?

(d) = ⟩ *'a*
     ?

(e) = ⟩ *a*
     ?

(f) = ⟩ *(eval 'a)*
     ?

(g) = ⟩ *(eval a)*
     ?

(h) = ⟩ *(eval (eval a))*
     ?

(i) = ⟩ *(eval (eval (eval a)))*
     ?

(j) = ⟩ *(eval (eval (eval (eval a))))*
     ?

(k) = ⟩ *(eval '(eval a))*
     ?

(l) = ⟩ *'(eval (eval a))*
     ?

(m) = ⟩ *(eval '(eval '(eval (eval a))))*
     ?

(n) = ⟩ *(eval (car (eval b)))*
     ?

(o) = ⟩ *(eval (cadr (eval b)))*
     ?

(p) = ⟩ *(caaddr b)*
     ?

(q) = ⟩ *(eval (eval (list (caadr b) b)))*
     ?

Applying a Function to Arguments

LISP provides another function, *apply*, that performs a somewhat different task than *eval*, but is also useful for building function calls. For example, suppose we have a list of lists such as *((a b c) (d e f) (g h i))*, and we want to merge the embedded lists to form the list *(a b c d e f g h i)*. We could use *do* to write an iterative function that performs this task, but we can accomplish our goal more easily with *apply*. The function *apply* takes two arguments, a function name and a list, and applies the named function to the elements in the list just as if that function had been called with the list elements as arguments. Thus we can merge the embedded lists in *((a b c) (d e f) (g h i))* with the following function call:

> => *(apply 'append '((a b c) (d e f) (g h i)))*
> (a b c d e f g h i)

which is equivalent to

> => *(append '(a b c) '(d e f) '(g h i))*
> (a b c d e f g h i)

As with other functions, both arguments to *apply* are evaluated before the named function is applied to the list elements. For example,

> => *(setq merge 'append)*
> append
> => *(setq args '((a b c) (d e f) (g h i)))*
> ((a b c) (d e f) (g h i))
> => *(apply merge args)*
> (a b c d e f g h i)

However, *apply* does not cause each of the elements of the list to be evaluated before applying the named function to them. Thus the following two function calls are equivalent:

> => *(apply 'cons '(a (b c)))*
> (a b c)
> => *(eval '(cons 'a '(b c)))*
> (a b c)

LISP Exercise

13.2 Try predicting what LISP will do in the following cases.

(a) => *(apply 'cons '(a (eval '(list 'a 'b))))*
 ?

(b) => *(eval '(cons 'a (apply 'list '(a b))))*
 ?

Let us consider some useful functions we can define with *apply*. For example, here is a very concise function to get the average of a list of numbers:

```
(defun list-mean (lis)
    (/ (apply '+ lis) (length lis)))
```

Applying + to the list calls + with as many arguments as there are in the list, thus computing the sum of all elements in the list. Dividing by the length of the list returns the average.

The function *apply* is also frequently used in conjunction with a *mapcar*. After we have mapped a function over a list with *mapcar*, we can apply another function to the resulting list with *apply*. For example, suppose we have a list of lists and we want to find the total number of elements in these lists. The following function performs this task:

```
(defun count-total-elements (lis)
    (apply '+ (mapcar 'length lis)))
```

Thus *(count-total-elements '((a b c) (d e f g) (h i))* would apply + to the list *(3 4 2)*, returning 9.

If we want a function called *countatoms* that counts all the atoms that appear at any level in a list, we can define it as follows:

```
(defun countatoms (lis)
    (cond ((null lis) 0)
          ((atom lis) 1)
          (t (apply '+ (mapcar 'countatoms lis)))))
```

Consider the following example:

```
=> (countatoms '(a (a (b) c) (d) e (f g)))
8
```

Since the argument is a nonempty list in this example, LISP evaluates the action *(apply '+ (mapcar 'countatoms lis))* in the third *cond* case. The *mapcar* in this expression calls *countatoms* recursively on the five elements in the argument *(a (a (b) c) (d) e (f g))*. When *countatoms* is applied to the first and fourth elements in the argument, which are atoms, it returns *1*. When *countatoms* is applied to each embedded list in the argument, it maps itself recursively over the elements in the embedded list and so on. Each call to *mapcar* returns a list of numbers and then + is applied to that list so that *countatoms* returns the number of all the atoms at all levels in its argument. (Compare this definition to the *car/cdr* recursive definition of *countatoms* that you wrote in Chapter 9.)

LISP Exercises

13.3 Write a new version of the function *flatten* from LISP Exercise 9.7 that uses *mapcar* and *apply*. Recall that *flatten* accepts one argument, which must be a list, and returns a new list containing all the atoms from the original list, but with no embedded lists. For example,

(flatten '(a (a (b) c) (d) (e f))) returns *(a a b c d e f)*.

13.4 Write a function called *add-operation* that does not accept any arguments. The function begins by printing the prompt *(what operation?)* and reading a user input, which must be a function name or *lambda* expression. Then the function repeatedly prints the prompt *(give me a set of arguments)* and reads a list of arguments typed by the user. The function applies the operation to each set of arguments the user types and when the user types *sum* in response to the prompt, the function prints a list that reports the sum of the operations (see the example). Then the function prints the prompt *(what operation?)* and proceeds through the steps again. The function returns *nil* when the user types *stop* in response to the prompt *(what operation?)*. For example,

```
= ) (add-operation)
    (what operation?) *
    (give me a set of arguments) (3 2)
    (give me a set of arguments) (4 5)
    (give me a set of arguments) (7 3)
    (give me a set of arguments) sum
    (47 is the sum)
    (what operation?) (lambda (x) (* x x x))
    (give me a set of arguments) (2)
    (give me a set of arguments) sum
    (8 is the sum)
    (what operation?) stop
nil
```

13.5 Define the function *every-p*, which takes two arguments — a predicate and a list. The function returns *t* if the predicate is true of each item in the list, and *nil* otherwise. For example,

(every-p 'oddp '(3 9 5 1)) = *t*.
(every-p 'atom '(a b (c) d)) = *nil*.

Hint: Think about using a logical function that takes as arguments the results of the individual tests.

In Chapters 10 and 11 you defined some functions that iterate through the elements in a list and return a list of just those elements that have a particular property. This is a very useful technique, called filtering. For example, you might want to save only the numbers in a list, only the atoms, or only the female members in a list of individuals, etc. We can combine *apply*, *append*, and *mapcar* in order to filter a list of items very easily. Consider the following definition of *save-numbers*:

```
(defun save-numbers (lis)
    (apply 'append (mapcar '(lambda (item)
                    (cond ((numberp item) (list item))
                          (t nil)))
        lis)))
```

The *lambda* expression in this function tests whether its argument is a number and if so, returns a list containing the argument; otherwise the *lambda* expression returns *nil*. When this *lambda* expression is mapped over a list, it returns a new list in which each of the original numbers now appears in a list, while all the non-numeric elements have been replaced by *nil*. For example, if we map this *lambda* expression over the list *(dog cat 2 4 horse 6)* it returns *(nil nil (2) (4) nil (6))*. Then, by applying *append* to that list, we get the desired result *(2 4 6)*.

LISP also has an additional mapping function called *mapcan*,* which is equivalent to applying *nconc* (the destructive version of *append*) to *mapcar*. Thus we can rewrite the function *save-numbers* as

```
(defun save-numbers (lis)
    (mapcan '(lambda (item)
                    (cond ((numberp item) (list item))
                          (t nil)))
        lis))
```

LISP Exercise

13.6 Write a new version of the the function *save-atoms* from LISP Exercise 10.7 without using *do*. Recall that *save-atoms* accepts one argument,

---

*This function is not found in the Interlisp dialect.

which must be a list, and returns a new list containing only the atoms from the original list. For example,

(save-atoms '((b j r) 34 (french english) car cdr cons))
    returns *(34 car cdr cons)*.

Using Backquote for List Construction

In this section we will discuss some additional special characters that provide control over the evaluation process. For example, suppose we want a simple program called *greet* that asks for the user's name and prints a greeting as follows:

```
= > (greet)
(What's your name?) Fred
(Hello Fred and how are you?)
```

At first glance, the function *greet* might seem to suit our needs:

```
(defun greet ()
    (let ((name nil))
        (print '(What's your name?))
        (setq name (read))
        (print '(Hello name and how are you?))))
```

Of course, the quote in front of the list to be printed would cause the entire list to be taken literally, so it would always print

```
(Hello name and how are you?)
```

and not print out the value of the local variable *name*. To solve this problem, we could construct the argument to *print* out of literal lists, variables, and function calls as follows:

```
(print (append '(Hello) (list name) '(and how are you?)))
```

However, this procedure for building expressions can be quite cumbersome when you intermix a large number of literal values and variables. LISP contains a mechanism for achieving the same result more simply. Instead of creating a list with *quote* we can build a list with the special symbol, `, called backquote, which allows us to specify which elements should be treated literally and which should be evaluated. When a list is backquoted, rather than quoted, LISP looks inside the list and evaluates any element that is preceded by a comma. Thus we could write *greet* as follows:

```
=> (defun greet ()
      (let ((name nil))
            (print '(What's your name?))
            (setq name (read))
            (print `(Hello ,name and how are you?))))
greet
=> (greet)
(What's your name?) John
(Hello John and how are you?)
(Hello John and how are you?)
```

There is one more special character, actually a pair of characters — ,@ — called comma-at, that is useful in backquoted lists. These characters can precede any element that evaluates to a list. Like the regular comma, comma-at causes the item following it to be evaluated, but the resulting list is not treated as an element of the backquoted list. Instead, LISP **splices** the evaluated item into the backquoted list; that is, the item is essentially merged with the other elements in the list. The following function calls demonstrate the distinction between , and ,@

```
=> (setq name '(John Robert Anderson))
(John Robert Anderson)
=> `(Hello ,name and how are you)
(Hello (John Robert Anderson) and how are you)
=> `(Hello ,@name and how are you)
(Hello John Robert Anderson and how are you)
```

LISP Exercises

13.7 Define a function *balance* that takes two arguments. The first argument should be a list holding the customer's name and the second argument should be a bank balance. The function calculates 10% interest on the balance and prints a message giving the name, balance, and interest as follows:

```
=> (balance '(John Robert Anderson) 130)
(We are pleased to inform you John Robert Anderson that you have 13 dollars interest
on your balance of 130 dollars for a new balance of 143 dollars)
```

13.8 You are probably familiar with the song that goes

> 99 bottles of beer on the wall
> 99 bottles of beer
> You take one down and pass it around
> 98 bottles of beer on the wall

and so on until the last verse

> 1 bottle of beer on the wall
> 1 bottle of beer
> You take one down and pass it around
> No bottles of beer on the wall.

Write a function called *beer* that accepts a positive integer as an argument and prints the lyrics of the song. The function should print all the verses beginning with the argument in the first verse and continuing down to the last verse. Remember, when you get down to 1 you will need to print the noun *bottle* rather than *bottles* and you should print *no bottles*, not *0 bottles* when you reach that point. To deal with this problem, write a helping function called *bottles* that accepts a positive integer as an argument and returns the appropriate phrase in the form (⟨*arg*⟩ *bottle[s]*). For example,

(bottles 0) returns (no bottles).
(bottles 1) returns (1 bottle).
(bottles 22) returns (22 bottles).

In testing *beer*, we suggest passing a number smaller than 99 unless you want a very long output.

Macros

In this section we will introduce an additional LISP construct called a **macro**, which allows us to write programs that construct function calls. Let us consider an example. By now we have had a great deal of experience writing functions, such as the *beer* function in Exercise 13.8, which perform an operation n times. For example, the function **blanks** issues n carriage returns to a terminal (to skip n lines in the screen output).

```
(defun blanks (n)
    (do ((count n (1- count)))
        ((zerop count) nil)
        (terpri)))
```

It would be nice if we could write a general-purpose program that can perform
any action a specified number of times instead of writing a different iterative
function for each action. When we call this general-purpose program we will
pass it a description of the action to be performed. If we name this general
purpose program *do-times*, the following call would cause it to issue four
carriage returns:

   (do-times '(terpri) 4)

If we wanted to print *hello* three times, we would call:

   (do-times '(print 'hello) 3)

We can already define *do-times* with the function *eval* as follows:

   (defun do-times (operation n)
    (do ((count n (1- count)))
     ((zerop count) nil)
    (eval operation)))

However, we can also accomplish our goal by defining *do-times* as a macro.
LISP provides the special form *defmacro* for creating macros and we can define
do-times as a macro with the following call:

   (defmacro do-times (operation n)
    ` *(do ((count ,n (1- count)))*
     ((zerop count) nil)
    ,operation))

As you can see, the form of a macro is similar to the form of a function, but
there are two ways in which LISP evaluates macros differently than it evaluates functions. First, LISP does not evaluate the arguments of a macro before
applying the macro to them. So, if *do-times* is defined as a macro rather than a
function, then we would call it as follows to print *hello* three times:

   (do-times (print 'hello) 3)

Second, when a macro is called, LISP evaluates the body of the macro and
then proceeds to evaluate the resulting expression. For example, suppose we
call *(do-times (print 'hello) 3)*. The body of the macro *do-times* is a backquoted list
that provides a template for the action we want to perform. The variables *n* and
operation are preceded by a comma in the body, so the body evaluates to a list in
which these variables have been replaced by their values:

   (do ((count 3 (1- count)))
    ((zerop count) nil)
    (print 'hello))

This list is then evaluated, and as as result LISP prints *hello* on the screen three times and *do-times* returns *nil*. Thus when a macro is called, the evaluation of the body of the macro essentially creates a function call, which is then executed. By the way, a macro does not require us to use backquote/comma notation. We can use any legal LISP expression as the body of a macro. For example, we could define *do-times* as follows:

```
(defmacro do-times (operation n)
   (list 'do
      (list (cons 'count (cons n '((1- count))))))
      '((zerop count) nil)
      operation))
```

As is apparent, however, it is much easier to construct the body of the macro with backquote/comma notation than to build it out of list function calls.

Of course, when we call a macro with different arguments, different function calls are created. For instance, if we call

```
(do-times (print count) 10)
```

then the following function call is constructed

```
(do ((count 10 (1- count)))
   ((zerop count) nil)
   (print count))
```

When it is evaluated, LISP prints the digits between 10 and 1.

LISP Exercises

13.9 The definition of *do-times* can be made more general if

1. We allowed for multiple operations.
2. We could initialize variables other than *count*.
3. We could perform one or more actions upon exiting.

Write a new version of the macro *do-times* that has a more general form. This macro will take four arguments: a list of operations, a list of additional initializations, a list of exiting actions, and a value for initializating the counter. When called, this macro will construct a call to *do* as described by the four arguments.

13.10 Write a new version of the function *factorial* from LISP Exercise 6.1 with your new version of *do-times*. Recall that *factorial* accepts a nonnegative integer as an argument and returns the factorial of that argument.

13.11 Use your new forms of *do-times* and *factorial* to define a function *print-factorial*. The function *print-factorial* accepts one argument, which must be a nonnegative integer, prints the factorial of every integer between the argument and 1 in descending order, and returns *nil*. For example,

```
=> (print-factorial 5)
     5       120
     4        24
     3         6
     2         2
     1         1
   nil
```

Creating Macros

There are three steps you can follow in defining a macro.

1. First, write down an example of the function you want the macro to create.
2. Decide which parts of the code will be common to all the functions you create with the macro and which parts will vary. For example, in *do-times* the same variable update and the same exit test will appear in every loop we create with the macro. The code that is constant across calls to the macro can be written literally into the body of the macro. The parts of the code that vary must be written into the body as variables; those parts of the code will be passed as arguments to the macro when it is called.
3. Define the macro that will create the function calls.

For example, suppose we want to define a macro called *terminating-search* that constructs function calls that perform a self-terminating search through a list. When the macro is called, the function it creates should apply a specified test to the elements of a specified list and return the first element that satisfies the test. Our first step is to specify an example function we want this macro to be able to create. For example, we might want a search function, *search-number*, that returns the first number it finds in the list. We could write the body of *search-number* as follows:

```
(do ((target lis (cdr target))
     (item (car lis) (car target)))
    ((null target) nil)
  (cond ((numberp item) (return item))))
```

Now we need to determine what parts of this code will be different if we create a different search function. One component that will vary is the value of *lis*, which is the list we are searching. A second component is the predicate we apply to each element of *lis* in the body of the function. If we were searching for the first atom in the list, our predicate would be *atom*, rather than *numberp*.

Now we should be ready to define our macro for creating self-terminating search functions. We will do that in the next exercise.

LISP Exercises

13.12 Write a macro called *terminating-search* that accepts two arguments. The first argument is a test predicate, and the second argument is the list to be searched. The macro should return the first element in the list that matches the predicate. If no element in the list matches the predicate, then the macro returns *nil*.

```
(terminating-search listp '(dog cat (a b c) box))
        returns (a b c).
```

(Make sure you understand why the second, but not the first, argument to *terminating-search* must be quoted.)

13.13 a. Use the macro *terminating-search* to define the function *search-number*. This function accepts one argument, which must be a list, and returns the first number in the list or else returns *nil* if none of the list elements are numbers. For example,

```
(search-number '(dog 67 (a b c) 89))
        returns 67.
```

b. Now, use *terminating-search* to define the function *nonempty-list*. This function accepts one list and returns the first element that is a nonempty list (or returns *nil* if there are none). For example,

```
(nonempty-list '(dog () 100 (s j) k))
        returns (s j).
```

Hint: You will have to create a test with a lambda expression that both tests for a list and tests that the list is not empty.

c. Use *terminating-search* to define the function *intersectionp*, which takes two lists and returns the first item in the first list that is also in the second list. If no element of the first list appears in the second, *intersectionp* returns *nil*. For example,

(intersectionp '(a b c) '(d b a))
     returns *a*.

13.14 Define a macro called *my-mapcar* using *do*. This macro should do what *mapcar* does. Like *mapcar*, *my-mapcar* should evaluate the arguments that are passed to it.

13.15 Optional. Define a template for car-cdr recursion with a macro and define *flatten* using that macro.

This chapter concludes our discussion of the basic capabilities of LISP. We have tried to describe the basic functions that are most useful and are generally common to the various dialects of LISP. However, each dialect of LISP provides many more built-in functions that we have not discussed. As a result, you may want to obtain a reference manual for your dialect of LISP as you begin to program seriously, and perhaps an advanced LISP text. In the remaining three chapters we will begin to describe some algorithms for performing reasoning and problem solving tasks based on the material we have covered in the preceding chapters.

Summary of LISP Functions

apply This function accepts two arguments — a function name and a list — and applies the named function to the elements of the list.

Example: *(apply '+ '(2 3 4)) = 9*.

defmacro This special form is similar to *defun*, but is used to define macros rather than functions. When a macro is called, it constructs and evaluates a function call.

Example:
(defmacro ex-or (test1 test2)
    `(or (and ,test1 (not ,test2))
        (and ,test2 (not ,test1)))).

eval This function accepts one argument and causes LISP to evaluate the value of the argument.

Example: *(eval '(+ 2 3 4))* = 9.

mapcan This function takes two arguments — a function and a list — and maps the function over the elements in the list. The function that is mapped must return a list, and the lists that result from this mapping are destructively spliced together.

Example: *(mapcan 'cdr '((a b c) (d e)))* = *(b c e)*.

quote This function takes one argument and forces LISP to treat the argument literally.

Example: *(quote a)* = *a*.

Note: *(quote a)* is equivalent to *'a*.

Glossary

macro A macro is a method of defining a template for a function definition. When the macro is evaluated, a function is created according to the template, and the function is evaluated.

splicing When list A is spliced into list B, the elements of A become elements of B (instead of A becoming an element of B).

Search Techniques

14

The first 13 chapters of this book introduced the basic programming features of LISP and discussed how to use these features to achieve various programming goals. Each dialect of LISP contains many more exotic features than we have described but with the material you have covered, you have already learned enough to achieve significant programming goals. The remaining three chapters provide examples of three significant artificial-intelligence problems and describe how LISP can be used to solve them. This chapter is devoted to the issue of search.

Search

Search is sometimes considered the fundamental problem of artificial intelligence. Throughout this chapter we will be discussing two closely related

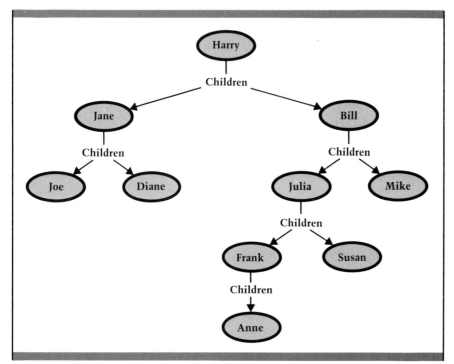

Figure 14.1

search tasks. One task is retrieving information from data structures like the one portrayed in Figure 14.1. As you can see, this tree represents parent–child relationships in a family. We can answer various questions about this family by searching this structure — for example, "Is Harry in the family?", or "Is Susan a descendant of Bill?"

The second task we will discuss is problem solving. For example, consider the "eight-puzzle," depicted in Figure 14.2. This is a familiar game with eight movable tiles arranged in 3-by-3 configuration with one open square. Tiles can be moved up, down, left, or right, into the open square, creating a new open square in the space that is vacated. The problem is to find a sequence of moves that converts the initial scrambled configuration of tiles into a goal configuration in which the tiles are arranged in numerical order. An alternative, more challenging task would be to find the shortest sequence of moves that achieves the goal. In this chapter we will develop techniques that enable us to solve problems like the eight-puzzle.

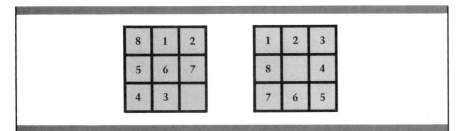

Figure 14.2

Trees and Networks

It may seem surprising that searching for items in a data structure is similar to solving a problem like the eight-puzzle, but they are closely related because the **search space** for a problem, that is, the collection of all possible sequences of moves, can be represented by a tree, or a similar network structure. A network is simply a structure that can be conveniently represented as a set of nodes connected by links. A tree is a special type of network, in which each node has only one node above it. Figure 14.3 shows a very small part of the search tree for the eight-puzzle.

Every node in this tree represents a **state** of the puzzle, that is, a configuration of the tiles. The root node corresponds to the **initial state** or initial config-

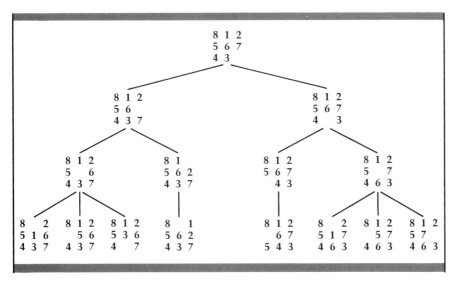

Figure 14.3

uration of tiles. Since it is possible to solve this eight-puzzle, somewhere in this tree there is at least one node, and possibly more, that represents the goal configuration or **goal state**. The task in problem solving is to find a route through the tree from the initial state to a goal state. Every link that descends from a node corresponds to a legal move, or operation, that can be applied in that problem state, so when we find a path through a problem-state tree, we are really describing a set of moves that takes us from the initial state to the goal state.

Creating Network Structures

The fact that we can use networks to characterize both fact-retrieval tasks and problem-solving tasks is an indication of the similarity of the two types of tasks, and we will be able to use the same basic algorithms to perform the tasks. However, there is also an important difference between the tasks concerning the network structures. In a fact-retrieval task we will be searching a **prestored network** structure: that is the network will be embodied in LISP data structures. For example, in Chapter 9 the function *bsearch* retrieved information from a network that was encoded as an assoc-list and in Chapter 11 *binary-search* searched a tree encoded by using properties as pointers between nodes.

In a problem-solving task, the tree structure exists only conceptually; it is not represented in LISP structures. The network in a problem-solving task will be **procedurally defined**; that is, we will essentially go along generating parts of the tree as we search it.

Before we begin describing the algorithms we can use to search both fact-retrieval trees and problem-solving trees, we will discuss functions we can use to encode a network in fact-retrieval tasks. A common way to represent network structures in LISP is to link atoms together with properties. Thus we can construct a network with a series of calls to *putprop*, in which the first argument corresponds to a node, the second argument represents immediate descendants of the first argument, and the third argument is the name of the link connecting the nodes.

For example, suppose we want to encode the following facts in LISP:

John is Mary's husband.

Mary is John's wife.

Herb and Al are Mary and John's children.

Mary is Herb and Al's mother.

John is Herb and Al's father.

Herb and Al are brothers.

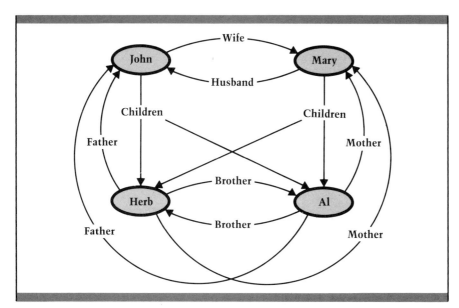

Figure 14.4

We can encode this information with the following set of calls to *putprop*:

```
(putprop 'Mary '(John) 'husband)
(putprop 'John '(Mary) 'wife)
(putprop 'Mary '(Al Herb) 'children)
(putprop 'John '(Al Herb) 'children)
(putprop 'Herb '(Mary) 'mother)
(putprop 'Al '(Mary) 'mother)
(putprop 'Herb '(John) 'father)
(putprop 'Al '(John) 'father)
(putprop 'Herb '(Al) 'brother)
(putprop 'Al '(Herb) 'brother)
```

Figure 14.4 portrays a network representation of this body of facts.

Since the second argument of these *putprops* specifies all the nodes that are linked to the first argument by a particular relationship, it is a list rather than a single atom. The links between nodes are frequently called pointers, because each of the connections is "one way" both semantically and functionally. For example, the link labeled "wife" connecting John and Mary indicates that Mary is the wife of John, but not that John is the wife of Mary. Furthermore, after encoding *(putprop 'John '(Mary) 'wife)*, we can find John's wife by calling *(get 'John 'wife)* but there is no corresponding call that will reveal Mary's husband. Thus we say the property "wife" points from John to Mary and not from Mary to John.

Adding Nodes to a Data Structure

When we are working with a prestored data structure, we may want to add nodes to the network to represent new facts. In our example, if a child is born we will want to add a node to the tree with the appropriate links. Once we have settled on a representation of nodes and links, writing functions that add nodes to a structure should be fairly straightforward. For example, the following function adds a child to a network like that in Figure 14.4.

```
(defun add-child (child mom dad)
    (putprop child (list mom) 'mother)
    (putprop child (list dad) 'father)
    (putprop mom (cons child (get mom 'children)) 'children)
    (putprop dad (cons child (get dad 'children)) 'children))
```

Notice that the first two calls to *putprop* simply assign new properties to the child, but the second two update the existing *children* property on the parents. We know that parents can have any number of children, and we do not want to erase any existing children while adding a new one. So, we call *(get mom 'children)* to get the list of children the mother already has, and *cons* the new child into that list. Finally, the resulting list is made the new value of the property. This relatively simple update will work only if the existing property value is a list rather than an atom. Thus when the property *children* is initially assigned to a parent, the value must be a list, even if the parent has only one child at the time.

LISP Exercise

14.1 Write a function *add-daughter* that will add a daughter node to a family structure. This function accepts three arguments: the girl's name, the mother's name, and the father's name. This function should do the same thing that *add-child* does, but it should also add *brother* and *sister* properties to the daughter node and it should update the *sister* property on the other children in the family. You should assume that each node in the tree has been assigned the property *sex* and that this property can have either the value *male* or *female*. You should also assume, for simplicity, that the mother and father have the same children. The function should simply return *t* when it is done.

Searching Networks

When we have information represented in either a prestored network or a procedurally defined network, we need to be able to search that network in order to use that information to perform tasks. There are three subtasks in search that we need to consider. First, we must be able to access all the nodes in the tree. In any given task we may not need to access all the nodes, but in principle we should have that ability. Second, we need to be able to generate the nodes in a systematic order, so we can be assured of an efficient and, if necessary, an exhaustive search. Third, we must be able to test the nodes we generate, to decide if they represent the goal of our search.

Expansion Functions: Accessing Nodes in a Tree Structure

In a search task we move from node to node in the tree structure until we reach a node that satisfies our goal. Therefore a fundamental subtask in search is to access all the nodes that are connected to a given node. For example, if we are searching the tree structure in Figure 14.1, we should be able to find all the children of any node in the tree. When given the node *Jane*, for example, we should be able to retrieve *Joe* and *Diane*. In the case of the eight-puzzle, if we are given one configuration of tiles, we should be able to generate every other configuration that can be formed by moving one tile. A function that accesses the nodes connected to a given node is called an **expansion function**.

In a data-retrieval task, the tree structure we need to search is actually encoded as a LISP data structure. If we have encoded the links between nodes as properties, then we can simply use the function *get* to access nodes in the network. Thus we could use the following expansion function to access all the children of a node in Figure 14.1.

```
(defun expand (person)
   (get person 'children))
```

For example, *(expand 'Jane)* would return *(Joe Diane)*.

In a problem-solving task, we are confronted with a different situation, because our network is not actually represented in a LISP data structure. We need to write an expansion function that can actually create all the nodes connected to a particular node in the tree. The exact nature of this function depends on the nature of the problem being solved. For example, consider our tic-tac-toe problem from Chapter 5. Each node in the problem-state tree for that problem corresponds to a configuration of *xs* and *os* on the board. The expansion function for that game would have to figure out all the legal moves that can be made given that configuration, and it would have to return a list of all the board configurations that result from the legal moves.

Let us consider a slightly simpler task, the "dog-cat" word-transformation game, and write an expansion function for this task. In this game the player is given a pair of three-letter words, such as "dog" and "cat." The task is to generate a sequence of words beginning with the first word and ending with the second word, by changing one letter at a time. Thus one solution to the pair "dog–cat" is

dog dot cot cat*

Since LISP does not know English, we will need to represent a vocabulary. A convenient way to do this is simply to assign a list of words to a global variable we can call *vocabulary*. For example,

```
=) (setq vocabulary '(dog cat ask boy cot dot eat fat
        gun hut ice jog hat kid lip mom not out pet rat
        sit top use vat why yes zap etc))
```

We will also need the ability to obtain the component letters of any word in this list. Fortunately, one can define a function *nthchar* that will do this. In Common LISP the function can be defined

```
(defun nthchar (word n)
    (prog1 (intern (string (char (string word) (1- n))))))
```

In other LISPs this function tends to be already defined or can be defined:

```
(defun nthchar (word n)
    (nth (1 − n) (explode word)))
```

It simply returns the specified letter of a word. So, *(nthchar 'dog 3)* returns *g*.

LISP Exercise

14.2 Write a function called *expand-word* for the dog–cat problem. This function should accept a single argument, which is a three-letter word, and return a list of all the words in the vocabulary that can be formed by changing any single letter in the argument. For example, given the list of words assigned to *vocabulary* above

(expand-word 'dog) returns (jog dot).

---

*For a more challenging task, try converting "ask" into "why," which is solvable.

Systematic Search

Now that we have described expansion functions, we need to discuss how to use an expansion function to search systematically through a tree. Let us consider an example. Suppose we are given the data structure in Figure 14.1 and want to find out if Susan is a descendant of Harry (i.e., a child, grandchild, etc.). Essentially, we need to see if Susan appears anywhere in the subtree below Harry. So, we need a function that will search systematically through the nodes in the subtree, either until we find Susan, or until we run out of nodes. In what order shall we search the nodes?

Figure 14.5a illustrates one common method for searching tree structures, called **breadth-first search**. In breadth-first search, we check all the nodes at a given level in the tree, before moving down to the next level. Thus with this method we would examine the two immediate descendants of Harry (Jane and Bill), before searching deeper in the tree.

Figure 14.5b illustrates a second common search method called **depth-first search**. In depth-first search, we always try to move down through the tree to get the next node before checking nodes at the same or a higher level. So we would consider all the descendants of Jane before considering Bill or any of his descendants.

The following iterative function, *depth*, implements the plan characterized in Figure 14.5b. This function accepts two arguments and performs a depth-first search to determine whether the second argument is a descendant of the first. Let us review what the function does, paying particular attention to the function *expand* and the variable *queue*.

```
(defun depth (person1 person2)
    (do ((queue (expand person1)
            (append (expand (car queue))(cdr queue))))
        ((null queue) nil)
        (cond ((equal (car queue) person2) (return t)))))

    (defun expand (person) (get person 'children))
=> (depth Bill Frank)
t
```

Note that the helping function *expand* is the same expansion function that we discussed earlier. It accepts one argument, which is a node in the tree, and returns a list of all the descendants of that node. The variable *queue* is used to save the list of all the nodes we have generated with the expansion function, but have not yet checked. If we consider what happens to *queue* in the function, we will see how it is used to implement a depth-first search.

240

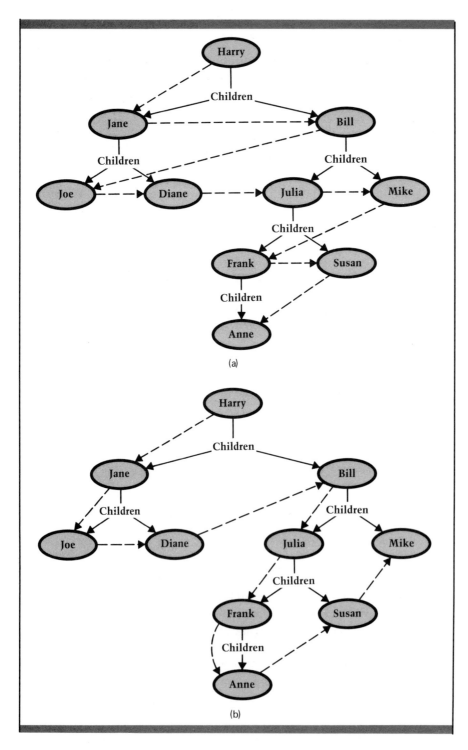

(a)

(b)

Figure 14.5

1. The function begins by expanding the value of *person1* and assigning the resulting list of descendants *(Jane Bill)* to the variable *queue*.
2. The exit test is executed next. If *queue* is empty, then *person1* has no descendants, so *person2* cannot be a descendant of the first. In that case, the function returns *nil*.
3. If *queue* is not empty, the function performs a goal test: It checks whether the *car* of *queue* is *equal* to *person2*. If so, then we have found *person2* among the descendants of *person1* and the function returns *t*.
4. If the test fails, the variable *queue* is updated. Since the first element in *queue* has just failed the test, we want to delete it from *queue*. However, before we delete that node, it is expanded so that we obtain a list of its descendants. That list is *append*ed in front of the *cdr* of *queue*. Thus as we discard the first node in *queue*, we add its descendants to the list of nodes to be searched.
5. We proceed to execute the exit test and the goal test and continue cycling around the loop, either until *queue* is empty or until we find the second argument among the descendants of the first argument.

It is important to note that the expansion is added to *front* of *queue*. That way, each time around the loop we will check a subnode of the last node we checked (if there are any). So, adding the expansion to the front of *queue* results in a depth-first search. If we were to add the elements to the back of *queue* we would get a breadth-first search. That is, we would consider all of the immediate children of a node before any grandchildren, and all of the grand-children before any great-grandchildren, etc.

LISP Exercises

14.3 Write a function called *breadth* which takes one argument: a root node in a tree. (The root node is the starting point in the tree.) The function should perform a breadth-first search of the tree and return the first node that has the property *success* with the value *t*. The function should return *nil* if no such node is found. Nodes will be connected to nodes below them by a property called *subnodes*. Below we have illustrated a simple network with an atom *a* as the root of the tree.

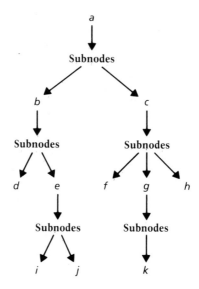

14.4 Write a function called *first-number* that does a depth first search for the first number that appears at any level in a list and returns that number. Note that this function implements *car-cdr* recursion iteratively.

14.5 Write a function *add-problem*, which will determine if any subset of digits in a list add to a specified sum. For example,

(add-problem '(1 2 3) 4) returns *t* since 1 + 3 = 4
(add-problem '(1 5 7) 4) returns *nil*.

To treat this as a search problem, encode each state as a list of a sum of some digits and an embedded list of remaining digits to be added. So, we would represent the initial state and the successors to the first state as

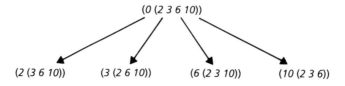

Note that expand must dynamically generate this tree structure rather than having it prestored.

Exhaustive Search

The search functions we have written so far perform self-terminating search; they return the first node they find that matches the goal. It is not difficult to modify the basic algorithm so that it exhaustively searches a tree and returns a list of all the nodes that satisfy a goal description. We simply need to add a result variable to our search function. Each time the function encounters a node that matches the goal, it will add that node to the list stored in the result variable, instead of immediately returning the node. When *queue* is finally empty, the function needs only to return the list stored in the result variable.

LISP Exercises

14.6 Write a function called *exhaustive*, which is an exhaustive version of the function *breadth* that you wrote for Exercise 14.3. The function *exhaustive* takes one argument, which is the root of a tree, and returns a list of all the nodes in the tree which have been assigned the property *success* with the value *t*.

14.7 Implement the *car-cdr* recursive function *flatten* from LISP Exercise 9.7 as an exhaustive search function. Recall that *flatten* accepts one argument, which must be a list, and returns a list containing all the atoms that appear at any level in the argument. For example,

(flatten '(a (b c (d) e f) g)) returns *(a b c d e f g)*.

Repeats and Cycles in Search

Search problems frequently involve networks that are not trees. Figure 14.6 illustrates two ways that networks can violate the definition of a tree.

First, we see that we can travel from the root node to node c by two paths, one through node a and one through node b. As a result, our search process may access c twice and repeat the process of testing it, expanding it, and checking the nodes below c, unless our search function guards against such repetitions. Second, notice that there is a cycle in the network. Node b leads to f, which leads to l, which leads back to b. When such a cycle exists in a network, the search routines we have been writing could wind up looping through and checking the nodes forever.

Both these problems can be solved in the same way — by keeping a list of all nodes that we have already tested and expanded. Each time we examine

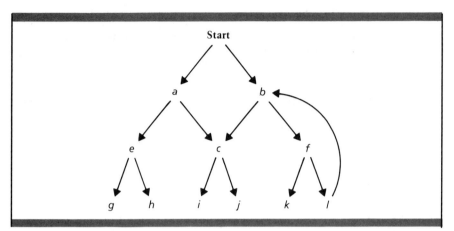

Start

a   b

e   c   f

g   h   i   j   k   l

Figure 14.6

another node, we will check if it is in the list of nodes we have already examined; if so, we simply will not expand the node again. The following function *network-depth* uses the variable *visited* to keep track of the nodes that have already been tested and expanded as it searches a network.

```
(defun network-depth (person1 person2)
    (do ((queue (expand person1)
            (cond ((member (car queue) visited)(cdr queue))
                  (t (append (expand (car queue))
                          (cdr queue)))))
        (visited nil (cons (car queue) visited)))
      ((null queue) nil)
      (cond ((equal (car queue) person2)(return t)))))
```

Notice that the structure of *network-depth* is very similar to the structure of *depth*. However, there are two important differences between the two functions. In the present function, each time we check the first node in *queue* and then update *queue*, we do not simply discard the first node. Instead, we add it to the variable *visited*, which holds a list of all the nodes already visited. At the same time, when we update *queue* we do not automatically add the expansion of the node we have just tested. Instead, we do a conditional update. If the node we have just tested has been visited previously, its expansion is not added to the queue. On the other hand, if this node has not been visited previously, then it is important to add its expansion to *queue* while we add it to the *visited* list.

LISP Exercises

14.8 Write a function, *pre-requisite*, which takes two arguments: a course name (an atom) and a list of courses which are the prerequisites of the first argument. The function should assign the list of prerequisites to the property *has-pre-req* on the first argument. The function should also add the first argument to the property *pre-req-for* on each course in the list of *prerequisites*. Test your function with the following calls to set up a prerequisite structure for the course *Automata*.

(pre-requisite 'Automata '(Systems CompFund CompLang))
(pre-requisite 'CompFund '(MathII Writing))
(pre-requisite 'Systems '(CompFund DataStruct))
(pre-requisite 'MathII '(MathI))

Here are some examples of the resulting property values after these calls have been evaluated.

(get 'Automata 'has-pre-req) returns *(Systems CompFund CompLang)*.
(get 'CompFund 'pre-req-for) returns *(Systems Automata)*.

14.9 Write a function *before* that accepts one argument which is the name of a course. The function returns a list of that course's prerequisites, each of the prerequisites' prerequisites, and so on. The function should return a list of unique course names (i.e. there should be no duplicate course names in the returned list). The order of the courses in the returned list is not important. For example,

(before 'Automata) returns
(MathI Writing MathII DataStruct CompLang CompFund Systems).

Solution Paths

So far we have discussed search functions that return either a node or a set of nodes in a network, or answer a true–false question about a network by returning *t* or *nil*. In most problem–solving situations, however, the goal is not to answer a true–false question or to return a node. Instead, we need to find a **solution path** — a chain of nodes connecting the root node and a goal node that corresponds to a sequence of moves or operations that solves the problem. Thus as we search through a network and expand nodes, we need to store information about the preceding nodes in the path, so that we can return the whole path when we reach the goal state.

We can represent a solution path as a list of the nodes that are on the path. Perhaps the most straightforward solution to storing path information is to modify the expansion function, so that instead of taking a node as its argument, it accepts a path. The expansion function expands the last node in the path, but instead of returning just a list of immediate descendants of that node, it returns a list of paths, each of which is generated by adding one descendant of the last node to the existing path.

For example, suppose we were given the tree structure in Figure 14.1, and wanted to find a path from Bill to Anne. The first time *expand* was called it would accept the list *(Bill)*, which represents a path with just one node in it. The expansion function would expand the last node in the path, *Bill*, and would obtain the descendants *Julia* and *Mike*. However, instead of returning that list of descendants, the function would return the paths leading to each descendent — that is, *((Julia Bill) (Mike Bill))*. Similarly, the function would accept *(Julia Bill)* as an argument and return paths to the descendants of Julia — i.e., *((Frank Julia Bill) (Susan Julia Bill))*.

Let us write a function, called *related* that performs the task we have just described: it takes two names and finds a path between them in the family tree displayed in Figure 14.1. We can do this by modifying our earlier function *network-depth* as follows:

```
(defun related (person1 person2)
    (do ((queue (list (list person1))
              (cond ((member (caar queue) visited)
                     (cdr queue))
                    (t (append (expand-path (car queue))
                               (cdr queue)))))
         (visited nil (cons (caar queue) visited)))
        ((null queue) nil)
        (cond ((equal (caar queue) person2)
               (return (reverse (car queue)))))))

(defun expand-path (path)
    (do ((temp (expand (car path)) (cdr temp))
         (result nil (cons (cons (car temp) path) result)))
        ((null temp) result)))

(defun expand (person)
    (get person 'children))

=> (related 'Bill 'Anne)
(Bill Julia Frank Anne)
```

The major difference between the function *related* and the earlier function *network-depth* is that *queue* now holds of a list of sublists where each sublist represents a path.

Initially, we have just one path, consisting of the first argument to the function. Every path is a list, so the function call *(list person1)* is used to create that path. Remember, however, that *queue* is a list of paths, so *queue* is initialized to *(list (list person1))*; in the case of our example function call, *queue* is initialized to *((Bill))*.

Each time through the loop we examine the first list in *queue*. Because of the way the paths are generated by *expand-path*, the most recent nodes are at the beginning of the list. So, to determine if a path has reached the goal, we just call *(equal (caar queue) person2)* to compare the first element in the list to the goal. If they are equal our path has reached the goal and we return it. Note that the path is reversed when it is returned, so that the root node is on the left.

When we generate a new node on a path we add it to the front of the existing path. (That is why we reverse the solution path when we finally return it.) Each time around the loop, we test a single node for success, as before, but now we need the function call *(caar queue)* to obtain the next node, (because *car queue* returns a path).

If that test fails, we update *queue* and *visited*, and go around the loop again. In updating *visited*, we add the node we have just checked, as before. If that node has already been visited, we simply discard the whole path leading up to that node from the queue. Otherwise, that path is passed to *expand-path*, and the new paths returned by *expand-path* are appended to the queue.

In updating *queue* we call a function *expand-path* rather than *expand*. The function *expand-path* accepts a path as its argument, and calls *expand* to obtain the immediate descendants of the most recent node in that path. Then *expand-path* inserts each of the descendants into a different copy of the original path to create new paths that are one node longer, and returns a list of those paths. As you can see, this list of paths is appended to the beginning of *queue*, so the function *related* is performing a depth-first search.

LISP Exercises

14.10 Given the *expand* function you wrote earlier for the dog–cat problem write a search function that will generate the minimum path solution to the dog–cat problem. A minimum-path solution is a solution that involves as few or fewer steps than any other solution. Note if you perform breadth-first search, you are guaranteed to find a minimum-path solution.

14.11 (Optional) Write a function called *waterjug* that solves waterjug problems. A waterjug problem specifies the capacities of three waterjugs (e.g., 6, 15, and 10 oz), and it assumes an unlimited source of water. The goal of the problem is to wind up with a specified quantity of water (e.g., 7 oz) in any one of the three jugs that is big enough to hold it. The legal moves are to fill jugs from the source of water, and to pour water from one jug to another jug. (The jugs do not have gradations. So, for example, you cannot pour exactly 12 oz of water directly into the 15-oz jug from the water source. However, you can put 12 oz into the 15-oz jug by filling the 6-oz jug twice and pouring it each time into the 15-oz jug.)

This function, called *waterjug*, takes four arguments — the capacities of three jugs and a desired quantity. It determines if the desired quantity can be obtained, and if it can, it prints out a sequence of moves that will produce a solution in the fewest steps. Note that the waterjug problem cannot be solved if the desired quantity is greater than the capacity of any of the jugs or if the greatest common divisor of the jugs' capacity does not divide evenly into the desired quantity. For example,

(waterjug 6 15 21 7) returns *cannot*.
(waterjug 6 15 10 7) returns *((fill a) (pour a b) (fill c)*
                                    (pour c b) (fill a) (pour a c)).
(waterjug 6 15 10 3) returns *((fill b) (pour b a) (empty a)*
                                    (pour b a)).

(Note: *a*, *b*, and *c* refer to the first, second and third jugs, respectively.)

Guided Search

The two search methods we have discussed, *depth-first* and *breadth-first* are examples of unguided search procedures. The order in which these methods examine nodes in a network is predetermined and is not guided by the actual contents of the network. Much of artificial intelligence is concerned with developing principles for guiding search down paths that are most likely to lead to a solution. Such methods do not just select the next node in the list to be expanded each time, but instead, assess all the remaining nodes and expand the one that seems most promising. Such methods are frequently referred to as **best-first search**. One common best-first search method is simply to expand the nodes that are closest, or most similar to the goal. Of course, such a method requires a measure of similarity. In the case of the dog–cat problem we could measure similarity between any node and the goal simply by counting how many letters differ between the two nodes. This measure will vary between 0 and 3; the lower the number the closer the two nodes are (a score of 0 means the two nodes are identical). Each time our search function selects a new node to expand, it could examine the list of nodes waiting to be expanded and select one that has the most letters in common with the goal. Let us write a best-first search function for the dog–cat problem as an exercise.

LISP Exercises

14.12 a. Define a function, *distance*, which measures the distance between two three-letter words for the dog–cat problem. The function should accept two three-letter words and return the number of letters that differ between the two words. For example,

(distance 'cat 'cog) returns 2.
(distance 'cat 'cat) returns 0.

b. Write a new version of the function *expand-path* that can be used in a best-first search. The previous version of this function accepted a list of nodes representing a path through a network and returned a list of all the paths in the network that extend the path by one node. The argument to the new version of *expand-path* will still be a list of nodes on a path, but the first element in the list will now be a number that represents the distance between the last node on the path and the goal. The new function should still return a list of paths in the network that extend the argument by one node, but the first element in each of these paths should be a measure of the distance from the last node in the path to the goal. Your new function should call the function *expand-word* so that you can use the new version of *expand-path* in the dog–cat problem. For example,

(expand-path '(2 dot dog)) returns ((1 cot dot dog) (2 not dot dog)
                                                              (3 dog dot dog))

c. In our previous search functions, we have selected the first element in *queue* to expand each time. We can also do this a best-first search if we order the paths in *queue* according to their distance from the goal with the paths closest to the goal at the front. Write a function called *interleave* that will take the list of paths returned by *expand-path* and insert them into *queue* according to the distance measure, such that the paths with the smallest distance-measure are closest to the front. This function takes two arguments: a list of paths that result from expanding one path in *queue* and the remaining paths in the *queue*. It should return a new version of the queue, with the new paths inserted in the appropriate position. For example, if *queue* holds *((2 dot dog) (2 cog dog))*, and the first path is expanded to yield *((1 cot dot dog) (2 not dot dog) (3 dog dot dog))*, then

(interleave '((1 cot dot dog) (2 not dot dog) (3 dog dot dog))
                '((2 cog dog))
returns ((1 cot dot dog) (2 not dot dog) (2 cog dog)
                (3 dog dot dog))

14.13 Write a new version of *dog-cat* that takes two three-letter words and performs a best-first search to find a minimum path solution to the problem. You should use the functions you defined in LISP Exercises 14.12.

14.14 a. Write a function *points-to*, which can be used to build a network representation with properties. The function takes three arguments: a node name (an atom), a distance (a number), and another node name (an atom). Each time it is called, the function builds a pointer from the first node to the second node by adding a list containing the distance and second node to the property *next* on the first node. (Note that the existence of a path from node 1 to node 2 does NOT imply that a path exists from node 2 to node 1, so the function does not build a pointer from the second node to the first). Try this function out by creating the following network:

(points-to 'a 10 'b)
(points-to 'a 30 'd)
(points-to 'a 100 'e)
(points-to 'b 50 'c)
(points-to 'c 10 'e)
(points-to 'd 20 'c)
(points-to 'd 60 'e)

b. Write a function called *minpath* that performs a best-first search on a network constructed by *points-to*. The function *minpath* takes two arguments: a starting node and an ending node. The function should return a list containing the nodes on the minimum path from the start node to the end node as measured by the total distance traveled between nodes, not the number of nodes on the path. For example, given the sample network in Exercise 14.14a,

(minpath 'a 'e) returns (a d c e).

14.15 (Optional) Write a function called *eight-puzzle* that employs a best-first search to solve eight-puzzle problems. The function should accept one argument that represents the initial state of the puzzle, find a solution path for the problem and print the successive puzzle states on that path. For example,

```
=> (eight-puzzle '((2 nil 3) (1 8 4) (7 6 5)))
2   3
1 8 4
7 6 5

  2 3
1 8 4
7 6 5

1 2 3
  8 4
7 6 5

nil
```

As you can see, in this example the initial puzzle state is represented as a list of three lists. Each of the embedded lists represents one of the rows in the puzzle and the blank space is represented by *nil*.

    To write *eight-puzzle* you will need to design an expansion function and find a way to measure the distance between problem states and the goal state. The goal in the eight-puzzle is to arrange the tiles in numerical order with the space in the middle and there are 16 configurations that satisfy this goal (since "1" can be in any of eight squares and the numbers can rise clockwise or counterclockwise). You will simplify the task of measuring distance if you select just one such configuration as your goal. Nilsson (1980) suggests using the following measure of the distance between puzzle states and the goal.

    For each tile count how many tiles it is away from its destination. Add to this measure 3 if the tile is in the center cell and add 6 if it is in the periphery and not followed by its successor. So, given

Problem State

2	8	1
4	6	3
7		5

Goal State

1	2	3
8		4
7	6	5

we get the following measures

Tile			
1 : 2 + 6	(out of sequence)	= 8
2 : 1 + 6	(out of sequence)	= 7
3 : 1 + 6	(out of sequence)	= 7
4 : 2 + 6	(out of sequence)	= 8
5 : 0 + 6	(out of sequence)	= 6
6 : 1 + 3	(center)	= 4
7 : 0 + 6	(out of sequence)	= 6
8 : 2 + 0	(followed by 1)	= 2
	TOTAL DISTANCE MEASURE	48

This chapter introduces an important concept in artificial intelligence. It describes how we can represent the search space in fact-retrieval tasks and problem-solving tasks as networks and it presents some basic algorithms for searching those networks. In Chapters 15 and 16 we will describe a second approach to artificial-intelligence tasks. Initially, we will describe how to retrieve information from unstructured data sets with pattern-matching techniques. Then we will describe a type of program called a production system that employs pattern matching to perform reasoning tasks.

Summary of LISP Functions

nthchar   This function takes two arguments — an atom and a number — and it returns the character that appears in the atom in the position specified by the number.

Example: *(nthchar 'house 4)* = *s*.

Glossary

best-first search   A method of search in which the nodes that appear closest to the goal are checked first.

breadth-first search   A method of search in which all the nodes at a particular level are checked before nodes at a deeper level.

depth-first search   A method of search in which the descendants of a node are checked before nodes at the same level as the node.

expansion function   A function that generates all the descendants of a node.

goal state   A node in the search space that represents a state in which the problem is solved.

initial state   The node in the search space that represents the problem state at the beginning of the problem.

prestored network   A network that is stored by some data structure, such as a property list.

procedurally defined network   A network that is generated dynamically by an expansion function.

search space   A representation of a problem by a network of paths, starting from the initial problem state and going to the various problem states that can be reached from that state.

solution path   A sequence of states and operations that goes from the initial problem state to a goal state.

state   A node in a search space that represents a state into which the problem can be transformed by a sequence of operations.

Pattern Matching

In Chapter 14 we examined search as one mechanism for solving problems. In this chapter we will describe an alternative approach to problem solving, called pattern matching. **Pattern matching** involves taking patterns or descriptions and finding elements in a data base that match the patterns. This turns out to be a powerful framework for problem solving. It is the basis of Prolog, which is a new artificial-intelligence programming language. Pattern matching is also the basis of production systems, which have proven useful for implementing models of human cognition and expert systems in artificial intelligence. We will discuss how to use pattern matching to implement production systems.

Data and Patterns

As an example of pattern matching, consider the following set of seven facts, which have been encoded in a list:

```
(setq database '((George is-father-of Fred)
                 (George is-father-of Donald)
                 (Mary is-mother-of Fred)
                 (Fred is-father-of Alice)
                 (Diane is-mother-of Tim)
                 (Donald is-father-of Mike)
                 (Alice is-mother-of Jill))))
```

As you can see, each fact has been encoded as an embedded list, which we will call a **clause**. Now suppose we want to find out who George's children are; we simply need to find every clause in the data base in which the first element is *George* and the second element is *is-father-of*. In other words, we need to find every clause that matches the following **pattern**:

(George is-father-of ⟨child⟩).

As you can see, a pattern is a type of template; it is a description of the information we are seeking in a data base. In pattern matching we access information in a data base by finding clauses that match such patterns. When we find a clause that matches our example pattern, the element that appears in the ⟨child⟩ position will be the name of one of George's children.

Notice that there are two types of components in the pattern above. Some components, like *George* or *is-father-of*, can match only to identical atoms in the data base. These components are called **pattern constants**. The other component ⟨child⟩ is like a wild card; it can match to any element in the data base. This type of pattern component is referred to as a **pattern variable**. We will adopt the convention of representing pattern variables by atoms that begin with an equal sign, like =x; any other atom that appears in a pattern is a constant.* Thus an actual pattern we could use to find George's children would be

(George is-father-of =x),

and this pattern would match to two clauses in our data base:

(George is-father-of Fred).
(George is-father-of Donald).

---

*The use of the term variable may be confusing in this context. A pattern variable is not the same thing as a LISP variable. A pattern is a literal list, and pattern variables are treated as literal atoms by LISP. The pattern-matching functions we write, however, treat atoms that begin with an equal sign as pattern variables and all other elements in the pattern as pattern constants.

A Simple Pattern-Matching Function

Let us write a basic function called *match*, which performs pattern matching. This function will accept one argument, a pattern clause, and will match the pattern to all the clauses in a data base stored in the global variable *database*. A pattern will not necessarily have a single variable in it, of course. For example, if we wanted to find all the father–child pairs in our data base, we would use a pattern with two variables, like *(= father is-father-of = child)*. On the other hand, we can submit a pattern with all constants, like *(George is-father-of Fred)*, in which case we are essentially asking a true–false question. Our pattern-matching function must be able to handle any legal pattern so that each time we seek information in the data base, we can simply write new patterns and will not need to write a new pattern-matching function.

Our function will return a list of all the matches it discovers. For each match, the function will report just the **variable bindings** in the pattern, i.e., the database components that match each variable. For example, if we find a clause in a data base that matches the pattern *(George is-father-of =x)*, we already know what the first two elements in that clause will be; they must be *George* and *is-father-of*. Thus our function will report only the third element in the data-base clause that binds to the variable *=x*. Here are some sample calls to *match*, and the match information that is returned:

> => (match '(George is-father-of =x))
>   (((=x Fred)) ((=x Donald)))

> => (match '(=x is-mother-of =y))
>   (((=x Mary)(=y Fred)) ((=x Diane)(=y Tim)) ((=x Alice)(=y Jill)))

As these examples show, *match* returns a list in which each match is represented by an embedded list. Each match is called an **instantiation** of the pattern. Each variable binding in a given match will in turn be represented as an embedded list of the match. In the first example, two matches were obtained, so the list returned by *match* contains two embedded lists. The pattern in this example contains only a single variable, *=x*, and so a single binding is reported for each of the two matches. In the second example, the pattern contains two variables, so two bindings are reported for each of the three clauses in the data base that match the pattern. Note that under this convention, if we submitted the pattern *(George is-father-of Donald)*, the function would return *(nil)*. This result is a list with one embedded list, *nil*, indicating that one match was found. However, since there are no variables in the pattern, there are no bindings to report, and so the embedded list is empty. On the other hand, when our pattern-matching function fails to find any matches, it just returns *nil*, regardless of the number of variables in the pattern.

The following function *match* is the top-level function in our pattern-matching program:

```
(defun match (pattern)
   (mapcan #'(lambda (x) (match-clause pattern x))
        database))
```

As described above, the function accepts one argument, which is a pattern clause. The function maps a helping function *match-clause* over the data base in order to compare the pattern to each clause in the data base. When a clause matches the pattern, *match-clause* returns a list of the variable bindings; when a pattern fails to match, *match-clause* returns *nil*. Thus if we called *match* with the pattern (George is-father-of =x), *match-clause* would return the following series of values on successive calls:

```
(((=x Fred)))
(((=x George)))
nil
nil
nil
nil
nil
```

The function *mapcan* will merge these lists together and thus will delete all of the *nil*s. The result returned by *match* will be (((=x Fred)) ((=x Donald))).

For now, let us make the simplifying assumption in defining the function *match-clause* that the pattern and data-base clauses each contain three elements. We can define *match-clause* as follows:

```
(defun match-clause (pat dat)
   (filter (list (elem-match (car pat) (car dat))
          (elem-match (cadr pat) (cadr dat))
          (elem-match (caddr pat) (caddr dat)))))
```

The function *match-clause* accepts two arguments — a pattern and a data-base clause. The function calls the helping function *elem-match* three times to compare each component of the pattern against the corresponding component of the data-base clause. The results of these three calls are placed in a list, and the function *filter* takes this result, checks for a complete match of all three elements, and if they all match, constructs a list of the variable bindings. If any of the three results is *nil* then there has been a mismatch and *filter* returns *nil*; otherwise, *filter* returns a list that contains a list of the variable bindings. The extra list is for purposes of appending by *mapcan* in *match*. Let us write the functions *elem-match* and *filter* as exercises.

LISP Exercises

15.1 Write a function called *elem-match* that accepts two arguments. The first argument is an element of a pattern, and the second argument is the corresponding component of a data-base clause. If the pattern element is a variable, the function should return a list of the two arguments — the variable followed by the data-base component (because a variable matches any constant). If the pattern component is a constant then the function should return *t* if the two arguments are equivalent and return *nil* otherwise. For example,

(elem-match '=x 'Donald) returns *(=x Donald)*.
(elem-match 'is-father-of 'is-father-of) returns *t*.
(elem-match 'George 'Alice) returns *nil*.

Hint: You can tell whether an atom is a variable or a constant by looking at the first character using the function *nthchar* from Chapter 14.

15.2 Write a function called *filter* that accepts a single argument, which is a list of three elements — the values returned by *elem-match* in matching the components of a clause. (Although the example we have used involves just three components in a clause, write *filter* to deal with arbitrary lists of elements.) If the argument indicates that the data-base clause did not match the pattern, *filter* should return *nil*. Otherwise, *filter* should return a list containing a list of the variable bindings for the match. For example, when *match-clause* is called with the pattern *(=x is-mother-of =y)* and the data-base clause *(Alice is-mother-of Jill)*, *filter* will then be called with the argument *((=x Alice) t (=y Jill))*. Since no *nil*s are present, all elements have been matched successfully. So,

(filter '((=x Alice) t (=y Jill))) returns *(((=x Alice) (=y Jill)))*.

On the other hand,

(filter '(t nil (=x Mary))) returns *nil*.

We have now defined the two helping functions used in *match-clause*, so we can test our complete *match* function. You should type in the definitions of *match-clause* and *match* given earlier. Set up the variable *database* and try calling *match* with some patterns. Here are some example matches using our *database*:

```
=> (match '(George is-father-of =child))
(((=child Fred)) ((=child Donald)))
```

```
=> (match '(=mom is-mother-of =child))
(((=mom Mary) (=child Fred)) ((=mom Diane) (=child Tim))
 ((=mom Alice) (=child Jill)))

=> (match '(=parent =relation Fred))
(((=parent George) (=relation is-father-of))
 ((=parent Mary) (=relation is-mother-of)))
```

In the exercises that follow, we will make our pattern matcher more flexible.

15.3 The function *match-clause* only matches patterns and clauses consisting of three elements. Write a new version of *match-clause* that will match patterns and clauses with any number of elements. This function will take two arguments — a pattern clause and a data-base clause. Just as in our previous version, if the data-base clause matches the pattern, the function should return a list of the list of variable bindings. If the two clauses do not match, the function should return *nil*. Note that if the pattern and data-base clauses have a different number of elements, they cannot match. For example,

```
(match-clause '(Joan is-mother-of =child =year)
             '(Joan is-mother-of Mary 1975))
returns (((=child Mary) (=year 1975))).

(match-clause '(Joan is-mother-of =child =year)
             '(Joan is-mother-of Mary))

returns nil.
```

Your new version of *match-clause* should still use the helping functions *filter* and *elem-match* as you defined them in LISP Exercises 15.1 and 15.2.

Multilevel Clauses

So far we have assumed that all components of pattern clauses and data-base clauses will be atoms. However, it is also possible for clause components to be embedded lists. For example, if our clauses represented mathematical expressions, some typical data-base clauses might look like this:

```
(setq database '(((4 + 3) * (3 - 2))
                 (7 + 3 + 2)
                 (4 * (2 + a))))
```

Some typical patterns we could match to the data base would look like this:

```
(=x * =y)
((=x + 3) * (3 - =y))
```

We can generalize our pattern-matching function to handle embedded lists by observing the following rules:

1. As before, a constant in a pattern can only match to an identical expression in the corresponding position of a data-base clause.
2. A variable in a pattern can bind to any single element, either an atom or an embedded list, that appears in the corresponding position of a data-base clause.
3. An embedded list in a pattern is itself treated as a pattern that must match to an embedded list in the corresponding position of a data-base clause.

Consider the following examples:

```
=> (match '((=x + 3) * (3 - =y)))
((((=x 4) (=y 2)))

=> (match '(=x * =y))
((((=x (4 + 3)) (=y (3 - 2))) ((=x 4) (=y (2 + a)))))
```

In the first example, the pattern, which has three components, matches the first clause in the data base — ((4 + 3) * (3 - 2)). The first component in the pattern is an embedded list, (=x + 3), which is itself treated as a pattern with three elements. That pattern matches to the first element in the first data-base clause and the variable =x binds to 4. The second element in the pattern is the constant *, which matches the corresponding element of the first data-base clause. Finally, the third pattern component is another embedded list, (3 - =y), which matches the third element of first data-base clause, and the variable =y binds to 2. The other two clauses in the data base do not match the pattern, so the function returns the two variable bindings for the single match it found.

In the second example, the pattern again has three components, but it contains no embedded lists. Here *match* found two matches. The pattern matches to the first clause in the data base, with the variable =x binding to the embedded list (4 + 3), and the variable =y binding to the embedded list (3 - 2). The pattern also matches the final clause in the data base. In this case, the variable =x binds to the atom 4, while the variable =y binds to the embedded list (2 + a).

LISP Exercise

15.4 Write a new definition of *match-clause* so that it can handle the examples just described. The function should accept two arguments, a pattern clause and a data-base clause, and behave just like the function you defined in LISP Exercise 15.3, except that it should be able to process pattern and data-base clauses that contain any level of embedded lists.

Multiple-Clause Patterns and Repeated Variables

So far we have assumed that our function *match* will match patterns consisting of a single clause, but frequently we need to match multiple-clause patterns. For example, suppose we want to find all of George's paternal grandchildren (i.e., the children of George's sons). We could obtain that information by matching the following two patterns simultaneously:

((George is-father-of =x)
  (=x is-father-of =y))

Of course, this method will yield the correct results only if *=x* is forced to bind to the same name each time. That is, the name bound to *=y* is the grandchild of George only if *=x* is bound to the same name when both patterns are matched.

Let us consider how each of these clauses would match individually to our sample data base of family relations.

Pattern	**Pattern**
(George is-father-of =x)	*(=x is-father-of =y)*
Bindings	**Bindings**
(((=x Fred))	*(((=x George) (=y Fred))*
((=x Donald)))	*((=x George) (=y Donald))*
	((=x Fred) (=y Alice))
	((=x Donald) (=y Mike)))

The task now is to find consistent bindings. In other words, we have to find all pairs consisting of one binding from the first column and one set of bindings from the second column in which *=x* is bound to the same name. This process of finding the consistent bindings is called **merging**. When we merge the bindings in this example, we obtain the following matches:

```
((( =x Fred) ( =y Alice))
 (( =x Donald) ( =y Mike)))
```

Given the way we set up our pattern, *Alice* and *Mike* (the names bound to the variable =y) are George's paternal grandchildren.

The following function *new-match* will match multiple-clause patterns to a data base:

```
(defun new-match (pattern)
      (do ((parts pattern (cdr parts))
          (answers (list nil)
                      (merge (match (car parts)) answers)))
         ((null parts) answers)
         (cond ((null answers) (return nil)))))
```

This function takes one argument, which is a list of pattern clauses. As you can see, *new-match* is a list-iteration function. The first variable in the function, *parts*, is the control variable, which is initialized to the list of pattern clauses. The second variable, *answers*, is a result variable that stores successful matches. Each time around the loop the first clause in *parts* is matched against all the clauses in the global variable *database* by the function *match*. This function has the same definition we gave it earlier, and it returns a list of variable bindings for successful matches. This list of bindings is then passed to the function *merge* along with the current contents of *answers*. As its name suggests, *merge* merges the new matches with prior matches and returns a list of all the consistent bindings. Note that there are two conditions under which we will exit the function *new-match*. The exit test for the loop checks to see if *parts* is empty. If so, there are no more pattern clauses to match, and the function returns the value of *answer*, which is a list of consistent matches. The body of the loop contains a second test, which checks to see if *answers* is empty. If so, then we have been unable to find any consistent matches to the pattern clauses we have checked so far. In that case, there can be no consistent matches to the complete pattern, so there is no point in looking further, and the function returns *nil*.

We still need to describe how the function *merge* works. In order to do that, let us consider a sample call to *new-match*:

```
= ) (new-match '((George is-father-of =x) (=x is-father-of =y)))
(((=y Alice) (=x Fred)) ((=y Mike) (=x Donald)))
```

As LISP evaluates *new-match*, *parts* is initialized to the pattern, and *answer* is initialized to *(nil)*. Then the exit test fails as does the test in the body of the loop, so the variables are updated. Let us examine how *answers* is updated the first time. First, *match* is called and that function finds two clauses in the data base that match the first clause in the pattern, so *match* returns the list *(((=x Fred)) ((=x Donald)))*. Then the function *merge* is called to merge these bindings with earlier matches. However, there have been no earlier matches, so *merge* simply returns the same list of bindings. After the variables are updated, the two tests in the loop fail again, and the variables are updated again. This time *match* matches the second pattern clause to the data base and returns the list

```
(((=x George) (=y Fred))
 ((=x George) (=y Donald))
 ((=x Fred) (=y Alice))
 ((=x Donald) (=y Mike)))
```

Thus the function *merge* is passed this list, and the current value of *answers*, which is *(((=x Fred)) ((=x Donald)))*. The function compares each match in the first list to each match in the second list. For example, it compares *((=x George) (=y Fred))* and *((=x Fred))*. If it finds the same variable in the two matches, it checks to see if the bindings are identical. In this example, *=x* appears in both of these matches, but the variable is bound to a different constant in each match, so the matches are not consistent. On the other hand, when *merge* checks the pair *((=x Fred) (=y Alice))* and *((=x Fred))*, it finds that *=x* is bound to the same constant in each match, and so these matches are consistent. When *merge* finds a consistent pair of matches, it combines all the bindings in the two matches to form an overall match. In the case of our example, when we combine our two matches we simply get *((=x Fred) (=y Alice))*. However, if *merge* compared the matches *((=x Fred) (=y Alice))* and *((=y Alice) (=z Jill))*, it would find they are consistent and return the new list *((=x Fred) (=y Alice) (=z Jill))*.

When *merge* has compared all the elements of the two lists, it will have found two consistent pairs of matches, and will return the list *(((=y Alice) (=x Fred)) ((=y Mike) (=x Donald)))*, which will be assigned to *answers*. Then the exit test will be performed again. Since there are only two clauses in our pattern, *parts* will now be empty, and the function will return the value of *answers*.

LISP Exercises

15.5 Define the function *merge* we just described. It should take two arguments. The first argument is a list of variable bindings for successful matches of a new pattern to the data base. The second argument is a list of consistent variable bindings from matching earlier pattern clauses to the data base. If the second argument is *(nil)*, the function should simply return the first argument. If the first argument is *nil*, the function should return *nil*. Otherwise, the function should compare each match in the first argument with each match in the second argument and return a list of variable bindings for all the consistent pairs of matches it finds. If the function does not find any consistent pairs, it should return *nil*.

After you have defined *merge* to handle the examples just described, try calling *new-match* with some multiple clause patterns. Using our family data base,

(new-match '((George is-father-of =x) (=x is-father-of =y)))
returns (((=y Alice) (=x Fred)) ((=y Mike) (=x Donald))).

(new-match '((=dad is-father-of =kid) (=mom is-mother-of =kid)))
returns (((=mom Mary) (=dad George) (=kid Fred))).

(new-match '((=grandmom is-mother-of =middle)
                    (=middle is-father-of =grandkid)))
returns (((=grandkid Alice) (=grandmom Mary) (=middle Fred))).

15.6 Our current definition of *new-match* allows a constant to bind to two different variables. For example, suppose we wanted to see whether *Mary* had two children. We could try the following:

=> (new-match '((Mary is-mother-of =x) (Mary is-mother-of =y)))
(((=y Fred) (=x Fred)))

Unfortunately, even though Mary has only one child, this pair of patterns matches anyway, because the variables =x and =y both bind to *Fred*. Modify your definition of *new-match* so that a given atom or list can bind only to one variable. After your modifications, you should get these results:

(new-match '((Mary is-mother-of =x) (Mary is-mother-of =y)))
returns *nil*.

(new-match '((=x is-father-of =y) (=y is-father-of =z)
                    (=x is-father-of =w)))
returns (((=w Donald) (=z Alice) (=x George) (=y Fred))
                    ((=w Fred) (=z Mike) (=x George) (=y Donald))).

(new-match '((George is-father-of =x) (George is-father-of =y)))
returns (((=y Donald) (=x Fred)) ((=y Fred) (=x Donald))).

Note that, as the third example makes clear, although different variables cannot bind to the same atom in a single instantiation, it still is possible for different variables to bind to the same atom in different instantiations.

Pattern-Matching Assessment

You should begin to notice that pattern matching can take a great deal of time. If we analyze what is happening, the reason becomes clear. Suppose we are matching a pattern that is p clauses long and a data base consisting of d clauses. If each clause has e elements, our function will have to compare $p * d * e$ pairs of elements, just to find all the clauses in the data base that match the pattern. In addition, we then have to worry about merging bindings. To merge m alternative bindings from a matching clause with a pre-existing set of n bindings requires $m * n$ merges. If each alternative binding from the match has k variables and each existing binding has l variables, then each merging is going to require $k * l$ comparisons. Thus to do the merging will require $m * n * k * l$ comparisons. Moreover, if a pattern has p clauses, we have to repeat this merging p times. Thus merging requires $p * m * n * k * l$ comparisons. Combining matching and merging, we come up with $p * (d * e + m * n * k * l)$ comparisons. For example, here are some values that are characteristic of the matches we have been considering:

$$p = \text{number of clauses in a pattern} = 2$$
$$d = \text{number of clauses in data base} = 7$$
$$e = \text{length of clauses} = 3$$
$$m, n = \text{number of instantiations} = 5$$
$$k, l = \text{number of bindings} = 2$$

Given these values, our pattern-matching function would have to perform

$2 * (7 * 3 + 5 * 5 * 2 * 2)$ or over 200 comparisons.

Thus a fairly modest pattern-matching task can require a substantial number of comparisons, and the number of comparisons can grow much larger as the data base and patterns grow in size. As a result, the issue of efficiency becomes very important. Fortunately, we can develop more efficient schemes for matching patterns than the one we have developed so far. One way to match patterns more efficiently is to write a function that directly matches a specific pattern. Thus to find the paternal grandchildren of George, we could write the following code:

```
(defun george ()
    (get-sons-with-children (get-father-clauses database)))

(defun get-father-clauses (data)
    (mapcan #'(lambda (clause)
                  (cond ((equal (relation clause) 'is-father-of)
                         (list clause))
                        (t nil)))
            data))
```

```
(defun get-sons-with-children (father-clauses)
    (mapcan
        #'(lambda (georgekid)
            (mapcan
                #'(lambda (clause) (is-father georgekid clause))
                father-clauses))
        (get-george-kids father-clauses)))

(defun is-father (target father-clause)
    (cond ((equal target (car father-clause))
            (list (list (list '=x target) (cons '=y (cddr father-clause)))))
        (t nil)))

(defun get-george-kids (clauses)
    (mapcan 'child-of-george clauses))

(defun child-of-george (clause)
    (cond ((equal (car clause) 'George) (list (caddr clause)))
        (t nil)))

(defun relation (clause) (cadr clause))
```

If you try this code, you will see that it returns the same bindings (although in a different order) as if you had used our pattern-matching function:

```
=> (new-match '((George is-father-of =x) (=x is-father-of =y)))
((((=y Mike) (=x Donald)) ((=y Alice) (=x Fred)))

=>(george)
((((=x Fred) (=y Alice)) ((=x Donald) (=y Mike)))
```

This special-purpose function is executed by LISP more quickly than our general-purpose pattern-matching function *new-match*. However, the function *george*, which can perform only a single task, requires almost as much code as the general-purpose function. It can become very time consuming to write a specific function for each of the matches you wish to perform. But, if you have a few patterns that are going to be repeatedly matched, then it may be worthwhile to write a specific matching function for those patterns.

LISP Exercises

15.7 Suppose we want to write a program that recognizes all the grandchildren of a person, not just the maternal or the paternal grandchildren. Since a parent might be related to a child by either an *is-father-of* or *is-mother-of* relation, this could not be written using our current pattern matcher. Instead, we need to be able to include an *or* in a pattern, so that *match* can report clauses that match either one pattern *or* another pattern. We will assume that a pattern can contain an *or* in the first position, followed by any number of patterns. When passed such a pattern, the function *match* should report all clauses that match any one of the patterns following the *or*. For example, the pattern

((or (=x is-father-of =y) (=x is-mother-of =y)))

will find all data-base clauses that contain *is-father-of* or *is-mother-of*. Similarly, the pattern

((or (=x is-father-of =y) (=x is-mother-of =y))
 (or (=y is-father-of =z) (=y is-mother-of =z)))

would find all cases in which $=x$ is a parent (mother or father) of $=y$, and $=y$ is a parent (again, either mother or father) of $=z$.

Redefine *match* so that it can handle patterns including *or*. (Your definition of *new-match* from LISP Exercise 15.6 does not need to be changed.) For example,

(new-match '((or (=x is-father-of =y) (=x is-mother-of =y))
                  (or (=y is-father-of =z) (=y is-mother-of =z))))
returns
(((=z Jill) (=x Fred) (=y Alice))
 ((=z Mike) (=x George) (=y Donald))
 ((=z Alice) (=x Mary) (=y Fred))
 ((=z Alice) (=x George) (=y Fred))).

Hint: The set of clauses in a data base that matches pattern *A* or pattern *B*, is the same as the set of clauses that match *A* and the set that match *B*.

15.8 Now write a specific LISP program called *gparent* to recognize the pattern

((or (=x is-father-of =y) (=x is-mother-of =y))
 (or (=y is-father-of =z) (=y is-mother-of =z)))

from the previous exercise, and compare its efficiency with the general pattern matcher. The function does not take any arguments and should return the same instantiations as the call to *new-match*, when passed this "grandparent" pattern, although the instantiations and the bindings within them may be in a different order.

Production Systems

Now that we have generated some functions that perform pattern matching, let us incorporate them into a complete system, called a **production system**, that can perform reasoning tasks. A production system has three basic components: (1) a data base of clauses that is generally called **working memory**; (2) a set of rules called **productions**; and (3) a program called a **rule interpreter** that applies the rules to the data base.

Each production is an **if–then** rule that is very similar to a *cond* case. An if–then rule specifies a test to be performed and an action to take if the test is satisfied. In a production the test takes the form of a pattern to match against working memory, and the action specifies a clause to add to working memory. The following is an example of a production rule:

```
IF ((=x is-father-of =y)
    (=z is-wife-of =x))
THEN (=z is-mother-of =y).
```

The pattern (IF part) matches a situation in which a person $=x$ is father of $=y$ and husband of $=z$. The action side (THEN part) infers that $=z$ then is mother of $=y$. We will encode this production by the following list structure, which will be the convention used in this textbook for representing productions:

```
(p1
    ((father =x =y)
     (wife =z =x))
 ==>
    (mother =z =y))
```

As you can see, a production takes the form of a list consisting of four elements.

1. The name of the production, in this case, *p1*.
2. A list containing one or more patterns that specifies a test. Note that in the test and action we have adopted the convention of placing the predicates (*father, wife, mother*) first, followed by the arguments. This will be convenient for later applications.
3. An arrow that separates the test from the action (so that the test can be easily distinguished from the action visually).
4. An action; more specifically, a pattern that describes a clause to be added to working memory.

The second element is frequently referred to as the **left-hand side** of the production and consists of a pattern like the ones we discussed in the section on pattern matching. If this pattern matches to clauses in working memory, then the production can be **fired** — that is, the action specified by the fourth element in the production can be executed. The fourth element is frequently referred to as the **right-hand side**. When the production fires, the pattern on the right-hand side is used to form a new clause; the variables in that pattern are replaced by the bindings they were assigned on the left-hand side and the resulting clause is added to working memory.

For example, suppose we apply the production *p1* to the following data base:

```
((father George Fred)
 (wife Alice George)
 (father Harry Mary)
 (mother Mary Alice))
```

We would obtain a single match in which $=x$ binds to *George*, $=y$ binds to *Fred*, and $=z$ binds to *Alice*, so the production would add the clause *(mother Alice Fred)* to working memory.

It is important to recognize that a single production can match to working memory in more than one way. For example, if we added the clause *(wife Susan Harry)* to our data base, then the production *p1* would match twice, yielding the following bindings:

```
(((=x George) (=y Fred) (=z Alice))
 ((=x Harry) (=y Mary) (=z Susan)))
```

Each successful match of a production to working memory is called an instantiation of the production. Thus after adding the clause *(wife Susan Harry)* to working memory, we obtained two instantiations of the production *p1*. The fact that a production can match more than once is important, because each instantiation of a production would write a different clause into working memory. In this case we would get *(mother Susan Mary)* as well as *(mother Alice Fred)*.

So far, we have discussed a single production, but a production system will generally contain a collection of productions to apply to working memory. This collection of productions is referred to as the **production set**. Table 15.1 contains a small production set that draws inferences about family relationships.

The Rule Interpreter: Applying Productions

We have discussed how a single production is applied; now let us discuss how our production system will work in performing a task. We will assume that our system employs two global variables, one that stores our production set and one that holds working memory. What we now need to discuss is the rule

Table 15.1. A set of productions

```
(setq productions '(
    (p1
     ((father =x =y)
      (wife =z =x))
     ==>
     (mother =z =y))
    (p2
     ((mother =x =y)
      (husband =z =x))
     ==>
     (father =z =y))
    (p3
     ((wife =x =y))
     ==>
     (husband =y =x))
    (p4
     ((husband =x =y))
     ==>
     (wife =y =x))
    (p5
     ((father =x =z)
      (mother =y =z))
     ==>
     (husband =x =y))
    (p6
     ((father =x =z)
      (mother =y =z))
     ==>
     (wife =y =z))
    (p7
     ((husband =x =y))
     ==>
     (male =x))
    (p8
     ((wife =x =y))
     ==>
     (female =x))))
```

interpreter, the program that applies the productions to the clauses in working memory.

The basic unit of processing in applying productions is a **cycle**, which is essentially equivalent to one pass through a loop. In each cycle, the rule interpreter performs three steps. First, it applies all the productions in the production set to working memory and finds all the productions whose conditions are satisfied (including multiple instantiations of a given production, if a production matches more than once with a different set of bindings). This set of matching productions is called the **conflict set**. Then the rule interpreter selects and fires one production from the conflict set, adding the specified clause to working memory. Finally, the rule interpreter prints a record of the production that fired and the clause that was added to working memory. After performing these steps, the rule interpreter proceeds to the next cycle and repeats them.

To specify when the production system will stop cycling, we need to add a constraint: we will not add a clause to working memory if that clause is already there. Thus when a production would add a clause to working memory that is already there, that production cannot fire. Given this constraint, we can specify an exit condition for our loop: we will exit when there are no productions that can fire. In other words, we exit the loop when there are no more clauses that can be added to working memory. Thus we have defined a system that accepts a set of facts (working memory) and a set of rules (the production set) and draws every possible inference that can be drawn based on the facts and rules.

Suppose we assign the following working memory to the global variable *database*:

```
(setq database '((male Fred)
                 (mother Diane Fred)
                 (father George Fred)
                 (father George Mary)
                 (wife Mary Tom)
                 (daughter Sally Tom)))
```

Let us consider what will happen when we start the production system running with the eight production rules in Table 15.1. In the first cycle, the following productions would match: *p3*, *p5*, *p6*, and *p8*. Only one production can fire in each cycle. To simplify things for this example, we will always select the first production in the conflict set, so *p3* would fire. As a result, the clause *(husband Tom Mary)* would be added to working memory, and our production system would print the following expression on the screen:

```
(firing p3 (husband Tom Mary)).
```

On the second cycle, the following productions would be in the conflict set: *p5*, *p6*, *p7*, and *p8*. Note that although the left-hand side of *p3* matches to a clause in working memory, the production is not in the conflict set, because the clause that the production would add is already in working memory. Similarly, although the left-hand side of *p4* matches a clause in working memory (the one added on the previous cycle), this production is also excluded from the conflict set for the same reason. Thus *p5* fires, adding the clause *(husband George Diane)* to working memory and printing the following expression on the screen:

(firing p5 (husband George Diane)).

If we allow our production system to run, the following output would appear on the screen (beginning with cycle 1):

```
(firing p3 (husband Tom Mary))
(firing p5 (husband George Diane))
(firing p4 (wife Diane George))
(firing p1 (mother Diane Mary))
(firing p7 (male Tom))
(firing p7 (male George))
(firing p8 (female Mary))
(firing p8 (female Diane))
done
```

In the ninth cycle none of the instantiations in the conflict set is able to add a new clause to working memory, so execution of the production system terminates.

Implementing the Rule Interpreter

Now let us write the code for the rule interpreter. The top-level function will be a loop that performs the following actions in each pass:

1. Apply the production set to working memory to get the conflict set.
2. Check to see if there are productions that can fire. If the conflict set is empty, return the atom *done*. If there are productions that can fire, then select a production from the conflict set and fire that production.
3. Print the name of the production that fired and the clause that was added to working memory. (This traces the firing of productions.)

We can code the top-level function *rule-interpreter* as follows:

```
(defun rule-interpreter ()
    (do ((cset (apply-prods) (apply-prods)))
        ((null cset) 'done)
        (perform-action (conflict-resolution cset))))

(defun conflict-resolution (cset) (car cset))

(defun perform-action (action)
    (print (cons 'firing action))
    (setq database (cons (cadr action) database)))
```

This function has a single local variable, *cset*, which holds the conflict set. As you can see, *rule-interpreter* calls the function *apply-prods* first to initialize *cset* and then to update *cset* in each cycle. The function *apply-prods* applies the production set to working memory and returns a list of all productions that are eligible to fire and the clauses they would add to working memory. For example, when *apply-prods* is called in the first cycle of our example above, it would return the following list:

```
((p3 (husband Tom Mary))
 (p5 (husband George Diane))
 (p6 (wife Diane Fred))
 (p8 (female Mary)))
```

After *cset* is updated, the exit test checks whether the conflict set is empty. If so, the function returns *done*; otherwise, the body of the loop is evaluated.

The body of the loop consists of two steps, one embedded within the other. First, a production is chosen to fire. The process of choosing a production is referred to as **conflict resolution**. There are many possible rules we can use to choose a production, but we will use a very simple one: We will just fire the first production in the conflict set. Second, the production chosen by *conflict-resolution* is passed to *perform-action*, which adds to working memory the clause that the production generates. In addition, *perform-action* prints the name of the production that fired along with the clause that was added to working memory.

We still need to write the helping function *apply-prods*, which is the heart of the production-system implementation. We will do this as a series of LISP exercises. We will work on its helping functions first, and then write *apply-prods*.

LISP Exercises

15.9 First, we need to write the function that, given a production instantiation, returns the clause that the production would insert into working memory. This function, *build-clause*, takes three arguments — the name of a production, the action of that production, and a list of variable bindings that represent an instantiation of the production. It should calculate the new clause that results when the variables in the action are replaced by the constants bound to the variables in the bindings list. Then it should check to see if this clause is already in the data base. If it is, we do not want to add it again, so *build-clause* should just return *nil*. If the clause is not in working memory, *build-clause* should return a list containing a list consisting of the name of the production and the action. (The extra list is needed because we will be appending this list to the clauses built from other production instantiations.) For example, if production *p7* matches to working memory, binding =*x* to *George* and =*y* to *Diane*, then,

(build-clause 'p7 '(male =x) '((=x George) (=y Diane)))
returns ((p7 (male George))).

The code for this exercise requires a call to *member* in which the first argument will be a list. Recall from Chapter 3 that *member* does not ordinarily recognize embedded lists in Common LISP. For example, *(member '(a) '((a) (b)))* returns *nil*. You can get *member* to recognize embedded lists in Common LISP, by adding the terms *:test 'equal* to the end of the function call, for example, *(member '(a) '((a) (b)) :test 'equal)*. These terms tell LISP to compare the first item to the list elements with an *equal* test rather than the usual *eql* test.

15.10 Now, write the helping function *match-prod*, which takes a production and returns a list of the actions of all its instantiations that successfully match working memory. Use the function *new-match* (from LISP Exercise 15.6 plus its helping functions from 15.7 and earlier exercises) to get a list of variable bindings for each successful match of the left-hand side of the production. For example, with our initial working memory,

(new-match '((father =x =y)))
returns (((=x George) (=y Mary)) ((=x George) (=y Fred))).

The function *match-prod* should go through this list and call the function *build-clause* to construct the clause that each instantiation would insert into working memory, and finally return the list of these constructed clauses.
For example, on the first cycle,

(match-prod '(p3 ((wife =x =y)) ==> (husband =y =x)))
returns ((p3 (husband Tom Mary))).

Make sure that *match-prod* returns all instantiations of a production. For example, if there are two *husband* clauses and neither of the two men are included in *male* clauses, then production *p7* would match with two different instantiations:

(match-prod '(p7 ((husband =x =y)) ==> (male =x)))
would return ((p7 (male George)) (p7 (male Tom))).

15.11 Now, we can write the function *apply-prods* to be used in *rule-interpreter*. This function should go through each production stored in the global variable *productions* and use *match-prod* to apply it to working memory. Recall that on the first cycle,

(apply-prods) returns
((p3 (husband Tom Mary)) (p5 (husband George Diane))
  (p6 (wife Diane Fred)) (p8 (female Mary)))).

Now that you have written the helping functions, type in the code for *conflict-resolution*, *perform-action*, and the top-level function *rule-interpreter* and try running the production system. You should get the trace presented earlier in this section. Try experimenting with adding some productions or using a different set of working-memory clauses.

Our earlier assessment of pattern matching essentially demonstrated that many comparisons are required to match even a single production to a relatively small set of working-memory clauses. As you can imagine, when we increase the size of the production set and working memory, our production system can take a very long time to run. However, it is possible to change our algorithm to make the production system much more efficient. In our simple algorithm, in each cycle each production is compared to the same working-memory clauses as in the previous cycle (plus one new clause). This algorithm makes the logic of production systems clear, but our system would run faster if we only compared each production to each working-memory clause one time and saved the results across cycles. In Chapter 16 we will introduce a much more efficient production-system algorithm that employs this idea.

Glossary   **clause**   An assertion, such as *(Mary is-mother-of Fred)*, that exists in a data base.

conflict resolution   The process of choosing a production instantiation from the conflict set to fire.

conflict set   The set of production instantiations that currently match and could fire.

cycle   A single pass in a production system consisting of matching productions, selecting one instantiation, and firing the instantiation.

firing a production   The process of updating working memory with the action produced by a production instantiation.

if–then rule   A rule that consists of a pattern that has the form: *if* a test (or tests) is satisfied, *then* perform a specified action (or actions).

instantiation   A representation of one way in which a pattern can match against a data base.

left-hand side   The part of an if–then rule that represents the pattern that must match against the data base.

merging   The process of finding consistent variable bindings when matching multiple pattern clauses to a data base.

pattern   A set of one or more clauses consisting of variables and/or constants that can be matched against clauses in a data base.

pattern constants   Terms in a pattern that must match to themselves in a data-base clause.

pattern matching   The process of matching a pattern against a data base.

pattern variables   Terms that can match to any constant in a data-base clause. By convention, in this text such terms are prefixed by =

production   An if–then rule in a production system.

production set   A set of production rules.

production system   A system consisting of a data base, a set of production rules, and a rule interpreter that applies the rules to the data base.

right-hand side   The part of an if–then rule that represents the inference to be made if the left-hand side matches the data base.

rule interpreter   A program that matches productions to a data base, selects productions to fire, and fires them.

variable bindings   A representation of the constants bound to variables in a pattern.

working memory   The data base in a production system.

Implementing a Complex System: An Efficient Production-System Interpreter

In Chapter 15 we discussed the concept of a production system and we wrote a rule interpreter. Recall that the algorithm for our rule interpreter was a direct translation into LISP of the production-system logic. In each cycle the rule interpreter matched a set of productions to the clauses in working memory and when it found a production whose conditions were satisfied, it fired that production. In the last section of that chapter, however, we observed that this straightforward algorithm is not very efficient. This algorithm is useful to demonstrate the logic of a production system, but we will want a much more efficient algorithm if we want to use production systems to perform reasoning tasks. In this chapter we will describe a much more efficient algorithm.

The algorithm that we will create is quite complex, and the set of functions we will write are equally complex. This illustrates the kind of program development that LISP programmers go through in real artificial-intelligence applications. This chapter is as much intended to illustrate the design of a complex artificial-intelligence system as it is to show how to implement production systems efficiently. This whole chapter is devoted to the step-by-step development of one program. Some of the code will be presented and explained in the text, while the rest will be assigned as exercises. The complete code to implement this production system will be given in the Answer Section. Functions that are required as answers to exercises will be marked as such.

A More Efficient Production System

The rule interpreter we wrote in the last chapter is inefficient because it performs many unnecessary operations. First, the same test clause may appear in multiple productions, and we wind up repeatedly matching the same test clause to the working-memory clauses. Second, in each cycle we start afresh matching our productions against all the clauses in working memory. As we enter each new cycle, however, all the working-memory clauses from the preceding cycle are carried over, while only one new clause is added. Thus most of the working-memory clauses we are matching were matched in the last cycle. Third, when we match a production against working memory a good deal of computation is required to merge test clauses and construct actions. Each time we match a production this computation is repeated. It is more efficient to have our program examine the productions before it begins matching, to determine which variables are repeated on the left-hand side and which appear on the right-hand side. Then the program can build LISP code for each production that will directly merge clauses and build actions.

In this chapter we will implement an alternative system, which has some of the features of the very efficient RETE pattern matcher developed for production systems by Forgy.*

The rule interpreter in this system does not start afresh in each cycle, matching all the productions against all the working-memory clauses. Instead, the rule interpreter processes only new working memory clauses in each cycle, storing information about the components of each clause. The rule interpreter checks to see if each new clause, in conjunction with the clauses entered earlier, completes a match to any productions. If so, then the instantiation is saved in a conflict set. This processing of new clauses is called entering clauses into the system. In the first cycle, all the initial working-memory clauses are

---

*This is described in Forgy C.L. RETE: A fast algorithm for the many pattern/many object pattern match problem. *Artificial Intelligence* 1982: *19*: 17–37. We will implement a slight variation and specialization of Forgy's algorithm. By greater abstraction, Forgy's algorithm achieves a considerable increase in generality and efficiency. However, the more concrete implementation here will illustrate the ideas of the RETE algorithm.

entered. In each succeeding cycle only one new clause is entered — the one that was added to working memory in the previous cycle.

After all the clauses have been entered in a cycle, one production in the conflict set is fired, and the remaining instantiations in the conflict set are saved. The instantiations that do not fire would turn up in the conflict set in the next cycle if the rule interpreter started matching again from scratch; so by saving those instantiations we can avoid duplicating all the matches that have already been performed. In the next cycle, the rule interpreter enters just one new clause and finds any instantiations that are completed by that clause. Those new instantiations are added to the conflict set saved from the previous cycle, and one instantiation in the conflict set is then fired and removed. If there are no instantiations in the conflict set after entering the new clause in a cycle (or after entering all the clauses in the first cycle) then there are no more inferences that can be drawn and execution terminates.

Here is the code for the top-level function in our production system:

```
(defun production-system ()
    (encode-productions)
    (rule-interpreter))
```

In writing this production system, we assume that the production set and working memory have the same format as in Chapter 15. Each clause will be a list containing a predicate, such as *mother*, followed by one argument or more. Each production will be a list with four components: the production name, the left-hand side condition, an arrow, and the right-hand side action. Before *production-system* starts the rule interpreter, however, the function *encode-productions* is called to preprocess the productions and store the information about the productions in a form that can be used efficiently. Then the function *rule-interpreter* is called. This function enters working-memory clauses into the system and fires productions until there are no more inferences to be drawn. Before we can describe the function *rule-interpreter*, we will need to describe the preprocessing that is done on the productions.

Encoding Productions

The function *encode-productions* performs a number of tasks that allow our production system to run more efficiently. First, the function assigns properties to each production name that store the predicates employed on the left-hand side of the production. For example, if we were encoding the production

```
(p1
  ((father =x =y)
   (wife =z =x))
  ==>
   (mother =z =y))
```

we would assign properties as follows:

```
(putprop 'p1 'father 'first)
(putprop 'p1 'wife 'second)
```

These properties indicate that the first test clause of the production
employs the predicate *father* and the second test clause of the production
employs the predicate *wife*. We will assume that each production employs
from one to three tests; if there were a third test, its predicate would be
assigned to the property *third*. The same properties, *first*, *second*, and *third* are
also assigned to the predicate; each time a predicate appears on the left-hand
side of a production in the first, second, or third clause, the function *encode-
productions* adds the name of the production to the corresponding property of
the predicate. Properties would be assigned as follows in encoding *p1*:

```
(putprop 'father (cons 'p1 (get 'father 'first)) 'first)
(putprop 'wife (cons 'p1 (get 'wife 'second)) 'second)
```

As you can see, predicates play a central role in storing information.
Setting up pointers between productions and predicates ahead of time allows
the rule interpreter to process working-memory clauses more efficiently. Each
time we enter a new clause into the system we can check what predicate it
employs and then retrieve the *first*, *second*, and *third* properties on the predicate
to find out what productions that new clause could match.

The function *encode-productions* assigns two other properties, *condition* and
action, to each production name. The property *condition* stores some LISP code
that determines whether the tests on the left-hand side of the production are
satisfied. The property *action* stores LISP code that can produce the appropriate
clause to be placed in working memory when the left-hand side is satisfied.
The code that is stored on each property is a *lambda* expression that is
constructed by *encode-productions*, based on the information contained in the
production set. We will *apply* the *lambda* expressions to the appropriate arguments when we need to execute it. As suggested in Chapter 15, the advantage
of writing specialized code for each production is that it can execute faster than
the equivalent general-purpose code.

After a production like *p1* has been processed by *encode-productions* our
final representation of the production will look like this:

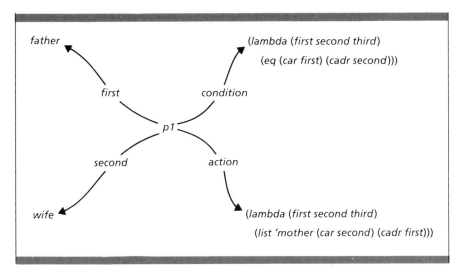

Figure 16.1

Here is the code for *encode-productions*:

```
(defun encode-productions ()
       (mapcar 'encode-a-production productions))
```

This function assumes that the production set is stored in the global variable *productions*. As you can see, *encode-productions* consists of a single function call that maps the function *encode-a-production* over the list of productions stored in *productions*.

Here is the code for the function *encode-a-production*:

```
(defun encode-a-production (production)
       (let ((name (car production))
             (condition (cadr production))
             (action (cadddr production)))
         (encode-condition condition name)
         (putprop name (build-action (mapcar 'cdr condition) action)
                  'action)))
```

This function accepts a single argument, which is a production. As you can see *encode-a-production* assigns the name, the left-hand side, and the right-hand side of the production to local variables, and then the function calls a helping function *encode-condition*. The function *encode-condition* builds the property pointers between the production and the predicates that appear on the left-hand side of the production, and it builds a *lambda* expression and stores it on the *condition* property of the production. Finally, *encode-a-production* calls the helping function *build-action* to construct the *lambda* expression that is assigned to the *action* property of the production. Here is the code for *encode-condition*:

```
(defun encode-condition (conditions production)
    (let (first second third)
        (setq first (car conditions))
        (update production (car first) 'first)
        (cond ((cdr conditions)
                (setq second (cadr conditions))
                (update production (car second) 'second)))
        (cond ((cddr conditions)
                (setq third (caddr conditions))
                (update production (car third) 'third)))
        (putprop production (build-condition (cdr first) (cdr second)
                                             (cdr third)) 'condition)))
```

This function takes two arguments, a list of test clauses and a production name. As you can see the function assigns the first test clause to the variable *first*, and then passes three arguments — the production name, the first-clause predicate, and the atom *first* — to the function *update*. The function *update* assigns the property *first* to the production with the first-clause predicate as its value. The function also updates the property *first* on the predicate, adding the production name to the list of productions stored there. Then *encode-a-production* checks for a second and a third test clause and if they exist, calls *update* accordingly. Finally, the function calls a helping function *build-condition* to construct the *lambda* expression that will determine if the left-hand side of the production has been satisfied. Before we discuss the function *build-condition* in more detail, let us define the function *update* as an exercise.

LISP Exercise

16.1 Define the helping function *update*. This function takes three arguments: a production name, a predicate, and the name of a property. This function should assign the property to the production with the predicate as the value of the property. The function should also add the production to the list of productions stored on the same property of the predicate.

Building Code to Detect Matches

To complete the code for *encode-condition* we need to define the function *build-condition*, which will construct a *lambda* expression that determines when the left-hand side of the production has been satisfied. Before we write the function *build-condition*, we need to specify more precisely what this *lambda* expression does. The *lambda* expression constructed for a production by *build-condition* will be called whenever the rule interpreter finds a set of working-memory clauses that match to the individual test clauses in the production. The *lambda* expression will check the set of clauses to see if it represents a consistent match to the production. For example, the clauses

(father George Donald)
(wife Mary George)

represent a consistent match to the pattern *((father =x =y) (wife =z =x))*. On the other hand, the clauses

(father George Donald)
(wife Alice John)

match the two test clauses of *p1* individually, but do not form a consistent match to *p1*. To match *p1* consistently, the first argument of the first clause must be identical to the second argument of the second clause, and that is not the case in this second example. This is the type of constraint that our *lambda* expression will check.

Here is the *lambda* expression that will be constructed for *p1*:

(lambda (first second third)
   (equal (car first) (cadr second)))

When the rule interpreter finds a set of working-memory clauses that match the test clauses in *p1*, the rule interpreter will *apply* this *lambda* expression to the arguments of those clauses. For example, suppose the rule interpreter finds these clauses in working memory.

(father George Donald)
(wife Mary George)

Then the rule interpreter will create the following list containing three sublists:

((George Donald) (Mary George) nil)

The first two sublists contain the arguments of the two working-memory clauses. Since *p1* only matches to two working memory clauses at a time, the third argument in this list is *nil*. Then the rule interpreter will *apply* the *lambda* expression to this list as follows:

(apply (get 'p1 'condition) '((George Donald) (Mary George) nil))

which is equivalent to

```
(apply '(lambda (first second third)
            (equal (car first) (cadr second)))
        '((George Donald) (Mary George) nil))
```

When this expression is evaluated, the three parameters of the *lambda* expression take on these bindings:

```
first = (George Donald)
second = (Mary George)
third = nil
```

As we stated earlier, to form a consistent match to *p1* the only constraint on the clauses is that the first argument in the first clause is identical to the second argument in the second clause. That is exactly what the *lambda* checks. If the *car* of the first argument is *equal* to the *cadr* of the second argument, the *lambda* expression returns *t*; otherwise, it returns *nil*.

Now let us consider the function *build-condition* more closely. This function accepts three lists as arguments, one for each possible test clause in a production. As you can see in the definition of *encode-condition*, each of the arguments is actually the *cdr* of the corresponding test clause. Thus each argument to *build-condition* is a list of just the clause arguments and not the predicate from the clause. If a production has only two test clauses, then the third argument to *build-condition* is *nil*. Similarly, if a production has just a single test clause, then the second and third arguments to *build-clause* are both *nil*. For example, since the left-hand side of the production *p1* contains two clauses,

```
((father =x =y)
 (wife =z =x))
```

the three arguments to *build-condition* for this production will be

```
(=x =y)
(=z =x)
nil
```

Here is the code for *build-condition*:

```
(defun build-condition (vars1 vars2 vars3)
    `(lambda (first second third) ,(build-test vars1 vars2 vars3)))
```

The function returns a list with three elements, which is a *lambda* expression. The first element in this list will be *lambda*, the second will be a parameter list *(first second third)*, and the third will be the body of the *lambda*, which is obtained by evaluating a call to the helping function *build-test*. This helping function is passed the three lists of test-clause arguments that were passed to *build-condition*. The function *build-test* compares the arguments in all possible pairs of the three lists. That is, it compares the arguments in the first and second clauses, the first and third clauses, and the second and third clauses. Whenever it finds the same variable in two clauses, it constructs an appropriate *equal* test that checks for that equality. In the case of our example, *build-test* determines that the variable =*x* appears in the first position of the first argument and in the second position of the second argument, and so it constructs the test

   (equal (car first) (cadr second))

This test can then be used in the *lambda* expression to check that two clauses that match the test clauses actually form a consistent match. The function *build-test* keeps a list of all the *equal* tests it constructs. If there is just one such test, as in our example, *build-test* returns that test. If there is more than one test in the list, *build-test* inserts *and* at the beginning of the list and returns the list. If there are no tests in the list, then *build-test* returns *t*.* Thus *(build-condition '((=x =y) '(=y =z) '(=z =w))* returns

      (lambda (first second third)
         (and (equal (cadr first) (car second))
            (equal (cadr second) (car third))))

and *(build-condition '(=x =y) nil nil)* returns

      (lambda (first second third)
         t)

Let us define *build-test* as an exercise.

LISP Exercise

16.2 Define the function *build-test*. This function accepts three arguments, which are lists. Each of these lists contains the arguments from the first, second, and third test clause of a production, respectively. The function returns a *lambda* expression that checks for consistent bindings of the variables in the clauses, as described above.

   In writing this function, you should define a helping function, which might be called *encode-pair*. This function should accept four arguments. Its first two arguments are lists that contain the arguments from two of the three test clauses. The second two arguments are atoms drawn from

---

*If there are no tests in the list, then any set of clauses that match the test clauses necessarily form a consistent match, so our *lambda* expression can simply return *t*.

the set *first*, *second*, *third*, that specify which clauses are being processed. This helping function should compare the arguments in the lists and if it finds the same variable in both clauses it should construct an appropriate *equal* test to check for that relationship. The function should return a list of all the tests it constructs in comparing the two clauses. If no variables appear in both clauses, the function should return *nil*.

For example:

(encode-pair '(=x) '(=y =x) 'first 'third)
returns (equal (car first) (cadr third)).

You may assume that all clauses have one or two arguments as in *(male =x)* and *(wife =y =x)* and that arguments are always variables.

Building Code to Perform Actions

Now we need to complete the code for the function *encode-a-production* by defining the function *build-action*. This function accepts two arguments. The first argument is a list of embedded lists containing the arguments for the test clauses in the production. In the case of *p1*, this list is *((=x =y) (=z =x))*. The second argument is the action clause of the production; in the case of *p1* this is *(mother =z =y)*. This function returns a *lambda* expression that will build a clause that can be inserted in working memory. In the case of *p1* the appropriate *lambda* expression is

(lambda (first second third)
  (list 'mother (car second) (cadr first)))

When the rule interpreter determines that the working memory-clauses *(father George Donald)* and *(wife Mary George)* form a consistent match to this production, the rule interpreter will *apply* this *lambda* expression to these clauses as follows:

(apply (get 'p1 'action) '((George Donald) (Mary George) nil))

which is equivalent to

(apply '(lambda (first second third)
       (list 'mother (car second) (cadr first)))
    '((George Donald) (Mary George) nil))

which returns

(mother Mary Donald)

16.3 To complete the function *encode-a-production*, define the helping function *build-action*, which builds the action associated with a production. This function accepts two arguments, as described above, and returns a *lambda* expression that will build a clause to be added to working memory. For example,

(build-action '((=x =y) (=z =x)) '(mother =z =y)) returns
(lambda (first second third) (list 'mother (car second) (cadr first))).

Hint: Note *(quote mother)* is equivalent to *'mother.*

Entering Clauses: The Rule Interpreter

We have now completed the code for *encode-productions* and can turn to the code for *rule-interpreter*. In each cycle, *rule-interpreter* will enter any new clauses in working memory into the system, add any new matching productions to the conflict set and fire one of the productions in the conflict set. This function will continue cycling until the conflict set is finally empty. The complex part of this function concerns the entering of new clauses. It is important to recognize that each time a new clause is entered, it may match to many different productions and can lead to multiple instantiations of the same production. Consider the following pair of productions and set of working-memory clauses.

```
(px ((father =x =y)
     (father =y =z))
 ==>
     (grandfather =x =z))

(py ((father =x =y)
     (brother =y =z))
 ==>
     (father =x =z))
```

working memory: *((father Fred Tom)*
(father George Bill)
(brother George Mary)
(brother George Alice))

After entering these four clauses, if we enter the additional clause *(father Tom George)* our matching process will yield two successful instantiations of both productions. Specifically,

production *px*

left-hand–side matches	right-hand–side action
(father Fred Tom) (father Tom George)	(grandfather Fred George)
(father Tom George) (father George Bill)	(grandfather Tom Bill)

production *py*

left-hand–side matches	right-hand–side action
(father Tom George) (brother George Mary)	(father Tom Mary)
(father Tom George) (brother George Alice)	(father Tom Alice)

Thus each time we enter a new clause from working memory, our task in the rule interpreter is to find all the new matches that are possible for each production.

Here is the code for *rule-interpreter*:

```
(defun rule-interpreter ()
     (let (choice)
          (do ((add-list database (cdr add-list))
               (conflict-set nil (append (enter-clause (car add-list))
                                         conflict-set)))
              ((and (null add-list)(null conflict-set)) database)
              (cond ((null add-list)
                 (setq choice (conflict-resolution conflict-set))
                 (perform-action choice)
                 (setq add-list (cdr choice))
                 (setq conflict-set (remove-repeats conflict-set
                                              (cadr choice))))))))

(defun conflict-resolution (conflict-set) (car conflict-set))

(defun perform-action (action)
     (print (cons 'firing action))
     (setq database (cons (cadr action) database)))
```

As you can see *rule-interpreter* is an iterative function that does not take any arguments. The function employs three local variables: *add-list*, *conflict-set*, and *choice*. The variable *add-list* holds the list of working-memory clauses that remain to be entered into the system. This variable is initialized to the value of the global variable *database*, which is assumed to hold a list of the initial working-memory clauses. The variable *conflict-set* holds a list of production instantiations that remain to be fired. This variable is initialized to *nil*, since initially no matching productions have been found. The variable *choice* is used to hold the production selected by *conflict-resolution*.

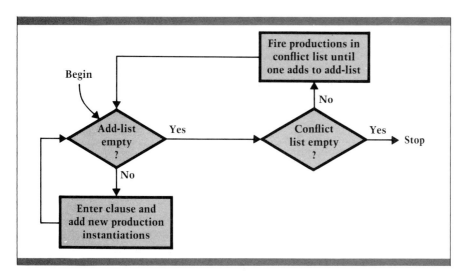

Figure 16.2

The diagram above illustrates the sequence of actions performed by this function. On each pass through the loop, *rule-interpreter* performs the following actions in the variable updates. The function calls *enter-clause* to enter the first working-memory clause in *add-list* into the system and *cdrs add-list* to delete that clause from *add-list*. The function *enter-clause* returns a list of all the new production matches it finds and that list of instantiations is added to the variable *conflict-set*.

The loop exit test checks to see if both *add-list* and *conflict-set* are empty. If so, then there are no more clauses to enter and no more productions to fire, so execution terminates and the final value of *database* is returned. Otherwise, a second test is performed in the body of the loop. If *add-list* is empty, then there are no more working-memory clauses to be entered into the system, so the function *conflict-resolution* is called to find an instantiation in the conflict set to fire. The function uses the same simple conflict resolution principle as *rule-interpreter* from Chapter 15. It also uses the same code for *perform-action*, which prints out a message and adds a clause to *database*. The instantiation that is selected is removed from *conflict-set* and the clause that the instantiation adds to working memory is assigned to the variable *add-list*. In the next pass through the loop, this new clause is entered into the system just as the original clauses were entered.

Let us consider the function *enter-clause* now. This function accepts a working-memory clause as an argument and performs two tasks. First, *enter-clause* adds a list containing the clause arguments to a property of the predicate called *bindings*. The *bindings* property for any predicate contains a record of all the working-memory clauses containing the predicate that have been entered into the system. For example, after the following working-memory clauses have been entered

```
(mother Alice Ellen)
(mother Alice George)
```

the function call *(get 'mother 'bindings)* would return

```
((Alice George) (Alice Ellen))
```

After storing the clause arguments on the *bindings* property, the function *enter-clause* checks to see if the new clause completes a match to any productions. Recall that every predicate has three properties, *first*, *second*, and *third*, which store lists of all the productions in which the predicate appears. The function *enter-clause* accesses these three lists and it accesses all the clauses that have already been entered into the system that match to the productions in these lists. Then the function finds all the complete instantiations that can be formed by adding the new working-memory clause to these previously entered clauses. Here is the code for *enter-clause*:

```
(defun enter-clause (clause)
       (let ((pred (car clause))
             (args (cdr clause)))
         (putprop pred (cons args (get pred 'bindings)) 'bindings)
         (append
              (mapcan #'(lambda (prod) (enter-first args prod))
                  (get pred 'first))
              (mapcan #'(lambda (prod) (enter-second args prod))
                  (get pred 'second))
              (mapcan #'(lambda (prod) (enter-third args prod))
                  (get pred 'third)))))
```

As you can see the function accepts one argument, which is a working-memory clause, and stores the arguments of the clause on the *bindings* property of the predicate. Then *enter-clause* creates a list of new instantiations to add to the conflict set by appending the results of three calls to *mapcan*.

Let us consider the first *mapcan* in more detail. This *mapcan* maps a *lambda* expression consisting of a call to *enter-first* over a list returned by the call *(get predicate 'first)*. The local variable *pred* holds the predicate of the new working-memory clause, so *(get pred 'first)* returns a list of all the productions in the system in which that predicate appears in the first test clause. The function *enter-first* takes two arguments — the list of arguments from the new working-memory clause — and a production name and returns a list of all instantiations of the production that can be completed with the addition of the new clause. Thus the *mapcan* returns a list of all instantiations of the productions stored on the property *first* that are completed by the new working-memory clause. The second and third *mapcan*s perform the same task for productions in which the predicate appears in the second test clause and for productions in which the predicate appears in the third test clause. Finally, *enter-clause append*s the results of these three *mapcan*s and returns the resulting list, which is appended to the conflict set. Given our example above, the function call *(enter-clause '(father Tom George))* would return the list

```
((px (grandfather Fred George))
 (px (grandfather Tom Bill))
 (py (father Tom Mary))
 (py (father Tom Alice)))
```

Let us now consider the code for *enter-first*.

```
(defun enter-first (args prod)
        (mapcan #'(lambda (x) (match-and-execute x prod))
                (cross-product (list args)
                               (clauses prod 'second)
                               (clauses prod 'third))))

(defun clauses (prod position)
        (or (get (get prod position) 'bindings) (list nil)))

(defun cross-product (lis1 lis2 lis3)
        (mapcan #'(lambda (x)
                    (mapcan #'(lambda (y)
                                (mapcar #'(lambda (z) (list x y z)) lis3))
                            lis2))
                lis1))
```

The function *enter-first* accepts two arguments — the first is a list of arguments from a working-memory clause and the second is a production name. This function calls a helping function *clauses* twice to obtain a list of previously entered working-memory clauses that match the predicate of the second test clause in the production and a list of those that match the third test clause. As you can see, *clauses* accepts a production name and a position as arguments. This function accesses the property on the production that stores the predicate from the test clause of the production in the specified position. Then the function accesses the *bindings* property of that predicate and returns its value, unless the value is *nil*. As discussed earlier, the *bindings* property stores a list of previously entered working-memory clauses that contain the predicate. Each working-memory clause is represented in the list as a sublist containing just the arguments from the clause. If there are no previous clauses that contain this predicate, the function returns *(nil)*. For instance, if *enter-first* were called with arguments *(Tom George)* and *py*, *(clauses 'py 'second)* might return *((George Mary) (George Alice))* and *(clauses 'py 'third)* might return *(nil)*.

At that point *cross-product* is called with three arguments — a list of the list of new clause arguments, and the results of two calls to *clauses*. The function *cross-product* constructs every possible three-item list that can be formed taking one item from the first list, one from the second, and one from the third. Thus, the call

> *(cross-product '((Tom George))'((George Mary) (George Alice)) '(nil))*

would return

> *(((Tom George) (George Mary) nil)*
> *((Tom George) (George Alice) nil))*

The function *enter-first* maps a helping function, *match-and-execute*, over this list returned by *cross-product*. The function *match-and-execute* checks to see if a set of working-memory clauses forms a consistent match to a production. The function *match-and-execute* accepts two arguments. The second argument is the name of a production and the first is a list of three lists, each of which represents a working-memory clause. The first embedded list contains the arguments from the clause currently being entered, the second embedded list contains arguments from a previous clause that matches the second test clause in the production, and the third embedded list contains arguments from a previous clause that matches to the third test clause in the production. The function *match-and-execute* accesses the *lambda* expression stored on the *condition* property of the production and applies it to the list of working-memory arguments. If the *lambda* expression returns *t*, then the working-memory clauses represent a consistent match. In that event, *match-and-execute* accesses the *lambda* expression stored on the *action* property of the production and applies it to the list of working-memory arguments in order to build a new clause. Finally, *match-and-execute* returns a list containing the production name and the new clause that has been constructed. If the list of working-memory arguments does not represent a consistent match to the production, then *match-and-execute* returns *nil*.

Let us consider an example; suppose we have the following production:

> *(px ((father =x =y)*
> *(father =y =z))*
> *= =>*
> *(grandfather =x =z))*

When this production is processed by *encode-productions*, the following *lambda* expression is stored on the *condition* property of *px*:

> (lambda (first second third)
>   (equal (cadr first) (car second)))

The following *lambda* expression is stored on the *action* property of the production:

> (lambda (first second third)
>   (list 'grandfather (car first) (cadr second)))

Then if *encode-clause* called

> (match-and-execute '((Fred Tom) (Tom George) nil) 'px)

the first *lambda* expression above would be retrieved from the *condition* property of *px* and applied to the list *((Fred Tom) (Tom George) nil)*. The *equal* test would return *t*, since the second element in the first sublist is equal to the first element in the second embedded list. As a result, the second *lambda* expression above would be retrieved from the *action* property of *px*. This *lambda* expression would be applied to the list of working-memory arguments, yielding the new clause *(grandfather Fred George)*. Thus *match-and-execute* would return the list *((px (grandfather Fred George)))*. Note *match-and-execute* returns a list of a list for purposes of the appending that will be done by *mapcan* in *enter-first*.

LISP Exercises

16.4 Define the function *match-and-execute*. To review, *match-and-execute* takes two arguments. The first is a list of arguments from three working-memory clauses and the second is the name of a production. The function checks to see if the working-memory clauses represent a consistent match to the production. If so, *match-and-execute* performs the action specified by the production. That is, the function builds a new clause and returns a doubly embedded list with two elements — the production name and the new clause. For example,

> (match-and-execute '((Fred Tom) (Tom George) nil) 'px)
>   returns ((px (grandfather Fred George))).

If the working-memory clauses do not represent a consistent match, *match-and-execute* returns *nil*. The appending done by *mapcan* in *enter-first* will delete these *nil*s. A final complication is that *match-and-execute* must check to make sure that the action created is not already in the data base. If it is, *match-and-execute* should return *nil*.

16.5 Define the functions *enter-second* and *enter-third*.

In this chapter we have implemented an efficient algorithm for a production system. Now that we have finished writing the code you should make up some productions rules and create a working memory and try the program. (The complete code for the program can be found in the Answer Section.) We have made some simplifying assumptions in writing this code. For example, we have assumed that no production will have more than three tests and we have assumed that each production will have a single action. However, we can generalize this algorithm without much difficulty if we wish to relax these assumptions. There are many ways in which we can make the production system more complex. For example, we frequently need to include productions that can remove clauses from working memory rather than adding them. That poses more of a problem for our algorithm, since we can no longer assume that any instantiation in the conflict set in one cycle will be in it again in the next cycle.

Conclusion

You have now completed your introduction to LISP and have gotten to the point where you have seen how a relatively complex system can be built. You should now try to make LISP part of your problem-solving repertoire by using it to help you solve whatever tasks you face — calculations, sorting of lists, or artificial-intelligence applications. LISP is a general programming language and can be used for any applications that other languages can.

If you want to use LISP for its special artificial-intelligence applications, you are strongly advised to learn more about artificial-intelligence applications, either through a textbook or a course. Among the things you need to learn more about are issues concerned with data structures, artificial-intelligence algorithms, and efficiency. One of the efficiency issues we have ignored is use of compilation to speed up computation. This varies a great deal from system to system, but you should inquire how to compile LISP code on your system. Another efficiency issue to become familiar with is the relative efficiency of various functions — e.g., *equal* versus *eql*. Again, consult the specifics of the documentation for your system. There are a great many textbooks and reference books on artificial intelligence. Some are listed below.

Barr A., Cohen P.R., Feigenbaum E.A., eds. (1981–1982) *The Handbook of Artificial Intelligence*, vols. 1–3. Los Altos, Calif. William Kaufmann.

Boden M. (1977) *Artificial Intelligence and Natural Man*. New York: Basic Books.

Charniak E., McDermott D. (1985) *Introduction to Artificial Intelligence*. Reading, Mass.: Addison–Wesley.

Nilsson N.J. (1980) *Principles of Artificial Intelligence*. Palo Alto, Ca.: Tioga.

Rich E. (1983) *Artificial Intelligence*. New York: McGraw–Hill.

Winston P.H. (1984) *Artificial Intelligence, 2nd ed.* Reading, Mass.: Addison–Wesley.

Winston P.H., Horn B.K.P. (1984) *LISP, 2nd ed.* Reading, Mass.: Addison–Wesley.

Answers to Exercises

Chapter 1

1.1 *(+ 3 2)*
1.2 *(/ 6 2)*
1.3 *(* 5 3 2)*
1.4 *(* (− 3 2) 5)*
1.5 *(/ (+ 60 40) 4)*
1.6 4, 5, 1, 3, 3, 7, 3, 0
1.7   i) No
    ii) No
1.8   i) *(a (b c))*
    ii) *d*
   iii) *(e (f (g)) (i j))*
   iv) *(e (f (g)) (i j))*
    v) 2
   vi) *(f (g))*

1.9 *(car '(c d e))*
1.10 *(cdr '(1 2 c))*
1.11 *(cons 'c '(e f))*
1.12 *(list '(3 2) '(b c))*
1.13 *(cons '(bike feet) '(car bus))*
1.14 *(+ (car '(4 3)) 2)*
1.15 *(car (cdr '(horse dog cat)))*
1.16 i) yes
  ii) no
  iii) no
  iv) yes
  v) no
  vi) yes
    For example,

    =⟩ *(setq x 'x)*
    x
    =⟩ *x*
    x

  vii) Yes
    For example,

    =⟩ *(setq x '(a b c))*
    (a b c)
    =⟩ *(setq y '(a b c))*
    (a b c)

1.17 *(setq x '(c (d e)))*
1.18 *(setq y (list 'a 'b))*
1.19 *(list 'd (car (cdr y)))*
   or
   (cons 'd (cdr y))
1.20 a. *(setq num 4)*
   b. *(setq num (+ num 1))*
   c. *(setq w '(a b c))*
   d. *(cons num (cdr w))*
1.21 a. *(cons (car x) y)*
   b. *(setq y (cons (car x) y))*
1.22 a. *(setq neworder '(coke pepsi))*
   b. *(setq neworder (list (car (cdr neworder)) (car neworder)))*
1.23 *(setq z (/ 18 (* 3 3)))*

1.24 a. *(setq data '(5 6))*
or
(setq data (list 5 6))
  b. *(+ 10 (car data))*

Chapter 2

2.1 i) There are two parameters: *item, oldlist*
  ii) There are two arguments: *'feet, units*
  iii) *'feet* evaluates to *feet*
    units evaluates to *(inches yards miles)*
  iv) a) The first parameter, *item* is assigned the value of the first argument: *feet*
    The second parameter, *oldlist*, is assigned the value of the second argument: *(inches yards miles)*
   b) *(car oldlist)* evaluates to *inches*
   c) *(cons item (cdr oldlist))* evaluates to *(feet yards miles)*
   d) *(cons (car oldlist) (cons item (cdr oldlist)))* evaluates to *(inches feet yards miles)*
   e) The call to *insert-second* returns *(inches feet yards miles)*.

2.2 *(defun first-elem (lis)*
    (car lis))
2.3 *(defun second-elem (lis)*
    (car (cdr lis)))
2.4 *(defun replace-first (item lis)*
    (cons item (cdr lis)))
2.5 *(defun ftoc (temp)*
    (/ (− temp 32) 1.8))
2.6 *(defun sqr (side)*
    (list (side 4) (* side side)))*
2.7 *(defun listone (item)*
    (cons item nil))
2.8 *(defun back (lis)*
    (append (reverse lis) (reverse lis)))
2.9 *(defun ends (lis)*
    (list (car lis) (car (reverse lis))))

or

(defun ends (lis)
    (list (car lis) (car (last lis))))

or
```
(defun ends (lis)
    (cons (car lis) (last lis)))
```
2.10 *(defun pal (lis)*
       (append lis (reverse lis)))
2.11 (a) *(defun snoc (item lis)*
          (append lis (list item)))
      (b) *(defun snoc (item lis)*
           (reverse (cons item (reverse lis))))
2.12 *(defun rotater (lis)*
        (append (last lis) (reverse (cdr (reverse lis)))))

or
```
(defun rotater (lis)
    (cons (car (reverse lis)) (reverse (cdr (reverse lis)))))
```

or
```
(defun rotater (lis)
    (cons (car (last lis)) (reverse (cdr (reverse lis)))))
```

Chapter 3
General comments

(a) Wherever the answer includes an "equal" test, the arguments could be in either order.

(b) Any occurrence of (< x y) could also be rewritten as (> y x). This is also true for >.

3.1 *(defun compare (num1 num2)*
       (> (+ num1 10) (num2 2)))*
3.2 *(defun palp (lis)*
       (equal lis (reverse lis)))
3.3 *(defun numline (item)*
       (list (zerop item) (< item 0)))
3.4 *(defun carlis (object)*
       (cond ((null object) nil)
             ((atom object) object)
             (t (car object))))

or
```
(defun carlis (object)
    (cond ((atom object) object)
          (t (car object))))
```

3.5 *(defun checktemp (temp)*
　　(cond ((> temp hightemp) 'hot)
　　　　((< temp lowtemp) 'cold)
　　　　(t 'medium)))

The order of the first two tests here does not matter, but the "medium" case must be last because there is no simple way to test whether *temp* is between *lowtemp* and *hightemp* using the functions you have learned so far.

3.6 *(defun make-list (item)*
　　(cond ((null item) nil)
　　　　((listp item) item)
　　　　(t (list item))))

Here again the code is clearer with three tests, but the first test could be taken out, since it is handled by the *listp* test. With three tests, the *null* must come before an *atom* test, otherwise *(make-list nil)* would be *(nil)* instead of *nil*.

3.7 *(defun classify (argument)*
　　(cond ((null argument) nil)
　　　　((listp argument) 'list)
　　　　((numberp argument) 'number)
　　　　(t 'atom)))

The *null* test must precede the *listp* test, and the *null* and *numberp* tests must precede the test for non-numeric atoms, which would employ the predicate *atom* if it were not in the "else" case.

3.8 *(defun numtype (num)*
　　(cond ((> num 0) 'positive)
　　　　((zerop num) 'zero)
　　　　(t 'negative)))

These three cases could be in any order. The test for the "negative" case is *(< num 0)* if you want to put one of the other cases last.

3.9 *(defun lisnump (argument)*
　　(or (numberp argument) (listp argument)))

3.10 *(defun samesign (num1 num2)*
　　(or (and (> num1 0) (> num2 0))
　　　　(and (> 0 num1) (> 0 num2))
　　　　(and (zerop num1) (zerop num2))))

The three "and" cases can be placed in any order.

3.11 *(defun classify-sentence (s)*
　　(cond ((or (equal (car s) 'why) (equal (car s) 'how)) 'question)
　　　　((and (member 'was s) (member 'by s)) 'passive)
　　　　(t 'active)))

3.12 *(defun my-not (val)*
(cond (val nil)
(t t)))

3.13 *(defun my-or (val1 val2)*
(cond (val1 val1)
(val2 val2)
(t nil)))

3.14 *(defun my-and (val1 val2)*
(cond (val1 (cond (val2 val2)
(t nil)))
(t nil)))

3.15 *(defun addbag (item bag)*
(cond ((not (member item bag)) (cons item bag))
(t bag)))
The two cases can be reversed.

3.16 *(defun safediv (num1 num2)*
(and (numberp num1)
(numberp num2)
(not (zerop num2))
(/ num1 num2)))
The first two tests could be reordered.

3.17 *(defun successor (target list)*
(cond ((not (member target list)) 'not-there)
((equal (last list) (member target list)) 'no-successor)
(t (car (cdr (member target list))))))

3.18 *(defun addit (item lis)*
(cond ((null item) lis)
((member item lis) 'found)
(t (append lis (list item)))))
The *null* test must come first. Instead of *(append lis (list item))*, you could also code the action as *(reverse (cons item (reverse lis)))*.

3.19 *(defun combine (x y)*
(cond ((or (null x) (null y)) nil)
((and (numberp x) (numberp y)) (+ x y))
((and (atom x) (atom y)) (list x y))
((and (listp x) (listp y)) (append x y))
((listp x) (cons y x))
(t (cons x y))))

Chapter 4

4.1 *(defun eqends (lis)*
      (cond ((null lis) nil)
            ((equal (car lis) (lastitem lis)) t)
            (t nil)))

 (defun lastitem (wholelist)
      (car (reverse wholelist)))

 or
 (defun lastitem (wholelist)
      (car (last wholelist)))

4.2 *(defun trim (lis)*
      (removelast (cdr lis)))

 or
 (defun trim (lis)
      (cdr (removelast lis)))

 (defun removelast (lis2)
      (reverse (cdr (reverse lis2))))

4.3 *(defun switch (lis1 lis2)*
      (append (removelast lis1) (last lis2)))

4.4 *(defun endsp (target lis)*
      (or (equal target (car lis))
          (equal target (lastitem lis))))

4.5 *(defun radius (x y)*
      (sqrt (+ (sqr x) (sqr y))))

 (defun sqr (num)
      (num num))*

4.6 *(defun evendiv (x y)*
      (cond ((< x y) (gooddiv y x))
            (t (gooddiv x y))))

 (defun gooddiv (num1 num2)
      (zerop (mod num1 num2)))

4.7 *(defun rightp (side1 side2 side3)*
      (< (abs (− (sumsq side1 side2) (sqr side3)))
         (pct 2 (sqr side3))))
 (defun sumsq (num1 num2)
      (+ (sqr num1) (sqr num2)))

 (defun pct (percentage base)
      ((/ percentage 100) base))*

Note: There are alternative ways to write *pct*, e.g., *(* .01 percentage base)*. Any code that in effect computes the product of *percentage* and *base* divided by 100 would be fine.

4.8 *(defun compute (equ)*
   (cond ((equal (cadr equ) '+) (+ (car equ) (caddr equ)))
      ((equal (cadr equ) '−) (− (car equ) (caddr equ)))
      ((equal (cadr equ) '*) (* (car equ) (caddr equ)))
      (t (/ (car equ) (caddr equ)))))

These four cases can appear in any order.

4.9 *(defun compound-sentence (s1 s2)*
   (and (equal (subject s1)
         (subject s2))
      (make-compound s1 s2)))

(defun subject (sentence)
   (cadar sentence))

(defun make-compound (sen1 sen2)
   (cond ((equal (cadr sen1) 1)
         (append (car sen1) '(and) (predicate sen2)))
      (t (append (car sen2) '(and) (predicate sen1)))))

(defun predicate (sentence)
   (cddar sentence))

4.10 *(defun winner (puzzle)*
   (winner-help (car puzzle) (cadr puzzle) (caddr puzzle)))

(defun winner-help (row1 row2 row3)
   (or (rows row1 row2 row3)
      (columns row1 row2 row3)
      (diagonals row1 row2 row3)))

(defun rows (row1 row2 row3)
   (or (check (car row1) (cadr row1) (caddr row1))
      (check (car row2) (cadr row2) (caddr row2))
      (check (car row3) (cadr row3) (caddr row3))))

(defun columns (row1 row2 row3)
   (or (check (car row1) (car row2) (car row3))
      (check (cadr row1) (cadr row2) (cadr row3))
      (check (caddr row1) (caddr row2) (caddr row3))))

```
(defun diagonals (row1 row2 row3)
   (or (check (car row1) (cadr row2) (caddr row3))
       (check (caddr row1) (cadr row2) (car row3))))

(defun check (cell1 cell2 cell3)
   (or (check-help cell1 cell2 cell3 'o)
       (check-help cell1 cell2 cell3 'x)))

(defun check-help (cell1 cell2 cell3 letter)
   (and (equal cell1 letter)
        (equal cell2 letter)
        (equal cell3 letter)
        letter))
```

4.11 The code for *add-one-pair* contains bugs. The correct code is

```
(defun add-one-pair (pair)
   (cond ((and (numberp (car pair)) (numberp (cadr pair)))
          (+ (car pair) (cadr pair)))
         (t 0)))
```

4.12 The functions *first-class*, *second-class*, and *third-class* all contain bugs. The correct code for each is

```
(defun first-class (sch) (cadr sch))
```

```
(defun second-class (sch) (caddr sch))
```

```
(defun third-class (sch) (car (last sch)))
```

Chapter 5

5.1
```
(defun read-aver-3 ()
   (/ (+ (read) (read) (read)) 3))
```
5.2
```
(defun read-combine (arg)
   (cons (car arg) (cdr (read))))
```
5.3
```
(defun print-pal (list1 list2)
   (print (append list1 (reverse list1)))
   (print (append list2 (reverse list2)))
   (print (append (append list1 list2)
                  (reverse (append list1 list2)))))
```
5.4
```
(defun read-check (arg)
   (print '(type an expression))
   (and (member (read) arg) t))
```

```
5.5 (defun print-nums ()
        (let (inp1 inp2)
            (print '(type two numbers))
            (setq inp1 (read))
            (setq inp2 (read))
            (print inp2)
            (print inp1)
            (print (+ inp1 inp2))))
5.6 (defun read-print (arg)
        (let (var)
            (print '(type an input))
            (print (read))
            (print '(type another input))
            (setq var (read))
            (print (list arg var))))
5.7 (defun longer-list (lis1 lis2)
        (let ((len1 (length lis1)) (len2 (length lis2)))
            (cond ((> len1 len2) lis1)
                  ((< len1 len2) lis2)
                  (t 'equal))))
5.8 (defun return-list ()
        (let ((input (read)))
            (cond ((listp input) input)
                  (t (list input)))))
5.9 (defun right-triangle (hyp side)
        (prog (side3)
            (cond ((> side hyp) (return 'impossible)))
            (setq side3 (sqrt (- (square hyp) (square side))))
            (print (list hyp side side3))
            (print (+ hyp side side3))))

    (defun square (num)
        (* num num))
5.10 (defun mean3 nil
        (let (sum)
            (print '(Type three numbers))
            (setq sum (read))
            (setq sum (+ sum (read)))
            (setq sum (+ sum (read)))
            (print sum)
            (print (/ sum 3))))
```

5.11 ```
(defun greet1 ()
    (let (name color)
        (princ "What is your name: ")
        (setq name (read))
        (terpri)
        (princ "Well, ")
        (princ name)
        (princ ", what is your favorite color: ")
        (setq color (read))
        (terpri)
        (princ "What a coincidence, ")
        (princ name)
        (princ "! ")
        (princ color)
        (princ " is my favorite color too.")))
```

**5.12**  ```
(defun tic-out (position)
    (printline (car position))
    (printline (cadr position))
    (printline (caddr position)))

(defun printline (line)
    (printchar (car line))
    (printchar (cadr line))
    (printchar (caddr line))
    (terpri))

(defun printchar (char)
    (cond ((null char) (princ "_"))
          (t (princ char))))
```

5.13 ```
(defun play-tic-tac-toe ()
    (let (ans)
        (princ "Do you want to be X or O: ")
        (setq ans (read))
        (terpri)
        (cond ((equal ans 'X) (play-role 'x 'o))
              ((equal ans 'O) (play-role 'o 'x))
              (t (princ "Bad answer") (terpri)))))
```
```

```
(defun play-role (user program)
    (prog (ans position)
        (setq position '((nil nil nil)(nil nil nil)(nil nil nil)))
        (setq position (get-input user position))
        (setq position (make-move program position))
        (setq position (get-input user position))
        (setq position (make-move program position))
        (setq position (get-input user position))
        (cond ((winner position) (return (congratulations))))
        (setq position (make-move program position))
        (cond ((winner position) (return (brag))))
        (setq position (get-input user position))
        (cond ((winner position) (return (congratulations))))
        (setq position (make-move program position))
        (cond ((winner position) (return (brag))))
        (setq position (get-input user position))
        (cond ((winner position) (return (congratulations))))
        (princ "Oh well. Maybe next time.")
        (terpri)))

(defun get-input (symbol position)
    (let (row column newposition)
        (princ "Enter the number of the row and then the column: ")
        (setq row (read))
        (setq column (read))
        (setq newposition (enter symbol row column position))
        (terpri)
        (tic-out newposition)
        (terpri)
        newposition))

(defun enter (symbol row column position)
    (cond ((equal row 1)
            (cons (enter-row symbol column (car position))
                (cdr position)))
        ((equal row 2)
            (list (car position)
                (enter-row symbol column (cadr position))
                (caddr position)))
        (t (list (car position) (cadr position)
                (enter-row symbol column (caddr position))))))
```

```
(defun enter-row (symbol column line)
    (cond ((equal column 1) (cons symbol (cdr line)))
          ((equal column 2) (list (car line) symbol (caddr line)))
          (t (list (car line) (cadr line) symbol))))
(defun congratulations ()
    (princ "Congratulations! You have won.")
    (terpri))

(defun brag ()
    (princ "HaHa! I won.")
    (terpri))

(defun make-move (symbol position)
    (let (newposition)
        (princ "Now I'll make my move:")
        (terpri)
        (setq newposition (choose-move symbol position))
        (tic-out newposition)
        (terpri)
        newposition))

(defun choose-move (symbol position)
    (cond ((null (cadr (cadr position))) (enter symbol 2 2 position))
          ((null (caar position)) (enter symbol 1 1 position))
          ((null (caddr (caddr position))) (enter symbol 3 3 position))
          ((null (caddr (car position))) (enter symbol 1 3 position))
          ((null (car (caddr position))) (enter symbol 3 1 position))
          ((null (cadr (car position))) (enter symbol 1 2 position))
          ((null (car (cadr position))) (enter symbol 2 1 position))
          ((null (caddr (car position))) (enter symbol 2 3 position))
          ((null (cadr (caddr position))) (enter symbol 3 2 position))))
```

Chapter 6

6.1
```
(defun factorial (num)
    (let ((counter 0) (product 1))
        (loop
            (cond ((equal counter num) (return product)))
            (setq counter (1+ counter))
            (setq product (* counter product)))))
```

6.2 Answers to questions about *int-multiply*:
  (a) *count*
  (b) *result*
  (c) *6*
  (d) The variable *count* is incremented by 1 on each pass through the loop.
  (e) 3 is added to the previous value of *result* on each pass through the loop.
  (f) None. The function will return *0* the first time the exit test is executed, without executing any variable updates in the loop.

6.3 *(defun num-sum (top)*
      (let ((count 0) (sum 0))
        (loop
          (cond ((equal count top) (return sum)))
          (setq count (1+ count))
          (princ "Enter the next number: ")
          (setq sum (+ (read) sum)))))

6.4 *(defun nth-item (n lis)*
      (let ((count 1))
        (loop
          (cond ((equal count n) (return (car lis))))
          (setq count (1+ count))
          (setq lis (cdr lis)))))

6.5 *(defun create-list (top)*
      (let ((counter top) (list-of-nums (list top)))
        (loop
          (cond ((equal counter 1) (return list-of-nums)))
          (setq counter (1- counter))
          (setq list-of-nums (cons counter list-of-nums)))))

6.6 *(defun add-negs (bottom)*
      (let ((count −1) (sum −1))
        (loop
          (cond ((equal count bottom) (return sum)))
          (setq count (1- count))
          (setq sum (+ count sum)))))

6.7 *(defun next-prime (start)*
      (let ((count start))
        (loop
          (cond ((primep count) (return count)))
          (setq count (1+ count)))))

6.8 *(defun add-threes (num)*
        (let ((count 0) (sum 0))
            (loop
                (cond ((> (+ count 3) num)
                        (return sum)))
                (setq count (+ count 3))
                (setq sum (+ count sum)))))
6.9 *(defun read-square ()*
        (let (item)
            (loop
                (princ "Enter the next number: ")
                (setq item (read))
                (cond ((not (numberp item)) (return 'done)))
                (print (square item)))))
    (defun square (num)
        (* num num))
6.10 *(defun read-sum ()*
        (let ((input) (sum 0))
            (loop
                (princ "Enter the next number: ")
                (setq input (read))
                (cond ((not (numberp input)) (return sum)))
                (setq sum (+ input sum)))))
In Problems 6.9, 6.10, 6.11, 6.12, and 6.13, the control variable could be
initialized to *nil* instead of the more concise answer given, if you wanted
to have lists of explicit variable–value pairs.
6.11 *(defun running-list ()*
        (let ((input) (lis nil))
            (loop
                (princ "Enter the next item for the list: ")
                (setq input (read))
                (cond ((numberp input) (return lis)))
                (setq lis (append lis (list input)))
                (print lis))))
6.12 *(defun diff-quot (constant)*
        (let (number)
            (loop
                (princ "Type a number: ")
                (setq number (read))
                (cond ((not (numberp number)) (return 'done)))
                (print (− constant number))
                (print (/ constant number)))))

6.13 *(defun withdrawals (balance)*
    (let ((amount) (totwith 0))
       (loop
          (princ "Type the next withdrawal: ")
          (setq amount (read))
          (cond ((equal amount 'statement)
               (return (list totwith (− balance totwith)))))
          (setq totwith (+ totwith amount)))))

Chapter 7

7.1 *(defun fact (n)*
    (cond ((zerop n) 1)
       (t (* n (fact (1− n))))))
7.2 *(defun power (m n)*
    (cond ((zerop n) 1)
       (t (* m (power m (1− n))))))
7.3 *(defun listnums (n)*
    (cond ((zerop n) nil)
       (t (cons n (listnums (1− n))))))
7.4 *(defun sortnums (n)*
    (cond ((zerop n) '(0))
       ((oddp n) (cons n (sortnums (1− n))))
       (t (append (sortnums (1− n)) (list n)))))
7.5 *(defun primep (n)*
    (check-divisions n (round (sqrt n))))

    (defun check-divisions (x count)
       (cond ((equal count 1) t)
         ((zerop (mod x count)) nil)
         (t (check-divisions x (1− count)))))
Make sure you understand why the first terminating case checks for 1, and not 0.
7.6 *(defun new-length (lis)*
    (cond ((null lis) 0)
       (t (1+ (new-length (cdr lis))))))
7.7 *(defun negnums (lis)*
    (cond ((null lis) nil)
       ((< (car lis) 0) (cons (car lis) (negnums (cdr lis))))
       (t (negnums (cdr lis)))))

7.8 *(defun greaternum (lis num)*
  (cond ((null lis) num)
    ((> (car lis) num) (car lis))
    (t (greaternum (cdr lis) num))))

7.9 *(defun add1nums (lis)*
  (cond ((null lis) nil)
    ((numberp (car lis)) (cons (1+ (car lis)) (add1nums (cdr lis))))
    (t (add1nums (cdr lis)))))

7.10 *(defun intersect (lis1 lis2)*
  (cond ((null lis1) nil)
    ((member (car lis1) lis2)
     (cons (car lis1) (intersect (cdr lis1) lis2)))
    (t (intersect (cdr lis1) lis2))))

7.11 *(defun carlist (lis)*
  (cond ((null lis) nil)
    (t (cons (car (car lis)) (carlist (cdr lis))))))

7.12 *(defun union (lis1 lis2)*
  (cond ((null lis1) lis2)
    ((member (car lis1) lis2) (union (cdr lis1) lis2))
    (t (cons (car lis1) (union (cdr lis1) lis2)))))

7.13 *(defun my-reverse (lis)*
  (cond ((null lis) nil)
    (t (append (my-reverse (cdr lis)) (list (car lis))))))

7.14 *(defun ackerman (n m)*
  (cond ((zerop n) (1+ m))
    ((zerop m) (ackerman (1- n) 1))
    (t (ackerman (1- n) (ackerman n (1- m))))))

7.15 *(defun rectangle (m n l)*
  (cond ((zerop n) nil)
    (t (printline m l)
     (rectangle m (1- n) l))))

 (defun printline (m l)
  (cond ((zerop m) (terpri))
    (t (princ l)
     (printline (1- m) l))))

7.16 *(defun diamond (n)*
  (triangle-top n 0)
  (triangle-bottom 0 n))

```
(defun triangle-top (n m)
    (cond (((< n 2) nil)
            (t (printout (1− n) (1+ (* m 2)))
                (triangle-top (1− n)(1+ m)))))))

(defun triangle-bottom (n m)
    (cond ((zerop m) nil)
            (t (printout n (1− (* m 2)))
                (triangle-bottom (1+ n)(1− m)))))))

(defun printout (n m)
    (cond ((zerop n) (printout1 m))
            (t (princ " ")
                (printout (1− n) m)))))

(defun printout1 (n)
    (cond ((zerop n) (terpri))
            (t (princ 'X)
                (printout1 (1− n)))))))
```

7.17
```
(defun sort (lis)
    (cond ((null lis) nil)
            (t (insert (car lis) (sort (cdr lis)))))))

(defun insert (item lis)
    (cond ((null lis) (list item))
            (((< item (car lis)) (cons item lis))
            (t (cons (car lis) (insert item (cdr lis))))))))
```

7.18
```
(defun powerset (lis)
    (cond ((null lis) (list nil))
            (t (append (addto (car lis) (powerset (cdr lis)))
                        (powerset (cdr lis)))))))

(defun addto (elem lis)
    (cond ((null lis) nil)
            (t (cons (cons elem (car lis))
                        (addto elem (cdr lis))))))))
```

Chapter 8

8.1
```
(defun list-sum (lis)
    (let ((sum 0))
        (loop
            (cond ((null lis) (return sum)))
            (setq sum (+ (car lis) sum))
            (setq lis (cdr lis)))))
```

8.2 *(defun list-car (lis)*
 (let ((carlist nil))
  (loop
   (cond ((null lis) (return carlist)))
   (setq carlist (append carlist (list (caar lis))))
   (setq lis (cdr lis)))))

8.3 *(defun new-member (item lis)*
 (let ()
  (loop
   (cond ((null lis) (return nil))
    ((equal item (car lis)) (return lis)))
   (setq lis (cdr lis)))))

8.4 *(defun make-sublists (lis)*
 (let ((numlis nil) (othlis nil))
  (loop
   (cond ((null lis) (return (list numlis othlis)))
    ((numberp (car lis))
     (setq numlis (append numlis (list (car lis)))))
    (t (setq othlis (append othlis (list (car lis))))))
   (setq lis (cdr lis)))))

8.5 *(defun remove-first (target lis)*
 (let ((newlist nil))
  (loop
   (cond ((null lis) (return newlist))
    ((equal target (car lis))
     (return (append newlist (cdr lis)))))
   (setq newlist (append newlist (list (car lis))))
   (setq lis (cdr lis)))))

8.6 *(defun save-negs (lis)*
 (let ((neglist nil))
  (loop
   (cond ((null lis) (return neglist))
    ((< (car lis) 0)
     (setq neglist (append neglist (list (car lis))))))
   (setq lis (cdr lis)))))

8.7 *(defun insertion-sort (lis)*
 (let ((sortedlist nil))
  (loop
   (cond ((null lis) (return sortedlist)))
   (setq sortedlist (numeric-insert (car lis) sortedlist))
   (setq lis (cdr lis)))))

```
(defun numeric-insert (item sorted)
    (let ((newlist nil))
        (loop
            (cond ((null sorted) (return (append newlist (list item))))
                  ((< item (car sorted))
                        (return (append newlist (cons item sorted)))))
            (setq newlist (append newlist (list (car sorted))))
            (setq sorted (cdr sorted)))))
```

8.8
```
(defun duplicates (lis)
    (let ((newlist nil))
        (loop
            (cond ((null lis)(return newlist))
                  ((member (car lis) (cdr lis))
                        (setq newlist (append newlist (list (car lis))))))
            (setq lis (remove (car lis) lis)))))
```

8.9
```
(defun intersection (lis1 lis2)
    (let ((result nil))
        (loop
            (cond ((null lis1) (return result))
                  ((member (car lis1) lis2)
                        (setq result (append result (list (car lis1))))))
            (setq lis1 (remove (car lis1) lis1)))))
```

Chapter 9

9.1
```
(defun addto (elt lis)
    (cond ((null lis) nil)
          (t (cons (cons elt (car lis)) (addto elt (cdr lis))))))
```

9.2
```
(defun addto (elt lis)
    (let ((result nil))
        (loop
            (cond ((null lis)(return result)))
            (setq result (cons (cons elt (car lis)) result))
            (setq lis (cdr lis))
        )))
```

9.3 a) ((b c) (b) (c) nil)

b) We can generate the powerset of a list by inserting the *car* of the list into each element of the powerset of the *cdr* of the list and merging the resulting list with the powerset of the *cdr* of the list.

c) *(nil)*

d) *(defun powerset (lis)*
  (cond ((null lis) '(nil))
    (t (append (addto (car lis) (powerset (cdr lis)))
      (powerset (cdr lis))))))

9.4 *(defun permut (lis)*
  (cond ((null lis) '(nil))
    (t (new-perms (car lis) (permut (cdr lis))))))

(defun new-perms (term lis-of-lis)
  (let ((result nil))
    (loop
      (cond ((null lis-of-lis) (return result)))
      (setq result (append (insert-thru term (car lis-of-lis))
        result))
      (setq lis-of-lis (cdr lis-of-lis)))))

(defun insert-thru (term lis)
  (let ((result nil) (pre nil))
    (loop
      (cond ((null lis) (return (cons (append pre (list term))
        result))))
      (setq result (cons (append pre (list term) lis)
        result))
      (setq pre (append pre (list (car lis))))
      (setq lis (cdr lis)))))

9.5 *(defun countatoms (lis)*
  (cond ((null lis) 0)
    ((atom (car lis)) (1+ (countatoms (cdr lis))))
    (t (+ (countatoms (car lis)) (countatoms (cdr lis))))))

9.6 *(defun delete-in (elt lis)*
  (cond ((null lis) nil)
    ((equal elt (car lis)) (delete-in elt (cdr lis)))
    ((atom (car lis)) (cons (car lis) (delete-in elt (cdr lis))))
    (t (cons (delete-in elt (car lis)) (delete-in elt (cdr lis))))))

9.7 *(defun flatten (lis)*
  (cond ((null lis) nil)
    ((atom (car lis)) (cons (car lis) (flatten (cdr lis))))
    (t (append (flatten (car lis)) (flatten (cdr lis))))))

9.8 *(defun skeleton (lis)*
  (cond ((null lis) nil)
    ((atom (car lis)) (skeleton (cdr lis)))
    (t (cons (skeleton (car lis)) (skeleton (cdr lis))))))

9.9 *(defun logic (exp)*
    (cond ((atom exp) exp)
        ((equal (car exp) '–) (not (logic (cadr exp))))
        ((equal (cadr exp) 'V)
           (or (logic (car exp)) (logic-help (cddr exp))))
        ((equal (cadr exp) '&)
          (and (logic (car exp)) (logic-help (cddr exp)))))))

    (defun logic-help (exp)
        (cond ((null (cdr exp)) (logic (car exp)))
        (t (logic exp))))

9.10 *(defun binary-search (key tree)*
    (cond ((null tree) nil)
        ((equal key (car tree)) t)
        ((< key (car tree)) (binary-search key (cadr tree)))
        (t (binary-search key (caddr tree)))))

9.11 *(defun bsearch (key root tree)*
    (cond ((null root) nil)
        ((equal root key) t)
        ((< key root)
          (bsearch key (cadr (assoc root tree)) tree))
        (t (bsearch key (caddr (assoc root tree)) tree))))

9.12 *(defun genset (lis)*
    (cond ((null lis) t)
        ((and (or (atom (car lis)) (genset (car lis)))
             (genset (cdr lis)))
          (not (inset (car lis) (cdr lis))))
        (t nil)))

    (defun inset (elem set)
        (cond ((null set) nil)
        ((atom elem) (member elem set))
        ((atom (car set)) (inset elem (cdr set)))
        ((eqset elem (car set)) t)
        (t (inset elem (cdr set)))))

    (defun eqset (set1 set2)
        (and (subset set1 set2)(subset set2 set1)))

    (defun subset (set1 set2)
        (cond ((null set1) t)
        ((inset (car set1) set2) (subset (cdr set1) set2))
        (t nil)))

Chapter 10

10.1 *(defun new-reverse (lis)*
　　(do ((oldlist lis (cdr oldlist))
　　　　(revlis nil (cons (car oldlist) revlis)))
　　　((null oldlist) revlis)))

10.2 *(defun list-avg (lis)*
　　(do ((oldlis lis (cdr oldlis))
　　　　(count 0 (1+ count))
　　　　(total 0 (+ total (car oldlis))))
　　　((null oldlis) (/ total count))))

You could also write this without counting up the number of elements, if you used *length* in the solution:

(defun list-avg (lis)
　　(do ((oldlis lis (cdr oldlis))
　　　　(total 0 (+ total (car oldlis))))
　　　((null oldlis) (/ total (length lis)))))

10.3 *(defun expon (base exponent)*
　　(do ((product 1 (product base))*
　　　　(count 0 (1+ count)))
　　　((equal count exponent) product)))

10.4 *(defun create-list (n)*
　　(do ((count 0 (1+ count))
　　　　(result nil (append result (list (1+ count)))))
　　　((equal count n) result)))

10.5 *(defun next-prime (n)*
　　(do ((count n (1+ count)))
　　　((primep count) count)))

10.6 *(defun sumall (n)*
　　(do ((count 0 (1+ count))
　　　　(result-sum 0 (+ result-sum (1+ count))))
　　　((equal count n) result-sum)))

10.7 *(defun save-atoms (lis)*
　　(do ((oldlis lis (cdr oldlis))
　　　　(atomlis nil (cond ((atom (car oldlis))
　　　　　　　　　　　　(append atomlis (list (car oldlis))))
　　　　　　　　(t atomlis))))
　　　((null oldlis) atomlis)))

10.8 *(defun sortnums (lis)*
        (do ((oldlis lis (cdr oldlis))
             (poslis nil (cond ((not (> 0 (car oldlis)))
                                 (append poslis (list (car oldlis))))
                        (t poslis)))
             (neglis nil (cond ((> 0 (car oldlis))
                                 (append neglis (list (car oldlis))))
                        (t neglis))))
             ((null oldlis) (list neglis poslis))))

10.9 *(defun rectangle (m n)*
        (do ((count m (1− count)))
             ((equal count 0) (return nil))
             (printline n)))

      (defun printline (n)
        (do ((count n (1− count)))
             ((equal count 0) (terpri))
             (princ 'x)))

10.10 *(defun printout (lis)*
        (do ((temp lis (cdr temp)))
             ((null temp) nil)
             (cond ((equal (car temp) 'ret) (terpri))
                   (t (princ (car temp)) (princ " ")))))

10.11 *(defun list-decrement (lis)*
        (mapcar '1− lis))

10.12 *(defun embed-lists (lis)*
        (mapcar 'list lis))

10.13 *(defun pair-up (list1 list2)*
        (mapcar 'list list1 list2))

10.14 *(defun add-to-lis (num numlis)*
        (mapcar #'(lambda (num2)
                    (+ num2 num))
                numlis))

10.15 *(defun covariance (lis1 lis2)*
        (/ (− (mean (mapcar ' lis1 lis2))*
              ((mean lis1) (mean lis2)))*
           (1− (length lis1))))

      (defun mean (lis)
        (do ((sum 0 (+ sum (car temp)))
             (temp lis (cdr temp)))
             ((null temp) (/ sum (length lis)))))

Chapter 11

11.1 *(defun buy (item name)*
(cond ((member item (get name 'goods)) (get name 'address))
(t nil)))

11.2 *(defun add-data (name ageval sexval)*
(putprop name ageval 'age)
(putprop name sexval 'sex))

11.3 *(defun childp (person1 person2)*
(cond ((member person1 (get person2 'children)) t)))

11.4 *(defun add-child (childarg motherarg fatherarg)*
(putprop childarg motherarg 'mother)
(putprop childarg fatherarg 'father)
(putprop motherarg (append (get motherarg 'children) (list childarg))
'children)
(putprop fatherarg (append (get fatherarg 'children) (list childarg))
'children))

11.5 *(defun list-props (lis)*
(mapcar '(lambda (item)
(list item (get item 'age) (get item 'sex)))
lis))

11.6 *(defun listsort (lis)*
(do ((oldlis lis (cdr oldlis))
(adultlis nil
(cond ((get (car oldlis) 'adult)
(append adultlis (list (car oldlis))))
(t adultlis)))
(childlis nil
(cond ((not (get (car oldlis) 'adult))
(append childlis (list (car oldlis))))
(t childlis))))
((null oldlis) (list childlis adultlis))))

11.7 *(defun encode-tree (root alist)*
(let ((lis (assoc root alist))
(node (newatom 'node)))
(putprop node (car lis) 'value)
(cond ((not (null (cadr lis)))
(putprop node (encode-tree (cadr lis) alist) 'lesser)))
(cond ((not (null (caddr lis)))
(putprop node (encode-tree (caddr lis) alist) 'greater)))
node))

11.8 *(defun binary-search (root target)*
(cond ((null root) nil)
((equal (get root 'value) target) t)
((< target (get root 'value)) (binary-search
(get root 'lesser) target))
(t (binary-search (get root 'greater) target))))

11.9 *(defun arraysum (len)*
(do ((index 0 (1+ index))
(sum 0 (+ (aref data index) sum)))
((equal index len) sum)))

11.10 *(defun array-switch (arrayname len)*
(do ((index 0 (1+ index)))
((equal index len) 'done)
(setf (aref arrayname index) (– 1 (aref arrayname index)))))*

11.11 *(defun array-search (name len)*
(do ((index 0 (1+ index))
(winners nil (cond ((equal (get (aref name index) 'score) 'won)
(append winners (list (aref name index))))
(t winners))))
((equal index len) winners)))

11.12 *(defun count-runs (len)*
(do ((index 0 (1+ index))
(totruns 0 (+ (get (aref stats index) 'runs) totruns)))
((equal index len) totruns)))

11.13 *(defun sort-by-sex (name len)*
(do ((index 0 (1+ index))
(flist nil (cond ((equal (get (aref name index) 'sex) 'female)
(append flist (list (aref name index))))
(t flist)))
(mlist nil (cond ((equal (get (aref name index) 'sex) 'male)
(append mlist (list (aref name index))))
(t mlist))))
((equal index len) (list flist mlist))))

11.14 *(defun matrix-add (array1 array2 m n)*
(let ((total (make-array (list m n))))
(do ((count 0 (1+ count)))
((equal count m) total)
(vector-add count n array1 array2 total))))

```
(defun vector-add (row length array1 array2 total)
    (do ((count 0 (1+ count)))
        ((equal count length) nil)
        (setf (aref total row count)
              (+ (aref array1 row count)(aref array2 row count)))))
```

Chapter 12

12.1   a.

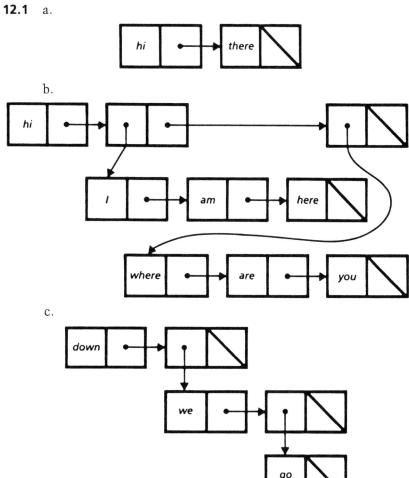

b.

c.

12.2 a. *(1 2 3)*
   b. *(((HI)))*

12.3 *(defun display-cons (lis hor vert)*
   (setq consarray (make-array (list hor vert)))
   (consfill lis 0 0)
   (printarray hor vert))

   (defun consfill (lis n1 n2)
   (cond ((null lis) (setf (aref consarray n1 n2) '\ ))
   ((atom lis) (setf (aref consarray n1 n2) lis))
   (t (setf (aref consarray n1 n2) " ")
   (carfill (car lis) (1+ n1) n2)
   (setf (aref consarray (+ n1 2) n2) "|")
   (cdrfill (cdr lis) (+ n1 3) n2)
   (setf (aref consarray (+ n1 4) n2) "]"))))

   (defun printarray (n1 n2)
   (do ((count 0 (1+ count)))
   ((equal count n2) nil)
   (printline n1 count)))

   (defun printline (n1 n2)
   (do ((count 0 (1+ count)))
   ((equal count n1) (terpri))
   (cond ((null (aref consarray count n2)) (princ " "))
   (t (princ (aref consarray count n2))))))

   (defun carfill (lis n1 n2)
   (cond ((atom lis) (consfill lis n1 n2))
   (t (setf (aref consarray n1 n2) ')*
   (setf (aref consarray n1 (1+ n2)) "|")
   (consfill lis n1 (+ n2 2)))))

   (defun cdrfill (lis n1 n2)
   (cond ((atom lis)(consfill lis n1 n2))
   (t (setf (aref consarray n1 n2) ')*
   (setf (aref consarray (+ n1 2) n2) " – ")
   (setf (aref consarray (+ n1 3) n2) " – ")
   (consfill lis (+ n1 4) n2))))

12.4 *(defun testsource (a b)*
   (cond ((eql a b) 'same-list)
   ((eql (cdr a) (cdr b)) 'same-tail)
   ((equal a b) 'same-value)
   (t 'different)))

12.5 *(defun equal* (a b)*
      (cond ((eql a b) t)
             (t (and (equal* (car a) (car b))
                      (equal* (cdr a) (cdr b))))))

12.6 *(defun copy1 (lis)*
      (cond ((null lis) nil)
             (t (cons (car lis) (copy1 (cdr lis))))))

12.7 *(defun copy2 (lis)*
      (cond ((null lis) nil)
             ((atom lis) lis)
             (t (cons (copy2 (car lis)) (copy2 (cdr lis))))))

12.8 a.   *(defun append2 (lis1 lis2)*
         (cond ((null lis1) lis2)
               (t (cons (car lis1) (append2 (cdr lis1) lis2)))))

     b.   *(defun append3 (lis1 lis2 lis3)*
         (append2 lis1 (append2 lis2 lis3)))

12.9 *(defun replace (old new lis)*
      (do ((point lis (cdr point)))
         ((null point) lis)
         (cond ((equal old (car point)) (rplaca point new)))))

12.10 *(defun splice-out (a lis)*
      (cond ((equal (car lis) a) (splice-out a (cdr lis)))
            (t (splice-out-helper a lis))))

      (defun splice-out-helper (a lis)
         (do ((point (cdr lis) (cdr point))
            (trail lis point))
         ((null point) lis)
         (cond ((equal a (car point))
               (rplacd trail (cddr trail))))))

12.11 *(defun insert (num lis)*
      (cond ((< num (car lis)) (cons num lis))
          (t (insert-helper num lis))))

      (defun insert-helper (num lis)
         (do ((point (cdr lis) (cdr point))
           (trail lis point)
           ((null point) (rplacd trail (list num)) lis)
           (cond ((< num (car point)) (rplacd trail (cons num point))
                        (return lis)))))

12.12 *(defun sorter (lis)*
          (do ((rest lis (cdr rest))
               (temp (car lis) (cadr rest))
               (min (minimum lis) (minimum (cdr rest))))
              ((null (cdr rest)) lis)
              (cond ((not (eq min rest))
                     (rplaca rest (car min)) (rplaca min temp)))))

   (defun minimum (lis)
          (do ((min lis (cond ((< (car rest) (car min*)) rest)*
                              ·(t min)))*
               (rest (cdr lis) (cdr rest)))
              ((null rest) min)))*

Chapter 13

13.1 (a) *dog*
        (b) *(list (quote a) (quote b))*
        (c) *b*
        (d) *a*
        (e) *dog*
        (f) *dog*
        (g) *b*
        (h) *(list (quote a) (quote b))*
        (i) *(a b)*
        (j) *Error: eval: Undefined function   a*
        (k) *b*
        (l) *(eval (eval a))*
        (m) *(list (quote a) (quote b))*
        (n) *dog*
        (o) *(list (quote a) (quote b))*
        (p) *quote*
        (q) *(a b)*
13.2 (a) *=⟩ (apply 'cons '(a (eval '(list 'a 'b))))*
             (a eval (quote (list (quote a) (quote b))))
        (b) *=⟩ (eval '(cons 'a (apply 'list '(a b))))*
             (a a b)
13.3 *(defun flatten (lis)*
          (cond ((null lis) nil)
                ((atom lis)(list lis))
                (t (apply 'append (mapcar 'flatten lis)))))

13.4 *(defun add-operation ()*
        (do ((input (get-operation) (get-operation)))
          ((equal input 'stop) nil)
          (do-operation input)))

    (defun get-operation ()
       (print '(what operation?))
       (read))

    (defun do-operation (op)
       (do ((input (get-args) (get-args))
         (sum 0 (+ sum (apply op input))))
         ((equal input 'sum) (print-sum sum))))

    (defun get-args ()
       (print '(give me a set of arguments))
       (read))

    (defun print-sum (num)
       (print (cons num '(is the sum))))

13.5 *(defun every-p (test lis)*
       (apply 'and (mapcar test lis)))

13.6 *(defun save-atoms (lis)*
       (mapcan '(lambda (item)
            (cond ((atom item)(list item))
                (t nil)))
          lis))

13.7 *(defun balance (name amount)*
       (print `(We are pleased to inform you ,@name that you have
          ,(* amount .1) dollars interest on your old balance of
          ,amount dollars for a new balance of ,(* amount 1.1)
          dollars)))

13.8 *(defun beer (n)*
       (do ((count n (1− count)))
         ((zerop count) nil)
         (print `(,@(bottles count) of beer on the wall))
         (print `(,@(bottles count) of beer))
         (print `(you take one down and pass it arround))
         (print `(,@(bottles (1− count)) of beer on the wall))
         (terpri)))

```
(defun bottles (n)
    (cond ((zerop n) '(no bottles))
          ((equal n 1) '(1 bottle))
          (t `(,n bottles))))
```

13.9
```
(defmacro do-times (operations initializations actions n)
    `(do ((count ,n (1- count))
          ,@initializations)
         ((zerop count) ,@actions)
       ,@operations))
```

13.10
```
(defun factorial (n)
    (do-times nil ((product 1 (* product count)))
       (product) n))
```

13.11
```
(defun print-factorial (n)
    (do-times ((princ count) (princ " ") (princ (factorial count)) (terpri))
       nil nil n))
```

13.12
```
(defmacro terminating-search (predicate lis)
    `(do ((target ,lis (cdr target)))
         ((null target) nil)
       (cond ((,predicate (car target)) (return (car target))))))
```

13.13   a.
```
(defun search-number (lis)
    (terminating-search numberp lis))
```
      b.
```
(defun non-empty-list (lis)
    (terminating-search (lambda (x)
                          (and (listp x) x))
      lis))
```
      c.
```
(defun intersectionp (lis1 lis2)
    (terminating-search (lambda (y)
                          (member y lis2))
      lis1))
```

13.14
```
(defmacro my-mapcar (fn l)
    `(do ((tasks ,l (cdr tasks))
          (result nil (append result (list (,fn (car tasks))))))
         ((null tasks) result)))
```

13.15
```
(defmacro car-cdr-macro (nullact speccases atomact combineact)
    `(cond ((null lis) ,nullact)
           ,@speccases
           ((atom (car lis)) ,atomact)
           (t ,combineact)))
```

```
(defun flatten (lis) (car-cdr-macro nil nil (cons (car lis)
                                                   (flatten (cdr lis)))
                            (append (flatten (car lis))
                                    (flatten (cdr lis)))))
```

Chapter 14

14.1
```
(defun add-daughter (child mom dad)
    (putprop child (list mom) 'mother)
    (putprop child (list dad) 'father)
    (putprop mom (cons child (get mom 'children)) 'children)
    (putprop dad (cons child (get dad 'children)) 'children)
    (add-siblings child (cdr (get mom 'children))))

(defun add-siblings (child siblings)
    (do ((lis siblings (cdr lis)))
        ((null lis) t)
        (cond ((equal 'male (get (car lis) 'sex))
                   (putprop child
                       (cons (car lis) (get child 'brothers))
                       'brothers))
              (t (putprop child
                      (cons (car lis) (get child 'sisters))
                      'sisters)))
        (putprop (car lis) (cons child (get (car lis) 'sisters)) 'sisters)))
```

14.2
```
(defun expand-word (word)
    (do ((candidates vocabulary (cdr candidates))
         (result nil
             (cond ((one-step word (car candidates))
                        (cons (car candidates) result))
                   (t result))))
        ((null candidates) result)))

(defun one-step (word1 word2)
    (and (not (equal word1 word2))
         (or (and (equal (nthchar word1 1) (nthchar word2 1))
                  (equal (nthchar word1 2) (nthchar word2 2)))
             (and (equal (nthchar word1 1) (nthchar word2 1))
                  (equal (nthchar word1 3) (nthchar word2 3)))
             (and (equal (nthchar word1 2) (nthchar word2 2))
                  (equal (nthchar word1 3) (nthchar word2 3))))))
```

14.3 *(defun breadth (start)*
(do ((queue (list start)
(append (cdr queue) (expand (car queue)))))
((null queue) nil)
(cond ((get (car queue) 'success) (return (car queue))))))

(defun expand (node)
(get node 'subnodes))

14.4 *(defun first-number (lis)*
(do ((queue lis (cond ((atom (car queue)) (cdr queue))
(t (append (car queue) (cdr queue))))))
((null queue) nil)
(cond ((numberp (car queue)) (return (car queue))))))

14.5 *(defun add-problem (lis sum)*
(do ((queue (list (list 0 lis))
(append (cdr queue) (expand (car queue)))))
((null queue) nil)
(cond ((equal (caar queue) sum) (return t)))))

(defun expand (state)
(let ((sum (car state))
(lis (cadr state)))
(do ((temp lis (cdr temp))
(result nil (append result
(list (list (+ sum (car temp))
(remove (car temp) lis))))))
((null temp) result))))

14.6 *(defun exhaustive (start)*
(do ((queue (list start)
(append (cdr queue) (expand (car queue))))
(result nil result))
((null queue) result)
(cond ((get (car queue) 'success)
(setq result (cons (car queue) result))))))

14.7 *(defun flatten (lis)*
(do ((queue lis (cond ((atom (car queue)) (cdr queue))
(t (append (car queue) (cdr queue)))))
(result nil result))
((null queue) (reverse result))
(cond ((not (listp (car queue))) (setq result
(cons (car queue) result))))))

14.8 *(defun pre-requisite (course pres)*
  (putprop course pres 'has-pre-req)
  (mapcar #'(lambda (x) (putprop x (cons course (get x 'pre-req-for))
            'pre-req-for)) pres))

14.9 *(defun before (course)*
  (do ((queue (expand course)
        (cond ((member (car queue) visited) (cdr queue))
          (t (append (cdr queue) (expand (car queue))))))
      (visited nil
        (cond ((member (car queue) visited) visited)
          (t (cons (car queue) visited)))))
      ((null queue) visited)))

(defun expand (course) (get course 'has-pre-req))

14.10 *(defun dog-cat (start goal)*
  (do ((paths (list (list start))
        (cond ((member (caar paths) visited) (cdr paths))
          (t (append (cdr paths) (expand-path (car paths))))))
      (visited nil (cons (caar paths) visited)))
      ((null paths) nil)
      (cond ((equal (caar paths) goal) (return (reverse (car paths)))))))

(defun expand-path (path)
  (do ((temp (expand-word (car path)) (cdr temp))
      (result nil (cons (cons (car temp) path) result)))
      ((null temp) result)))

14.11 *(defun waterjug (a b c g)*
  (cond ((not (legal a b c g)) 'cannot)
    (t (do ((paths (list (list (list 0 0 0)))
          (cond ((member (caar paths) visited) (cdr paths))
            (t (append paths (expand
              (list a b c)
              (list 'a 'b 'c)
              (car paths)))))))
        (visited nil (cons (caar paths) visited)))
        ((null paths) nil)
        (cond ((member g (caar paths)) (return (reverse
                      (cdar paths))))))))))

```
(defun expand (capacities names path)
    (let ((values (car path))
          (ops (cdr path)))
        (mapcar #'(lambda (x) (append x ops))
            (append
                (fill-jugs capacities names values)
                (empty capacities names values)
                (pour capacities names values)))))

(defun fill-jugs (capacities names values)
    (do ((cset capacities (cdr cset))
         (nset names (cdr nset))
         (vset values (cdr vset))
         (pre-val nil (append pre-val (list (car vset))))
         (result nil
             (cond ((zerop (car vset)) (cons (list
                         (append pre-val (cons (car cset) (cdr vset)))
                         (list 'fill (car nset))) result))
                   (t result))))
        ((null vset) result)))

(defun empty (capacities names values)
    (do ((cset capacities (cdr cset))
         (nset names (cdr nset))
         (vset values (cdr vset))
         (pre-val nil (append pre-val (list (car vset))))
         (result nil
             (cond ((not (zerop (car vset))) (cons (list
                         (append pre-val (cons 0 (cdr vset)))
                         (list 'empty (car nset))) result))
                   (t result))))
        ((null vset) result)))

(defun pour (capacities names values)
    (do ((cset1 capacities (cdr cset1))
         (nset1 names (cdr nset1))
         (vset1 values (cdr vset1))
         (pre-val1 nil (append pre-val1 (list (car vset1))))
         (result nil (append result (pour-h cset1 nset1 vset1 pre-val1))))
        ((null (cdr vset1)) result)))
```

```
(defun pour-h (cset1 nset1 vset1 prefix)
    (do ((cap1 (car cset1 (car cset1)))
         (name1 (car nset1 (car nset1)))
         (value1 (car vset1 (car vset1)))
         (cset2 (cdr cset1) (cdr cset2))
         (nset2 (cdr nset1) (cdr nset2))
         (vset2 (cdr vset1) (cdr vset2))
         (pre-val nil (append pre-val (list (car vset2))))
         (result nil (append result (pour-both prefix pre-val (cdr vset2)
             cap1 name1 value1 (car cset2) (car nset2) (car vset2)))))
        ((null vset2) result)))

(defun pour-both (pre1 pre2 rest cap1 name1 value1 cap2 name2 value2)
    (let ((result nil))
       (cond ((and (> value1 0) (< value2 cap2))
                    (setq result (cons (list (append pre1 (cons
                        (pour-from value1 value2 cap2) pre2) (cons
                        (pour-to value1 value2 cap2) rest))
                                                (list 'pour name1 name2))
                                result))))
       (cond ((and (> value2 0) (< value1 cap1))
                    (setq result (cons (list (append pre1 (cons
                        (pour-to value2 value1 cap1) pre2) (cons
                        (pour-from value2 value1 cap1) rest))
                                                (list 'pour name2 name1))
                                result))))
    result))

(defun pour-to (fvalue tvalue tcap)
    (cond ((> (+ fvalue tvalue) tcap) tcap)
          (t (+ fvalue tvalue))))

(defun pour-from (fvalue tvalue tcap)
    (cond ((> (+ fvalue tvalue) tcap) (- (+ fvalue tvalue) tcap))
          (t 0)))

(defun legal (a b c g)
    (and (or (not (> g a))
             (not (> g b))
             (not (> g c)))
         (zerop (mod g (gcd (gcd a b) c)))))
```

14.12 a. (defun distance (word1 word2)
    (let ((n 3))
      (cond ((equal (nthchar word1 1) (nthchar word2 1))
          (setq n (1− n))))
      (cond ((equal (nthchar word1 2) (nthchar word2 2))
          (setq n (1− n))))
      (cond ((equal (nthchar word1 3) (nthchar word2 3))
          (setq n (1−) n))
      (t n))))

b. (defun expand-path (path goal)
    (mapcar #'(lambda (x) (cons (distance x goal) (cons x (cdr path))))
    (expand-state (cadr path))))

c. (defun interleave (new old)
    (do ((tasks new (cdr tasks))
      (result old (insert (car tasks) result)))
    ((null tasks) result)))

(defun insert (item list)
    (do ((tail list (cdr tail))
      (pre nil (append pre (list (car tail)))))
    ((null tail) (append pre (list item)))
    (cond ((not (< (caar tail) (car item)))
      (return (append pre (list item) tail))))))

14.13 (defun dog-cat (start goal)
    (do ((paths (list (list (distance start goal) start))
      (cond ((member (cadar paths) visited) (cdr paths))
      (t (interleave (expand-path (car paths) goal)
        (cdr paths)))))
    (visited nil (cons (cadar paths) visited)))
    ((null paths) nil)
    (cond ((equal (cadar paths) goal) (return
        (reverse (cdar paths)))))))

14.14 a. (defun points-to (node1 distance node2)
    (putprop node1 (cons (list distance node2)
      (get node1 'next)) 'next))

b. (defun minpath (start goal)
    (do ((paths (list (list 0 start))
      (cond ((member (cadar paths) visited) (cdr paths))
      (t (interleave (expand-nodepaths (car paths))
        (cdr paths)))))
    (visited nil (cons (cadar paths) visited)))
    ((null paths) nil)
    (cond ((equal (cadar paths) goal) (return
        (reverse (cdar paths)))))))

```
(defun expand-nodepaths (path)
    (mapcar #'(lambda (x) (cons (+ (car x) (car path))
                            (cons (cadr x) (cdr path))))
        (get (cadr path) 'next)))
```

14.15
```
(defun eight-puzzle (start)
    (do ((paths (list (list (distance start) start))
                (cond ((member (cadar paths) visited) (cdr paths))
                    (t (interleave (expand-paths (car paths))
                            (cdr paths)))))
        (visited nil (cons (cadar paths) visited)))
        ((null paths) nil)
        (cond ((zerop (caar paths)) (return
                            (output (reverse (cdar paths))))))))
```

```
(defun newcode (state)
    (append (car state)
            (cddr (cadr state))
            (reverse (caddr state))
            (list (caadr state) (caar state))))
```

```
(defun distance (state)
    (do ((sequence (newcode state) sequence)
        (measure (center (cadr (cadr state))) (+ measure
                                    (periphery position
                                        sequence)))
        (position 1 (1+ position)))
        ((equal position 9) measure)))
```

```
(defun center (tile)
    (cond ((null tile) 0)
        ((member tile '(2 4 6 8)) 4)
        (t 5)))
```

```
(defun periphery (position sequence)
    (let ((cell (nthcell position sequence))
        (next (nthcell (1+ position) sequence)))
        (cond ((null cell) 0)
            ((null next) (+ 6 (steps cell position sequence)))
            ((or (equal cell (1- next))
                (and (equal cell 8) (equal next 1)))
                (steps cell position sequence))
            (t (+ 6 (steps cell position sequence))))))
```

```
(defun steps (cell position sequence)
  (let ((distance (abs (- cell position))))
    (cond ((< distance 4) distance)
          ((> distance 4) (- 8 distance))
          ((member cell '(1 3 5 7)) 4)
          (t 2))))

(defun nthcell (n lis)
  (do ((rest lis (cdr rest))
       (count 1 (1+ count)))
      ((equal count n) (car rest))))

(defun expand-paths (path)
  (mapcar #'(lambda (x) (cons (distance x) (cons x (cdr path))))
          (expand-state (cadr path))))

(defun expand-state (state)
  (append (expandline state)
          (mapcar 'transverse (expandline (transverse state)))))

(defun expandline (state)
  (cond ((member nil (car state))
         (mapcar #'(lambda (x) (cons x (cdr state)))
                 (shuffle (car state))))
        ((member nil (cadr state))
         (mapcar #'(lambda (x) (cons (car state)
                                     (cons x (cddr state))))
                 (shuffle (cadr state))))
        ((member nil (caddr state))
         (mapcar #'(lambda (x) (list (car state) (cadr state) x))
                 (shuffle (caddr state))))))

(defun transverse (lis)
  (let ((first (car lis)) (second (cadr lis)) (third (caddr lis)))
    (list (list (car first) (car second) (car third))
          (list (cadr first) (cadr second) (cadr third))
          (list (caddr first) (caddr second) (caddr third)))))

(defun shuffle (line)
  (cond ((null (car line)) (list (list (cadr line) (car line) (caddr line))))
        ((null (cadr line)) (list (list (cadr line) (car line) (caddr line))
                                  (list (car line) (caddr line) (cadr line))))
        (t (list (list (car line) (caddr line) (cadr line))))))
```

```
(defun output (lis)
    (do ((queue lis (cdr queue)))
        ((null queue) nil)
        (mapcar 'output-help (caar queue)) (terpri)
        (mapcar 'output-help (cadar queue)) (terpri)
        (mapcar 'output-help (caddar queue)) (terpri)
        (terpri)))

(defun output-help (item)
    (cond ((null item) (princ " ") (princ " "))
          (t (princ item) (princ " "))))
```

Chapter 15

15.1
```
(defun elem-match (pattern data)
    (cond ((variablep pattern) (list pattern data))
          ((equal pattern data) t)
          (t nil)))

(defun variablep (term)
    (equal (nthchar term 1) '=))
```
15.2
```
(defun filter (lis)
    (cond ((member nil lis) nil)
          (t (list (delete-ts lis)))))

(defun delete-ts (lis)
    (mapcan '(lambda (item) (cond ((equal item t) nil)
                                  (t (list item))))
            lis))
```
15.3
```
(defun match-clause (pat dat)
    (cond ((equal (length pat) (length dat))
              (filter (mapcar 'elem-match pat dat)))
          (t nil)))
```
15.4
```
(defun match-clause (pat dat)
    (filter (match-recursive pat dat)))

(defun filter (lis)
    (cond ((null lis) nil)
          (t (list (delete-ts lis)))))
```

```
(defun match-recursive (pat dat)
    (cond ((equal pat dat) (list t))
          ((variablep pat) (list (list pat dat)))
          ((or (atom pat) (atom dat)) nil)
          (t (combine (match-recursive (car pat) (car dat))
                      (cdr pat) (cdr dat)))))

(defun variablep (term)
    (and (atom term)
         (equal (nthchar term 1) '=)))

(defun combine (match pat dat)
    (cond ((not match) nil)
          (t (let ((newmatch (match-recursive pat dat)))
                  (cond ((not newmatch) nil)
                        (t (append match newmatch)))))))
```

15.5
```
(defun merge (new old)
    (cond ((null new) nil)
          ((equal old '(nil)) new)
          (t (mapcan #'(lambda (x) (merge-old x old)) new))))

(defun merge-old (ins old)
    (mapcan #'(lambda (y) (merge-pair ins y)) old))

(defun merge-pair (ins1 ins2)
    (cond ((or (null ins1) (null ins2)) (list (or ins1 ins2)))
          (t
              (do ((chores ins1 (cdr chores))
                   (result ins2 (merge-ins result (car chores))))
                  ((null chores) (cond (result (list result))
                                       (t nil)))
                  (cond ((null result) (return nil)))))))

(defun merge-ins (ins pair)
    (cond ((assoc (car pair) ins)
           (cond ((equal (cadr pair) (cadr (assoc (car pair) ins))) ins)
                 (t nil)))
          (t (cons pair ins))))
```

15.6
```
(defun new-match (pattern)
    (do ((parts pattern (cdr parts))
         (answers (list nil) (merge (match (car parts)) answers)))
        ((null parts) (fdups answers))
        (cond ((null answers) (return nil)))))
```

```
(defun fdups (lis)
    (do ((chores lis (cdr chores))
         (result nil
                 (cond ((duptest (car chores)) result)
                       (t (cons (car chores) result)))))
        ((null chores) result)))

(defun duptest (pairs)
    (do ((chores pairs (cdr chores))
         (set nil (cons (next-value chores) set)))
        ((null chores) nil)
        (cond ((member (next-value chores) set) (return t)))))

(defun next-value (lis)
    (cadar lis))
```

15.7
```
(defun match (clause)
    (cond ((equal (car clause) 'or)
           (mapcan #'(lambda (x) (match x))
                   (cdr clause)))
          (t (mapcan #'(lambda (x) (match-clause clause x)) database))))
```

15.8
```
(defun gparent ()
    (gparent1 (parents database)))

(defun parents (dbase)
    (do ((targets dbase (cdr targets))
         (results nil
                  (cond ((member (get-relation targets)
                                 '(is-mother-of is-father-of))
                         (cons (list (get-first targets)
                                     (get-third targets))
                               results))
                        (t results))))
        ((null targets) results)))

(defun get-relation (lis)
    (cadar lis))

(defun get-first (lis)
    (caar lis))

(defun get-third (lis)
    (caddar lis))
```

```
(defun gparent1 (pairs)
  (mapcan #'(lambda (x)
                (mapcan #'(lambda (y) (gtest x y)) pairs))
           pairs))

(defun gtest (pair1 pair2)
  (cond ((equal (cadr pair1) (car pair2))
          (list (list (list '=x (car pair1))
                      (list '=y (car pair2))
                      (list '=z (cadr pair2)))))
        (t nil)))
```

15.9
```
(defun build-clause (prod clause bindings)
  (do ((old-clause clause (cdr old-clause))
       (new-clause nil (append new-clause
                        (list (or (associate (assoc (car old-clause)
                                                    bindings))
                                  (car old-clause))))))
      ((null old-clause) (edit-old prod new-clause))))

(defun edit-old (prod clause)
  (cond ((member clause database :test 'equal) nil)
        (t (list (list prod clause)))))

(defun associate (lis)
  (cadr lis))
```

15.10
```
(defun match-prod (prod)
  (do ((instans (new-match (get-test prod)) (cdr instans))
       (result nil (append result (build-clause (prod-name prod)
                                                 (act-pattern prod)
                                                 (car instans)))))
      ((null instans) result)))

(defun prod-name (prod) (car prod))

(defun get-test (prod) (cadr prod))

(defun act-pattern (prod) (cadddr prod))
```

15.11
```
(defun apply-prods ()
  (do ((plist productions (cdr plist))
       (result nil (append result (match-prod (car plist)))))
      ((null plist) result)))
```

Chapter 16

```
(defun production-system ()
    (encode-productions)
    (rule-interpreter))

(defun encode-productions ()
    (mapcar 'encode-a-production productions))

(defun encode-a-production (production)
    (let ((name (car production))
          (condition (cadr production))
          (action (cadddr production)))
        (encode-condition condition name)
        (putprop name (build-action (mapcar 'cdr condition) action)
            'action)))

(defun encode-condition (conditions prodname)
    (let (first second third)
        (setq first (car conditions))
        (update prodname (car first) 'first)
        (cond ((cdr conditions)
               (setq second (cadr conditions))
               (update prodname (car second) 'second)))
        (cond ((cddr conditions)
               (setq third (caddr conditions))
               (update prodname (car third) 'third)))
        (putprop prodname (build-condition (cdr first) (cdr second)
                              (cdr third)) 'condition)))
```

16.1
```
(defun update (prodname pred relation)
    (putprop prodname pred relation)
    (putprop pred (cons prodname (get pred relation)) relation))
```

```
(defun build-condition (vars1 vars2 vars3)
    `(lambda (first second third) ,(build-test vars1 vars2 vars3)))
```

16.2
```
(defun build-test (vars1 vars2 vars3)
    (let ((test (append (encode-pair vars1 vars2 'first 'second)
                        (encode-pair vars1 vars3 'first 'third)
                        (encode-pair vars2 vars3 'second 'third))))
        (cond ((null test) t)
              ((null (cdr test)) (car test))
              (t (cons 'and test)))))
```

```
(defun encode-pair (vars1 vars2 name1 name2)
    (and vars1 vars2
        (cond ((eq (car vars1) (car vars2))
                `((eq (car ,name1) (car ,name2))))
              ((and (cdr vars1) (eq (cadr vars1) (car vars2)))
                `((eq (cadr ,name1) (car ,name2))))
              ((and (cdr vars2) (eq (car vars1) (cadr vars2)))
                `((eq (car ,name1) (cadr ,name2))))
              ((and (cdr vars1) (cdr vars2) (eq (cadr vars1) (cadr vars2)))
                `((eq (cadr ,name1) (cadr ,name2)))))))
```

16.3
```
(defun build-action (condition action)
    `(lambda (first second third)
        (list (quote ,(car action))
            ,@(describe-args condition (cdr action)))))

(defun describe-args (condition action)
    (let ((args1 (car condition))
          (args2 (cadr condition))
          (args3 (caddr condition)))
        (mapcar
          #'(lambda (x)
                (cond ((equal x (car args1)) '(car first))
                      ((and (cdr args1)
                            (equal x (cadr args1))) '(cadr first))
                      ((equal x (car args2)) '(car second))
                      ((and (cdr args2)
                            (equal x (cadr args2))) '(cadr second))
                      ((equal x (car args3)) '(car third))
                      ((and (cdr args3)
                            (equal x (cadr args3))) '(cadr third))))
          action)))

(defun rule-interpreter ()
    (let (choice)
        (do ((add-list database (cdr add-list))
             (conflict-set nil (append (enter-clause (car add-list))
                                       conflict-set)))
            ((and (null add-list) (null conflict-set)) database)
            (cond ((null add-list)
                    (setq choice (conflict-resolution conflict-set))
                    (perform-action choice)
                    (setq add-list (cdr choice))
                    (setq conflict-set (remove-repeats conflict-set
                                       (cadr choice))))))))
```

```
(defun conflict-resolution (conflict-set) (car conflict-set))

(defun perform-action (action)
    (print (cons 'firing action))
    (setq database (cons (cadr action) database)))

(defun remove-repeats (conflict-set action)
        (do ((temp conflict-set (cdr temp))
                (result nil (cond ((equal (cadar temp) action) result)
                                    (t (cons (car temp) result)))))
            ((null temp) result)))
(defun enter-clause (clause)
        (let ((pred (car clause))
            (args (cdr clause)))
            (putprop pred (cons args (get pred 'bindings)) 'bindings)
            (append
                (mapcan #'(lambda (prod) (enter-first args prod))
                            (get pred 'first))
                (mapcan #'(lambda (prod) (enter-second args prod))
                            (get pred 'second))
                (mapcan #'(lambda (prod) (enter-third args prod))
                            (get pred 'third)))))

(defun enter-first (args prod)
        (mapcan #'(lambda (x) (match-and-execute x prod))
                (cross-product (list args)
                        (clauses prod 'second)
                        (clauses prod 'third))))

(defun clauses (prod position)
        (or (get (get prod position) 'bindings) (list nil)))

(defun cross-product (lis1 lis2 lis3)
        (mapcan #'(lambda (x)
                        (mapcan #'(lambda (y)
                                        (mapcar #'(lambda (z) (list x y z)) lis3))
                            lis2))
            lis1))
```

16.4
```
(defun match-and-execute (args prod)
        (cond ((apply (get prod 'condition) args)
                    (check-for-dups prod (apply (get prod 'action) args)))
            (t nil)))
```

```
(defun check-for-dups (prod action)
    (cond ((member* action database) nil)
          (t (list (list prod action)))))

(defun member* (target lis)
    (do ((temp lis (cdr temp)))
        ((null temp) nil)
        (cond ((equal (car temp) target) (return temp)))))
```

16.5
```
(defun enter-second (args prod)
    (mapcan #'(lambda (x) (match-and-execute x prod))
        (cross-product (clauses prod 'first)
                       (list args)
                       (clauses prod 'third))))

(defun enter-third (args prod)
    (mapcan #'(lambda (x) (match-and-execute x prod))
        (cross-product (clauses prod 'first)
                       (clauses prod 'second)
                       (list args))))

(defun putprop (atom value property)
    (setf (get atom property) value))
```

Index